Beyond Multiculturalism

McMaster Divinity College Press
McMaster Ministry Studies Series, Volume 6

Beyond Multiculturalism
Intentional Intercultural Congregations as an Expression of the Kingdom

EDITED BY
CHARLES A. COOK,
LORAJOY TIRA-DIMANGONDAYAO,
AND
LAUREN UMBACH

FOREWORD BY
MINHO SONG

☙PICKWICK *Publications* · Eugene, Oregon

BEYOND MULTICULTURALISM
Intentional Intercultural Congregations as an Expression of the Kingdom

McMaster Ministry Studies Series, Volume 6
McMaster Divinity College Press

Copyright © 2024 Wipf and Stock Publishers. All rights reserved. Except for brief quotations in critical publications or reviews, no part of this book may be reproduced in any manner without prior written permission from the publisher. Write: Permissions, Wipf and Stock Publishers, 199 W. 8th Ave., Suite 3, Eugene, OR 97401.

Pickwick Publications
An Imprint of Wipf and Stock Publishers
199 W. 8th Ave., Suite 3
Eugene, OR 97401

McMaster Divinity College Press
1280 Main Street West
Hamilton, Ontario, Canada
L8S 4K1

www.wipfandstock.com

PAPERBACK ISBN: 978-1-6667-8370-4
HARDCOVER ISBN: 978-1-6667-8371-1
EBOOK ISBN: 978-1-6667-8372-8

McMaster Ministry Studies Series
ISSN 2564-4386 (Print)
ISSN 2564-4394 (Ebook)

Cataloguing-in-Publication data:

Names: Charles A. Cook, editor. | Lorajoy Tira-Dimangondayao, editor. | Lauren Umbach, editor.

Title: Beyond multiculturalism : intentional intercultural congregations as an expression of the kingdom / edited by Charles A. Cook, Lorajoy Tira-Dimangondayao, and Lauren Umbach.

Description: Eugene, OR: Pickwick Publications, 2024 | McMaster Ministry Studies Series 6. | Includes bibliographical references and index.

Identifiers: ISBN 978-1-6667-8370-4 (paperback). | ISBN 978-1-6667-8371-1 (hardcover).| ISBN 978-1-6667-8372-8 (ebook).

Subjects: LCSH: Church. | Church and minorities. | Cultural fusion. | Communities—Religious aspects—Christianity.

Classification: BV600.3 .C66 2024 (print). | BV600.3 (ebook).

09/25/24

Contents

Lists of Contributors | ix
Foreword by Minho Song | xv
Preface | xvii
Acknowledgements | xxi
Introduction by Charles A. Cook | xxiii

PART ONE: FOR KING OR COUNTRY? | 1

Shifting from Multicultural Churches
to an Intercultural Ecclesiology | 3
    SHERMAN LAU

Multicultural Churches as Counter-Narrative in Pluralist Canada:
Our Role as Sign and Foretaste of an Alternative People/Nation | 11
    DAN SHEFFIELD

Changing World, Changing Church | 20
    AMANDA ROSS

PART TWO: TOWARDS KINGDOM CULTURES | 27

What the Peoples of St. Barnabas Church Have Taught Me about Intercultural Preaching: Interruptions, Incarnations, and Invocations | 29
    JENNIFER A. SINGH

Towards a More Intercultural Church: Lessons Learned
from the Royal Canadian Chaplain Service | 40
    THICH TRUONG

The Means of Grace and the Mission of the Church | 51
    JUSTIN BRADBURY

Seeing What the Father is Doing: A Practical and Theological Vineyard Approach to Moving beyond Multiculturalism | 65
    BETH M. STOVELL AND MELT VAN DER SPUY

PART THREE: KINGDOM COLLABORATIONS | 79

Multivocational Ministry in Multicultural Canada | 81
    JAMES W. WATSON

My Journey to Planting a Church of All Nations | 89
    JORGE LIN

A Case Study of Crosspoint Church | 95
    ROB CHARTRAND

Willingdon Church: A Case Study of an Intercultural Church Family | 103
    JOHN BEST

City Church of Winnipeg: A Case Study of a First Generation Intentionally Intercultural Church | 111
    TIM AND SUE NIELSEN

Cross-Congregational and Cross-Generational Ministries: An Intentional Shift for the Canadian Chinese Church | 118
    CALVIN SUN

PART FOUR: FOR KING AND KIN | 127

Diversity: A Means to a Greater End | 129
    ASHWIN RAMANI

The Body of Christ—Becoming Who God Is Calling Us To Be | 135
    VANIA LEVANS

The Correlation between Forgiveness, Reconciliation, and the Trinitarian Unity of the Church and its Impact on Missional Efficacy | 142
    CLINT MIX

The Intercultural Leader | 154
    SAM OWUSU

The Stories We Share: An Intersectional Approach towards Family and Home | 161
    LORAJOY TIRA-DIMANGONDAYAO

Conclusion | 173
    Lorajoy Tira-Dimangondayao and Lauren Umbach

Index of Modern Authors | 177
Index of Ancient Sources | 181

Lists of Contributors

John Best (MDiv), Pastor at Willingdon Church, Burnaby, BC since 2014. His roles have included oversight of International Language Ministries, Global Mission, Online Ministry, and Worship Arts. He has an MDiv from ACTS Seminaries, is married to Christy and has three teenaged children.

Justin Bradbury (PhD), Regional Director for the Wesleyan Church in Western Canada based in Calgary, AB. Previously he and his family organized the International Place of Friendship in Winnipeg, MB, out of which a new multicultural church was planted. His passion is to help position Canadian Christians to embrace new immigrants in friendship and service, and Christian diasporas in shared mission in their new homeland.

Rob Chartrand (DMin), Assistant Professor and Program Coordinator of Christian Ministry at Briercrest College, Caronport, SK. He is the founder and former Lead Pastor of Crosspoint Church in Edmonton, AB. As a Metis Canadian, he is familiar with living in the third-culture space and is passionate about growing multiethnic churches that live in the tension between unity and diversity. He is a graduate of Canadian Theological Seminary (MA in Religion), Briercrest Seminary (MA in Leadership and Management), and Asbury Theological Seminary (DMin).

Charles A. Cook (PhD), Executive Director of the Jaffray Centre for Global Initiatives and Professor of Global Studies and Mission at Ambrose University since 1989. Born to Canadian international workers, he was raised in Colombia, Ecuador, and Peru. Charlie is involved in global Jaffray-related initiatives.

Sherman Lau (PhD), Lead Pastor of Killarney Park MB Church, an intentionally intercultural church in Vancouver, BC and Program Director

Lists of Contributors

of Intercultural Ministry at Pacific Life Bible College in Surrey, BC. He completed a Doctor of Intercultural Studies from Western Seminary in Oregon in 2022.

Vania Levans (MDiv), Pastor, spiritual director, teacher, musician. She graduated in 2006 with an MDiv from Regent College, where she served as the Music and Worship Coordinator 2011–2014. Vania is passionate about encouraging and nurturing sanctification—the life-long process of maturing in Christ and sharing the good news of Christ with others. She enjoys working with and learning from people of other cultures, socio-economic statuses, and ages. She currently serves as the Lead Pastor at Marineview Chapel Christian Community Church in Vancouver, BC.

Jorge Lin, Argentine-Taiwanese-Canadian who is a Church Planting Missionary with the Evangelical Free Church of Canada in New Westminster, BC. Jorge has moved from his heritage in Buddhism to the Christian faith through friends and a series of profound encounters with God, leading to a *mathematical* conclusion that God is real.

Clint Mix (DMin) has served in three denominational roles across Canada with both The Alliance Canada and the Canadian Baptists of Ontario and Quebec. His primary focus has been in the areas of leader and church development and church planting. Additionally, Clint serves as a sessional lecturer at Tyndale, Ambrose, and other seminaries.

Tim and Sue Nielsen were the lead couple in planting City Church of Winnipeg in 2008. They have continued to pastor the church since its inception. The Nielsens have been involved in full time cross-cultural ministry in Winnipeg for the past thirty-four years. Originally, they embraced the ethnic-specific model of church planting, but working in a multicultural city eventually caused them to question both the theological basis and the practical implications of this model. They have spent the past seventeen years working with newly arriving refugees and, in 2017, they were the lead couple in birthing Naomi House, a ministry of City Church that serves as a seven-bedroom transitional home for newly arriving refugees. Naomi House also offers programming and is a Sponsorship Agreement Holder with the Canadian Government.

Sam Owusu (PhD), Founding Senior Pastor of Calvary Worship Center, an international church comprised of 110 nations in Surrey, BC. He is a national and international speaker on culture and change, regularly speaking at Billy Graham Association conferences. Sam is also an Adjunct Professor at Trinity Western University.

Ashwin Ramani (MDiv), Associate Teaching and Community Pastor at Centre Street Church in Calgary, AB. He grew up in South India and came to faith in Christ at the age of seventeen from a Hindu family. Ashwin and his wife Aboli came to Canada in 2009 to pursue his education at Ambrose Seminary. Ashwin has a passion to reach out to people of various faith backgrounds with the gospel. Ashwin and Aboli have four children—Adarsh, Aarav, Amos, and Aviva.

Amanda Ross, pursuing a PhD in Theological Studies at Wycliffe. She is a Euro-Canadian with several years of church and parachurch ministry experience, has witnessed the growing need for a more integrated approach to intercultural and multicultural ministry. Her emerging research in this changing landscape calls upon established communities to respond with humility and a willingness to allow previous viewpoints to be sharpened in light of broadening perspectives and worldwide. She completed an MDiv at Ambrose University in Calgary, AB and a ThM at Wycliffe College in the University of Toronto.

Dan Sheffield, Pastor of a culturally diverse congregation in St. Catharines, ON. Before this current pastorate, he planted a multicultural congregation in post-Apartheid South Africa, researched and wrote a book trying to figure out what they did right and wrong (*The Multicultural Leader*), spent fifteen years as Director of Global & Intercultural Ministries for The Free Methodist Church in Canada, and led a house church community in Hamilton for eight years. He is a McMaster Divinity College graduate and has been an adjunct lecturer at Tyndale Seminary since 2007.

Jennifer Singh (PhD), Assistant Professor of intercultural studies at Ambrose University. Prior to this, Jennifer was involved in international development work and served with Samaritan's Purse Canada, the International Christian Alliance on Prostitution, and Ellilta Women at Risk in a variety of countries, including Cambodia, Uganda, and Ethiopia.

Melt van der Spuy (DMin), Senior Pastor of the multicultural Yellowknife Vineyard Church in the Northwest Territories of Canada and Regional Team Leader of the thirteen Vineyard Churches in the Prairies and Northern Region of Canada. He has served as the Catalyst for theological education of AVC Canada and serves on the National Leadership team

Lists of Contributors

of Vineyard Canada. Melt is a former first-class Rugby player in South Africa, holds an MTh in missions from the University of Stellenbosch and graduated with a DMin from Fuller Seminary in 2021. He has served Senior Pastorates in Kenilworth Vineyard Church in Cape Town and in Yellowknife. He served terms as the Principal of the Evangelical Seminary of Southern Africa and as the Regional Director for Development Associates International (DAI) South Africa. His academic discipline is in the practical theologies of preaching, mission, leadership, and pastoral care. He is a husband to Anida, father to Marie, Simone, Emma, Anele, and Fezisa, and grandfather to Elan.

Beth M. Stovell (PhD), Professor of Old Testament and Chair of General Theological Studies at Ambrose Seminary of Ambrose University. In ministry for over twenty-five years, she works with her husband, Jon, as a national theological consultant for Vineyard Canada. Beth is involved with the Canadian Poverty Institute and the Calgary Alliance for the Common Good.

Calvin Sun, English Pastoral Intern at South Calgary Chinese Evangelical Free Church. He has been a member of the English congregation since 2006 and started interning at his home church in 2019. Before transitioning to full-time church ministry, he was an art director and motion designer for two decades. Calvin was born in Hong Kong but grew up in Canada. As a pastor's kid who moved from city to city, he experienced different Canadian Chinese Church contexts and has a passion for the next generation of Asian Canadian Christians. He is particularly interested in the intersection between faith, technology, art, and play.

Lorajoy Tira-Dimangondayao (BTh) is interested in religion vis-à-vis migration in the Canadian context and is passionate about faith formation in diaspora youth communities. Born in Manila and raised in the Canadian prairies, she is a "1.75 Generation" Filipino Canadian and is fluent in Franglaistaglishspagalog.

Thich Truong, Canadian Armed Forces Chaplain. He is an ordained minister with the Christian and Missionary Alliance in Canada. He served in churches across Canada prior to joining the Canadian Armed Forces in 2017. He started his military career as a part-time Reservist Chaplain with the Calgary Highlanders and transferred to the full-time Regular Force in 2019. He has served at bases in Alberta, Nova Scotia, and now at the CF Chaplain School and Centre in Ontario, training chaplains in military chaplaincy. His foundation in Intercultural Studies at Ambrose Seminary has continued to be an asset to his work as a chaplain as he advocates for the needs and well-being of the diverse soldiers that he serves and cares for in the Canadian Armed Forces.

Lauren Umbach (MA), Research and Program Coordinator for the Jaffray Centre for Global Initiatives at Ambrose University. Prior to this, she worked in Asia for four years. Born in Edmonton, and now living and working in Calgary, Lauren is third-generation German Canadian.

James Watson (PhD) works for The Salvation Army, graduated from McMaster Divinity College with a MDiv, and completed a PhD from Fuller Theological Seminary. He has been involved in national research on immigration, churches, and tentmakers. He lives in Kitchener, ON and teaches in areas of mission and leadership at Tyndale University.

Foreword

Minho Song

More than thirty years ago, when my faith community (Young Nak Korean Presbyterian Church of Toronto) was renting worship space from a primarily Caucasian group of believers in East York, we were at the receiving end of their mercy. We were not the best tenants because our children often ran around rambunctiously in the church, and we adults gave off a strong smell of Kimchi whenever we had our traditional food. Each time the idea of *eviction* came up in the members' meeting, it was Rev. McDonald who came to our rescue. He had been born in Hamhung, North Korea, to a couple serving as Canadian missionaries.

Our church was in East York for fourteen years before we purchased our facility and moved out. We are forever grateful for the hospitality the Canadian congregation has shown us. We now extend our hospitality to several immigrant groups meeting at our church. However, we made clear from the beginning that it would not be a tenant-landlord relationship with them. We have remained as fellow brothers and sisters following the same Master, and we like it! Instead of a set rental fee, they give us free will offerings for missions from time to time. When they give, we accept them and pass them on to needy places. So far, everything has worked out well. Some of them have grown very dear to us.

Beyond Multiculturalism is a sequel to *Beyond Hospitality*. The book addresses the critical topic of going beyond hospitality and multiculturalism. Living in a multicultural society, we constantly ask, "How do we get along as brothers and sisters who are different from us?" or "How do we work with those who are different from us for the sake of the gospel?"

Ultimately, we want to share the gospel in a multicultural society by becoming intentionally intercultural congregations; that is, training our people to intersect with those who are not like us by deliberately entering their lives. Some church members have been practising this *deliberate entering* business. An opportunity came up four years ago to help Yazidi refugees living in the Greater Toronto Area. Our church organized a team and learned about the needs of these refugees. For the past four years, even during the pandemic, the team has been faithful in reaching out to the refugees. The Yazidi team members tell us the importance of intentionally crossing the cultural barrier, without which there cannot be an incarnational ministry.

Multiculturalism can be both a blessing and a curse. While it teaches us to respect and protect those who are different, it can also reinforce staying within our ethnic enclaves. I am glad that *Beyond Multiculturalism* is out. It is timely as it will encourage us to examine what it means to cross cultures without crossing borders. Hopefully, our examination will lead to more meaningful ministries inside and outside our churches.

Preface

ONLY FAMILY MEMBERS CAN know what unfolds in a home and only family members can really know the extent of the stories shared. In Canada, like families, intentionally intercultural congregations forge together relationships with members from diverse worlds as expressions of the kingdom. This, like family, requires that members are encouraged to share their voices, that stories are told in safe places, so that we may join voices to one song. "We cannot know where we are going if we do not know where we are. We cannot chart a future together if we do not know where we are from," counsels Sadiri Joy Tira, diaspora missiology specialist at the Jaffray Centre for Global Initiatives at Ambrose University. We listen to each other's voices as we share our stories so that we may join our stories to one.

Joy Tira's counsel surfaces as we reflect on the stories told and voices heard at the 2021 JaffrayAng Symposium (jaffrayangsymposium.com), convened at the height of the COVID-19 pandemic. In the months following the symposium, Canada's own *family* stories were exposed for all the world to see. In 2021, Canada was forced into *awareness*, and Canada's politeness was revealed to be pretentious. Touting a proudly diverse society on the global stage, Canada, it turns out, does not have adequate *hospitality* to build a home for the peoples of the world who have come together. Contrary to Prime Minister Justin Trudeau's 2015 statement "Diversity is our strength," increasing racial and ethnic diversity has left us with a weed-like plot of increased racial tension, if allowed to establish roots. How does a nation go beyond a reified sense of hospitality and multiculturalism to a people bound together by a sense of community? Of significance to us is the question: How does a local Christian congregation go beyond *government-mandated multiculturalism and hospitality* towards something *more*? How do we cultivate intentional intercultural

Preface

congregations? How does a local congregation go from being a *hospice* to a *home*?

There is an ongoing call by many for local congregations to "go beyond multicultural" particularly as *hospitality* in the service of government-mandated multiculturalism proves incapable of nurturing local church families. The Christian community must expand the modern understanding of hospitality which tends to be a temporary space before one is released into the next phase. Congregations need to move beyond the government labels (e.g., "visible minority") and start using the language of family as we work together to hear all the voices—established Canadians and New Canadians from shore to shore—in our boardrooms, on our platforms, at our dining tables as well as in our pews.

In his 2019 Cadbury Lectures at the University of Birmingham, Protestant theologian Miroslav Volf expounds the concept of "home." He suggests that current society lives in a state of "modern homelessness" with individuals and communities longing for *home* in its greatest sense—a place of dynamic relationships, resonance, wholeness, and fulfilment, a place where one is known and loved. Volf suggests further that, this place, more than a bounded physical and social space, is where Christ followers work together with God to build the ultimate *home* where God dwells with and in people.

In a society known for its pluralism and diversity, for people striving to move beyond the *ships of empire* on a land still reverberating from the trauma of colonialism, how does the local body of Christ followers go *beyond multiculturalism* towards something *more,* towards the *family home*? How can local congregations *go beyond* government mandated multiculturalism to a sense of the ultimate *home*?

The chapters considered in this volume suggest that the intent of reconciled relationships and making a home for all in a postcolonial age prescribes—to use Kwok Pui-Lan's language—a "'pluriphonic,' 'multivocal,' 'symphony,' or 'assembly of voices'" mode of dialogue. Demonstrating an emphasis on multivocality, this book does not aim to articulate a single theory nor does it claim to be an exhaustive study. Rather, it will communicate a variety of perspectives from Canadians, with intentionality as a mode of communicating in a multivocal fashion. This volume, just as we are advocating for our congregations, seeks to be intercultural in nature. More than being a digest of diverse perspectives on going *beyond multiculturalism*, it celebrates a developing song of the Canadian church that is located at the nexus of the national Canadian church, the

Preface

local Evangelical congregation, New Canadians, and the need for *belonging in Christian family*.

It is our greatest hope that in the fullness of time, these preliminary thoughts, lent by multiple voices united in one song, will inform a reflective and robust practice, firmly rooted in the work of Jesus Christ and in his church, for—what Christians believe is—the advance of the kingdom of Christ Jesus. Though the volume may at times appear to read *uneven* from chapter to chapter and may not follow the traditional form of conventional works of academic writing, it has at its aim a goal to communicate authentically and effectively the developing thoughts of the Canadian church family.

Acknowledgements

As with any project of this magnitude, there are many people who have contributed in countless ways to the publication of this book. We are particularly grateful to Dr. Sam Owusu for cohosting the JaffrayAng Beyond Multiculturalism symposium (2021). Dr. Owusu has faithfully advocated for the development of intentional intercultural congregations in Canada and encouraged the Jaffray Centre to explore what it means for the church to move beyond multiculturalism. The Calvary Worship Centre, in Surrey, BC stands as a testimony to his long obedience in nurturing an intentional intercultural community of faith.

A special word of appreciation also goes out to Michael and Rosario Ang family for their lasting contribution to the Jaffray Centre. The JaffrayAng Symposium recognizes the Ang family's rich legacy of domestic and international missional influence through their transnational work. In many ways, the ideas and concerns addressed in this book represent several of the realities they faced over years as New Canadians.

To those who supported this project behind the scenes, we are deeply indebted for their valuable contribution. We are particularly grateful to the Jaffray Centre's Diaspora Network convener, Dr. Sadiri Joy Tira, for his ongoing passion to see greater integration of diaspora Christian community into our national dialogue. To that end, we are also indebted to each of the presenters and participants to the 2021 JaffrayAng Symposium for their engagement with the material online during the height of the COVID pandemic. The commitment to prepare, present, and then share their work is appreciated.

Finally, we acknowledge our gratitude to the folks at McMaster Divinity College Press for their encouragement and assistance in bringing this little volume to fruition. We trust that *Beyond Multiculturalism* will contribute to the ongoing dialogue regarding the complex issues

Acknowledgements

associated with developing intentional intercultural church in multicultural Canada.

Charles A. Cook,
Lorajoy Tira-Dimangondayao,
and Lauren Umbach

Introduction

Charles A. Cook

Perhaps my church is a lot like yours—an increasing multicultural mosaic of Jesus followers from a variety of places around the globe. For the better part of fifty years, Canadian churches have quietly benefited from the gradual influence of immigrant believers who, having come to Canada for various reasons, have brought with them a vibrant faith in God.

We are living at a time where the currents of global Christianity no longer flow as robustly through Canada and other Western nations as they once did. Therefore, it should not come as a surprise that, at this point in history, the face of Christianity is changing. Today the *typical* contemporary Christian is more likely to be a woman living in a village in Nigeria or in a Brazilian *favela*. Kenyan scholar John Mbiti reminds us that "the centers of the church's universality [are] no longer in Geneva, Rome, Athens, Paris, London, New York, but in Kinshasa, Buenos Aires, Addis Ababa, and Manila."[1] All indications are that Christianity has moved to the Global South and is doing very well—not just holding its own but growing.

As the church in Canada continues to recalibrate for mission and ministry in the twenty-first century, it needs to be attentive to a number of shifting new realities. Migration in Canada continues to increase, and so too does diversity. Ongoing immigration coupled with growing ethnic tensions are compelling congregations to reflect and confront a number of accelerating new realities; realities that have converged and

---

1. Jenkins, *Next Christendom*, 2.

are shaping a dynamic new conversation around the necessity to explore what becoming intentionally intercultural churches might look like in a multicultural Canada.

EMERGENCE OF WORLD CHRISTIANITY

The twentieth century saw the Christian centre gradually shift from the northern regions of our world to Africa, Asia, and Latin America. Lesslie Newbigin observed that the modern missionary movement took its rise in a period when the tide of political power, of economic and cultural expansion, was flowing out from Western Europe and North America into other parts of the world.[2] That flow steadily diminished throughout the latter half of the twentieth century, as the church in the Majority World took on new life and established itself as a genuine global faith.

Unquestionably, one of the more significant influences has been the southern global expansion of Christianity over the last quarter century. The growth of the church in the Global South has spawned the emergence of a younger, larger, indigenous church that is outpacing the church in the Global North. This shift has meant that the historic Euro-Canadian church has had to learn to navigate an increasingly flat, more interconnected world, in concert with our global church family. In essence, the past recipients of the gospel are now co-labours and partners as together we engage in the work of God around the globe.

MIGRATION AND CULTURAL DIVERSITY

The emergence of world Christianity coupled with an increase in global migration has created a unique situation for the church in Canada. We live in a world where millions of people are on the move, living in countries other than where they were originally born. Increasingly, many Christians from the Global South, looking for a better life for their families, are migrating to the north. The effect is that the mission of God in the twenty-first century is no longer primarily a western enterprise, but a collaborative global effort. Mission is now from "everywhere to everyone."[3]

Nowhere is this more evident than here in Canada. As a nation of immigrants, the Canadian socio-cultural landscape continues to change

2. Newbigin, *Word in Season*, 7.
3. See Escobar, *New Global Mission*.

Introduction

as immigration shapes the makeup of our country. The 2021 Canadian census highlighted that nearly one-in-four Canadians were born outside of the country accounting for 23 percent of the population.[4] In 2016, that percentage had been 21.9 percent, and statistics suggest that this upward trend will continue. It is anticipated, by 2041, over one third of Canadians, or 34 percent, will be foreign-born.[5] Interestingly, many New Canadians will continue to come from Christian regions of the world.

Further influencing our national reality is the fact that non-Christian faiths are also on the move. Once in Canada, New Canadian immigrants also assert their influence in a nation that celebrates multiculturalism and accepts pluralism. The continual steady flow of New Canadians bringing their cultural diversity and religious perspectives is forcing the church in Canada to develop a deeper understanding of their faith. This calls many Christians to a renewed commitment to a life in Christ that is authentic, and to develop the skills and knowledge needed to articulate the claims of Christ in meaningful ways to a culturally and religiously diverse population right in their own neighborhoods.

RESPONSE TO CULTURAL DIVERSITY

Given this new environment, Canadian congregations must be more attentive in their response to these shifting realities. Perhaps a starting point might be to identify how the church can engage around the conversation of ethnic diversity.

Multiculturalism has been part of the Canadian narrative for the better part of half a century. Often framed as a "Canadian advantage," multiculturalism is an ideal that has caused us to stand out as a desired destination for many immigrants. In many ways, the Canadian government policy has provided a framework that encourages Canadians to be accepting and welcoming of the Other. Multiculturalism provides the church with an opportunity to live out its faith by moving beyond the rhetoric of multiculturalism to a deeper level of embrace of the ethnic Other in an intentional act of intercultural mutuality.

I propose that the only institution in society which has *any chance of developing the intercultural framework* is the church—a *spirit-filled church* under the *lordship of Jesus* infused *with the kingdom values* able to address

4. "Immigrants."
5. "Canada in 2041."

Introduction

many of society's intractable challenges. After all, the message emanating from the cross and the empty grave is that Christ overcame and destroyed all barriers, including the barriers caused by culture. The church, the community of faith, is the only institution in contemporary society with the spirit and the means to embrace the cultural Other and break through the power of cultural fragmentation. Building an intercultural community then, requires that we engage the Other by seeking to understand their worldview. Being attentive, we can apply Christ's inexhaustible wisdom to understanding the strengths and weaknesses of cultures as a means of being able to take on the full measure of what God has intended our life in Christ to be. Perhaps then, society would take notice of the church in a more positive light.

EPHESIAN MOMENT

All these twenty-first-century realities have coalesced to set the stage for what late missiologist Andrew Walls suggested might be a *return of the Ephesian moment*.[6] Reflecting on the book of Ephesians, he makes a compelling argument for the importance of diversity in the local church. Local communities of faith, Walls believes, are enriched when they move beyond their culture-specific understanding of God to embrace a much richer, fuller understanding of the Father in more diverse intercultural communities. Diverse communities which focus on our mutual edification in Christ, and intentional interpersonal communion (around meals and fellowship), nurture a more mature, shared, understanding of Christ. For Walls, "The full-grown humanity of Christ requires all Christian generations, just as it embodies all the cultural variety that six continents can bring."[7] That, in essence, we only fully understand the fullness of Christ by interacting with Christians of other cultures.

While Walls acknowledges that we still need to be ourselves, he also believed that the welcoming of the *Ephesian moment* highlights the fact that we need to move beyond our primarily monocultural communities to welcome the ethnic Other; as we in our congregations work to fully grasp the fullness of Christ and multi-faceted grandeur of God.

---

6. See Walls's essay titled "Ephesian Moment" (*Cross-Cultural Process*, 72–81).
7. Walls, *Missionary Movement*, xvii.

Introduction

NEW BREED OF INBETWEENER

In order to embrace the Ephesian moment, we need a new breed of Jesus follower. People willing to stand up as *inbetweeners* to advocate for intentional intercultural congregations. This idea of being an "inbetweener" flows from the reality that we need to extend the gift of understanding and make space in our lives to develop friendship with those who are the Other. After all, the Other, like us, is created in the image of God and is of infinite value to God.

A candid assessment of our own attitudes would likely reveal that all too often we allow the spirit of the age rather than the essence of the gospel to shape our attitudes towards the Other. This tendency manifests itself in who we give deference to, who assumes power, and who—individuals or groups—exerts unfair privilege over another. Yet these human-centred approaches that exalt one group over another need to be challenged and measured against the message of the gospel. Jesus ultimately calls us to be servants not masters. To be concerned for the Other and not to be consumed with ourselves: this is the role of the inbetweener.

So, why become an inbetweener? The short answer: Love. The apostle Paul reminds us that Christ's love is what ultimately compels us to be concerned for the Other (2 Cor 5:14). If we belong to Christ, his love is at work in us. Jesus, early on in the Gospels, summarizes the teaching of the law in terms of the greatest commandments—Love God and love others (see Matt 22:37–39). In Jesus, the love of God was expressed towards us, his fallen and alienated creation. Our acknowledgement of his love at work in and through us enables us to express compassion and generosity towards the Other. This is a truth so aptly expressed in that great neighbor loving passage, the parable of the Good Samaritan (Luke 10:25–37).

A CANADIAN RESPONSE TO MOVE US BEYOND THE MULTICULTURAL CHURCH

The question becomes how do we live this out in our churches? Communities of faith have largely approached this diversity through an ethic of hospitality: Euro-Canadians have readily welcomed newcomers into existing congregations. However, with this approach, newcomers are rarely fully integrated into the life and leadership of the congregation. In this volume we suggest that Christians need to move beyond hospitality towards understanding what welcoming the Other means for us today. But,

Introduction

as varied cultural expressions of Christianity emerge across Canada, new and established Canadian congregations alike, need to explore innovative ways to move beyond historic cultural, linguistic, and racial silos towards greater collaboration and deeper covenantal unity so that the world will see and believe the transforming nature of the gospel.

Most Canadian churches have diverse congregations, and many intentionally celebrate the cultures of their congregants. They have adopted a multicultural perspective, recognizing diversity as a "fundamental characteristic of Canadian society," and participating in "preserv[ing] and enhanc[ing] [Canadian] multicultural heritage."[8] However, while they may have multiple ethnicities represented within their congregations, most churches tend to be organized and led by one prominent ethnic or cultural value system (Euro-Canadian, Chinese Canadian, etc.). Although these churches may value tolerance and celebrate one another's cultural distinctiveness, the engagement tends toward superficial and polite social interaction. Because of this lack of deep cultural understanding of the Other, power differentials are often not addressed reducing the opportunity for authentic and meaningful exchanges between cultural groups. Inadvertently, then, these churches reinforce tendencies toward tribalism and prejudices latent in western culture. Congregations need to move beyond traditional Canadian understandings of multiculturalism and work towards becoming intentionally intercultural; demonstrating that multicultural diversity can be inclusive.

These intercultural—not simply multicultural—congregations create spaces where all are welcomed and valued equally, and where all are involved in designing, developing, and leading the community. This means congregations need to look beyond their own cultural perspectives about how they do church and engage with the Other. Intercultural congregations take us deeper than multicultural models of community, as there is more comprehensive mutuality, reciprocity, and equality. The social structures and everyday interactions of an intercultural church revolve around relationship building. Deep connections, mutual respect, and learning from one another are intentionally fostered, and people of different cultures are welcomed into positions of authority and encouraged to bring their unique cultural perspectives to the table.

---

8. *Canadian Multiculturalism Act.*

Introduction

THE TRAJECTORY OF THIS BOOK

Beyond Multiculturalism, in many ways, continues to engage the themes discussed in our previous volume *Beyond Hospitality*. There we advocated for communities of faith that moved beyond simple acts of hospitality in an effort to engage more intentionally with immigrants and welcome them into vibrant congregational communities. Continuing to reflect on intentionally welcoming the Other, in *Beyond Multiculturalism*, we examine what this might look like as communities of faith move beyond a multicultural posture in order to become more intentionally intercultural communities of faith.

Before we delve into this theme, let me simply begin by making two observations. First, we want to underscore that the intercultural church is but one of many expressions of the church, and that these other expressions have served, and no doubt will continue to serve, their communities. Secondly, I recognize that this theme is perhaps not top of mind for many church leaders. Nevertheless, it is an important conversation we need to be having within the community of faith in Canada, particularly given the continuing changes.

The topics discussed in this volume are designed to move a much-needed conversation in the church further. It is an encouragement to get church leaders and congregants to examine closely held assumptions. How can intentionally intercultural congregations move us beyond multiculturalism towards inclusive communities of faith who reflect kingdom life? This curated collection intentionally includes a diverse range of voices, both new and established. These authors represent different generations, genders, ethnicities, regions in Canada, academic and vocational experiences, and denominational backgrounds, among other unique factors. We are convinced that it is only in giving voice to diversity within our communities that valuable insights are generated, which enables us to work together to bridge across differences and break down divisions. It is through the process of sharing stories and our diverse experiences that we can learn and grow together as an inclusive and welcoming Church.

Beyond Multiculturalism presents various theological, sociological, and pragmatic elements churches need to attend to as they seek to move toward greater relevancy; catching the wave of what God is doing across Canada and around the world. The book is divided into four sections, each reflecting on different aspects of what it means to go beyond multiculturalism. In Part One: For King or Country? the authors explore our

Introduction

allegiance to King Jesus and the reality of kingdom values expressed as family, as opposed to Canadian values espoused by the country. As you read these chapters challenging us to think deeper and differently about the multicultural church, we invite you to reflect on how this applies to your ministry context. In Part Two: Towards Kingdom Cultures, you will hear the voices of authors who describe Kingdom cultures in their communities, highlighting the integral roles of mutuality and multivocality. Although their ministry contexts may look very different than yours, what concepts could be applied to your community? The third section, Part Three: Kingdom Collaborations, is a collection of stories reflecting the experiences of several communities of faith in different stages of moving towards being intentionally intercultural congregations. As you read their stories where they share the joys and challenges of their journeys, we invite you to reflect on what you can learn from their experiences. Finally, in Part Four: For King and Kin, several authors present a call for honest, though difficult, introspection, as well as Spirit-guided action. This is a simple yet profound undertaking—requiring self-giving action that prefers the model of King Jesus and preferences kin in Christ over self and tribe. How can we take intentional steps to move towards greater unity in the body of Christ?

As you read these voices and chapters, we invite you to join us in the conversation and reflect on how the authors' stories, insights, and experiences relate to your own and can influence and shape your own life and ministry in your multicultural contexts.

BIBLIOGRAPHY

"Canada in 2041: A Larger, More Diverse Population with Greater Differences between Regions." *Statistics Canada*. No pages. Online: https://www150.statcan.gc.ca/n1/daily-quotidien/220908/dq220908a-eng.htm.

Escobar, Samuel. *The New Global Mission: The Gospel from Everywhere to Everyone*. Downers Grove, IL: InterVarsity, 2003.

"Immigrants Make Up the Largest Share of the Population in over 150 Years and Continue to Shape Who We Are as Canadians." *Statistics Canada*. No pages. Online: https://www150.statcan.gc.ca/n1/daily-quotidien/221026/dq221026a-eng.htm.

Jenkins, Philip. *The Next Christendom: The Coming of Global Christianity*. New York: Oxford University Press, 2002.

Multiculturalism and Citizenship Canada. *The Canadian Multiculturalism Act*. Ottawa: Ministry of Justice, 1985.

Introduction

Newbigin, Lesslie. *A Word in Season: Perspectives on Christian World Missions*. Grand Rapids: Eerdmans, 1994.
Walls, Andrew F. *The Cross-Cultural Process in Christian History: Studies in the Transmission and Appropriation of Faith*. Maryknoll, NY: Orbis, 2002.
———. *The Missionary Movement in Christian History: Studies in the Transmission of Faith*. Maryknoll, NY: Orbis, 1996.

Part One

For King or Country?

Some have suggested that in Canada "diversity is our strength"; in actuality, however, our increasing racial and ethnic diversity may have us positioned on a precarious path, which unattended or ignored, leaves our nation and congregations open to increased multicultural tension. The lack of social cohesion is increasingly apparent in local churches as Christians from non-European backgrounds become more vocal about their need to be heard, and as Euro-Canadian Christians are being held accountable for historic power differentials. In light of this discussion, there is a need for local congregations to *go beyond multicultural*. There must be something *more* to our communities of faith than the modern understanding of *hospitality*. How do we live counter-culturally and genuinely welcome the other into our communities as equal participants?

The chapters in the first section explore our allegiance to King Jesus and the reality of kingdom values expressed as family, as opposed to Canadian values espoused by the country. As you read these chapters challenging us to think deeper and differently about the multicultural church, we invite you to reflect on how this applies to your ministry context.

Shifting from Multicultural Churches to an Intercultural Ecclesiology

Sherman Lau

THE MULTICULTURAL CHURCH DEBATE

THE EFFICACY AND RELEVANCE of the multicultural church[1] has been debated for close to twenty years, as such ecclesial expressions are few and far between, as well as short-lived. Mark Naylor of the Center for Intercultural Leadership Development, for example, states, "While applauding this vision, supporting the effort, and sympathizing with the intercultural struggles that inevitably arise, I would like to take issue with those who promote this form of local church as more in conformity with the New Testament ideal than other less ethnically diverse churches."[2] He contends that upholding multicultural congregations as the *true* church over and against monocultural congregations promotes an "either/or" approach instead of the body of Christ as *both* universal church *and* local congregation which allows for a *truer multicultural* expression of the

1. Advocates for the multicultural or multiethnic church, such as Mark DeYmaz, author of *Building a Healthy Multi-ethnic Church*, and Soong-Chan Rah, author of *Many Colors* and *Next Evangelicalism*, propose that the future of the Christian church in North America will lie with multicultural churches. The terms are used interchangeably to describe diverse congregations which are not segregated by ethnicity, gender, nor economics status.

2. Naylor refers to the move towards intentionally "multicultural churches" based on the eschatological vision of Rev 5:9 and 7:9 to become a microcosm of that grand event in this age ("Navigating the Multicultural Maze").

Christian faith. In contrast, Sam Owusu, lead pastor of Calvary Worship Center, the largest multicultural church in greater Vancouver, BC, presented the following apologetic at the Symposium for Intentionally Multicultural Churches in 2002:

> What does it mean for the church of Jesus Christ to live and make its witness in a multicultural world? Our world, our nation, and our communities are rapidly changing around us. And the church finds itself as the bewildered cultural bystander to this multicultural change . . . Why bewildered? If the truth were told, most Christian congregations are homogeneous and ethnocentric . . . How the church of Jesus Christ deals with the rapidity and the complexity of this multicultural, postmodern ethos will tell the world whether it has reason to listen to the message we proclaim . . . We should not pursue racial or cultural diversity simply because it is politically correct, or it is the latest theological fad. We should do it because it is the gospel.[3]

Owusu's idea of the multicultural church is appealing and overdue in the Canadian context *for the sake of the gospel*. Multicultural churches do serve as pragmatic witnesses of God's heart for the nations. Moreover, our governments, hospitals, schools, and corporations have already incorporated the Canadian mosaic of ethnic diversity through the policy of multiculturalism; ergo, we would expect our churches to follow suit. However, unlike the institutions identified above, the multicultural fellowship of the saints does not merely serve as an illustration of inclusion. *Rather, it is the representation and living testimony of God's people who are intentionally living out kingdom unity amidst diversity in Jesus Christ, evidenced by our commitment to "one Lord, one faith, one baptism"* (Eph 4:5, ESV).

The challenge for Canadian churches to experience kingdom unity amidst diversity lies with the ontological reality and social policy of multiculturalism, which, ironically, is what motivates us to be hospitable and welcoming to the alien and stranger. However, the values of Canadian multiculturalism—accommodation, tolerance, and co-existence—are contrary to achieving a kingdom-inspired intercultural community. Reflect on these values as follows: *accommodation* is functionally to make or share space with the stranger without creating a sense of belonging; *tolerance* is the acknowledgment of the other's values, beliefs, or practices without true acceptance or understanding; and *co-existence* promotes the

---

3. Owusu, "What Color Is your God?" 3.

idea of equality at the cost of genuine commonality. Thus, Canada's multicultural policy creates a false solidarity amongst Christians in Canada, *promoting instead Christian ethnocentrism coupled with a historical legacy of ethnic marginalization.*

CANADA'S JOURNEY TO MULTICULTURALISM

Adopted in 1971, the "Canadian Multiculturalism Act" formalized the government's commitment to promote "the full and *equitable* participation of individuals and communities of all origins in the continuing evolution and shaping of all aspects of Canadian society."[4] Functionally, the Act, "presented multiculturalism as a positive instrument of change, to *remove barriers* that preclude the involvement, equity, and representation of all citizens in Canadian institutions, as well access to these institutions."[5] Incidentally, the Act coincided with a shift in immigration trends for 1971, as, for the first time, the majority of new immigrants were of non-European ancestry, a precedent that has persisted ever since.[6]

The "Canadian Multiculturalism Act" was then integrated into the "Canadian Charter of Rights and Freedoms" on July 21, 1988. This policy not only recognized the diversity of Canada both in ethnicity and culture, but also placed multiculturalism as a high value: clauses 3(1)(a) and 3(1)(b) of "Bill C–93," which recognizes the cultural diversity of Canada, state that Canadians are free to *preserve and share their cultural heritage* and affirm that multiculturalism is a fundamental characteristic of Canadian identity.[7] In short, to be Canadian is to be multicultural.

However, there is a dark side and inconsistency to the story of Canada's journey towards multiculturalism and policy of accommodation which is the myth of equality. The legacy of systemic racism endured by Indigenous peoples, black, Chinese, South Asian, and Japanese communities before, during, and after the country's founding is well documented. Moreover, in British Columbia, the global coronavirus pandemic revived anti-Asian racism, as incidents of verbal harassment, hate crimes, and violence surged by 717 percent towards individuals of Asian descent.[8]

4. Jedwab, "Multiculturalism" (italics mine).
5. Brousseau and Dewing, *Canadian Multiculturalism*, 4 (italics original).
6. Jedwab, "Multiculturalism" (italics mine).
7. *Canadian Multiculturalism Act*, 13 (italics mine).
8. "Canada Has a Serious Anti-Asian Racism Problem."

Part One: For King or Country?

The sad reality of Canada's multicultural policy is that it is adhered to in principle but not necessarily in practice. Said another way, *that Canada has a multicultural policy does not necessarily mean that every person is multicultural.* The most common charge against multiculturalism is that it undermines the cohesion and shared identity that a society needs, which is antithetical to its purpose. Furthermore, "multiculturalist provisions privilege some communities at the expense of others, and they depart from the liberal-democratic commitments to the equal treatment of all individuals and to individual rights and liberties."[9]

The main contention of immigrants by "established" English or French speaking Canadians is that they choose to speak their own ethnic languages or wear traditional dress in public. They tend to see immigrants as ignorant of Canadian cultural practices and unwilling to "act like Canadians," and they express discomfort with the changes in Canadian society that have been brought about by immigration.[10] This last reaction has seen legislation introduced in Quebec, known as "Bill 21," which bans public servants from wearing "religious symbols" and has been interpreted as discrimination against Muslims and Sikhs, for whom the *hijab* and *kirpan* are not only part of their religious identity but also something that defines their ethnic identity.[11] Whose natural rights and freedoms do we protect in this instance?

Safwat Marzouk, author of *Intercultural Church*, states, "Although multiculturalism is a great step towards accepting cultural and linguistic difference, the concern is that people will end up forming islands within the same community while avoiding deep engagement with one another."[12] Studying the epistemology of multiculturalism, especially within the Canadian context, it is not in the best interest of the Canadian church to form—by ensuring that our individual religious rights and freedoms are protected—accommodating and tolerant congregations that co-exist together. Our interest should be in formulating an intercultural ecclesiology which is a "church that fosters a just diversity, integrates different cultural articulations of faith and worship, and embodies in the world an alternative to the politics of assimilation and segregation."[13]

---

9. Crowder, *Theories of Multiculturalism*, 11.
10. Francis et al., *Destinies*, 454.
11. Wells, "Battle."
12. Marzouk, *Intercultural Church*, 118–19.
13. Marzouk, *Intercultural Church*, 3.

INVOLVEMENT, EMPATHY, AND COMMONNESS

Canada's multicultural policy is something to appreciate and be proud of. But it falls short of the kingdom ideal that God has for his *ecclesia* (or "called out" ones [Mark 3:13]). As Jesus' disciples, we have been called out from our ethnocentrism to be his representatives and ambassadors (2 Cor 5:20). Furthermore, we are no longer to be conformed to this world but to be transformed by the renewing of our minds (Rom 12:2). God's expectation is that his people do not merely incorporate the ways of the world in thought and action but will choose to do better. The disciples as *ecclesia* were called out from Jerusalem to be witnesses of the good news, crossing ethnic, social, and religious barriers in order to establish an intercultural relationship with God. This is the cost of following Jesus (Luke 9:23). Thus, the alternative to the cultural values of accommodation, tolerance, and co-existence are the kingdom practices of involvement, empathy, and commonness.

A review of the Old and New Testaments will reveal that the God of the Israelites was very involved in his creation and with his people. In the garden of Eden, God is described as interacting with Adam, and he is so concerned that Adam has no suitable mate; so, he creates one for him (Gen 2:18). Later, the Exodus narrative describes in detail God's promise to Abraham by rescuing his descendants from Egypt, protecting them in the desert and providing them with a land to call their own. At the consecration of the priests, God proclaims that he will dwell among the people of Israel and will be their God (Exod 29:45). However, the Israelites demand a human king and forsake God; yet he remains involved as he counsels Samuel on the selection process (1 Sam 9). Despite the Israelites' continued disobedience and rejection, God continues to send prophets to call them to repentance and to turn from their evil ways (Zech 1:4). God warns of judgment and sorrow, and yet proclaims the coming of the Savior who will redeem both the Israelites and the world from their sin (Zech 9:9–13). God's involvement is not limited to his interaction with his people but also extended to an expectation of his people towards the sojourner. God commands the Israelites, his chosen people, to show respect and love to the sojourner who lived amongst them (Lev 19:33). This ethic of mercy contrasted with the norm to take advantage of or exploit the sojourner. Furthermore, the foreigner is to be afforded the same rights and freedoms as inhabitants of the host culture (Deut 17:9).

PART ONE: FOR KING OR COUNTRY?

Moreover, John 4:1–42 encapsulates the importance of empathy in building acceptance and, ultimately, trust. Jesus does not stand on accepted protocol but instead crosses geographic, gender, and cultural barriers to intentionally interact with the Samaritan woman at the well. This involvement would have made Jesus unclean and required stringent temple cleansing rites to be "made right" before God. The good news of this narrative is that Jesus focused on the person rather than the circumstance and provided space for them to be loved by God. In the same way, sojourners and aliens in our midst who already feel excluded, exploited, or oppressed and for the church to continue to do so, contributes to their further feelings of rejection. *Communities of faith need to do better at creating not only welcoming spaces but belonging spaces.*

Lastly, Canadian multiculturalism encourages citizens to preserve and share their ethnic heritages. Thus, we celebrate Ramadan, the Lunar New Year, Diwali, Hanukkah, Christmas, Kwanza, Greek Day, Italian Day, and other numerous religious or cultural holidays. In participating in these festivities, we are introduced to the foods, language, and culture of the mosaic of Canada. Churches who have incorporated this multicultural practice of integration host international potlucks, invite members to share their ethnic culture, and even invite them to pray in their mother tongue. These opportunities are wonderful approaches to building community, but do they *really* disciple us to be intercultural persons or establish genuine commonness?

In John 11:1–44, Jesus goes to see Mary and Martha because their brother Lazarus had died. The theme of death prevails throughout the Old and New Testaments, especially after the disobedience of Adam and Eve. Immediately after their expulsion, there is death in the family, with the murder of Abel by Cain. God, however, spares Cain's life (Gen 3:15). This is the first post-Fall instance of God's mercy, not wrath. Later chapters of Genesis record the narrative of the Flood that caused the deaths of thousands. But God saves Noah and his family to repopulate the earth. In Exod 12, we learn of the origins of Passover—God struck Egypt with the tenth plague killing all firstborn male children. God instructs Moses on how to protect the children of Israel with the sacrifice of a lamb and to spread its blood on the doorposts, that the Spirit may "pass over." It is with this final plague that Pharaoh relents and releases the Hebrews.

However, through the prophet Ezekiel, we know that death is not the final word for God's people. God imparts Ezekiel with a vision of the valley of dry bones, which represents the dead body of Israel. It is God's breath that will restore these dry bones to life, and this restoration of the nation will be cause for *true* celebration (Ezek 37:11–14). It is Jesus' breath who restores Lazarus to life when he cries out, "Lazarus, come out" (John 11:43, ESV). The death and resurrection of Lazarus is a precursor to the death and resurrection of Jesus that is witnessed by Mary, Martha, and his disciples, once again, showing God's involvement in his creation. In his earthly form, Jesus did not merely co-exist with his family, disciples, his close friends, or the crowd. He built genuine commonness, and nothing is more common to all than death. For genuine commonness to exist in an intercultural ministry, we must heed his command: "If anyone would come after me, let him deny himself and take up his cross daily and follow me. For whoever would save his life will lose it, but whoever loses his life for my sake will save it" (Luke 9:23–24, ESV).

Again, celebrating the foods, language, and culture that make up the mosaic of Canada is wonderful. But churches who aspire to a kingdom-inspired intercultural ethic also need to put to death our ethno-cultural approaches to homily and liturgy, tribalism, and fear. It gives us fear when we think that our ethnic heritage will be forgotten or assimilated. That's why we settle for co-existence to protect our identity. However, as the verses above have shown, for God, death is not the end but the opportunity for something new to arise, which is so much better. Genuine commonness is achieved when, in dialogue, we share our fears as well as hopes.

This chapter has addressed the efficacy of multicultural congregations when they are influenced by the Canadian multicultural values of accommodation, tolerance, and co-existence. By incorporating these multicultural values, these congregations attempt to make space, acknowledge differing values, beliefs, and practices while treating one another as equals *except when there is a power imbalance*. Intercultural ecclesiology in the Canadian multicultural context is achieved when we shift from accommodation to involvement, tolerance to empathy, and co-existence to commonness. The body of Christ was not called to be tolerant or accommodating, nor to, least of all, co-exist with one another. Rather, the body as God's New humanity is to be a diverse community, called out from our ethnocentrism as witnesses to the power of God to redeem and restore broken relationships with him and one another in a multi-ethnic and multi-faith reality.

PART ONE: FOR KING OR COUNTRY?

BIBLIOGRAPHY

Brousseau, Laurence, and Michael Dewing. *Canadian Multiculturalism*. Ottawa: Library of Parliament, 2018.

"Canada Has a Serious Anti-Asian Racism Problem and It's Time to Address It." *Daily Hive*, March 30, 2021. No pages. Online: https://dailyhive.com/vancouver/anti-asian-racism-canada.

Multiculturalism and Citizenship Canada. *The Canadian Multiculturalism Act: A Guide for Canadians*. Ottawa: Ministry of Justice, 1990.

Crowder, George. *Theories of Multiculturalism: An Introduction*. Cambridge: Polity, 2013.

DeYmaz, Mark. *Building a Healthy Multi-Ethnic Church: Mandate, Commitments, and Practices of a Diverse Congregation*. San Francisco: Jossey-Bass, 2007.

Francis, R. Douglas, et al. *Destinies: Canadian History Since Confederation*. 5th ed. Toronto: Nelson, 2004.

Jedwab, Jack. "Multiculturalism." *The Canadian Encyclopedia*. (Mar 20, 2020). No pages. Online: https://www.thecanadianencyclopedia.ca/en/article/multiculturalism.

Marzouk, Safwat. *Intercultural Church: A Biblical Vision for an Age of Migration*. Minneapolis: Fortress, 2019.

Naylor, Mark. "Navigating the Multicultural Maze: Setting an Intercultural Agenda for FEBBC/Y Churches." In *Being Church: Explorations in Christian Community*, edited by Larry Perkins, 13–42. Langley, BC: Northwest Baptist Seminary, 2007.

Owusu, Sam. "What Color Is your God?" Paper presented at the Symposium on Intentionally Multicultural Churches, Langley, BC, June 7, 2002.

Rah, Soong-Chan. *Many Colors: Cultural Intelligence for a Changing Church*. Chicago, Moody, 2010.

———. *The Next Evangelicalism: Freeing the Church from Western Cultural Captivity*. Downers Grove, IL: InterVarsity, 2009.

Wells, Paul. "The Battle against Quebec's Bill 21." *MacLean's*, November 8, 2019. No pages. Online: https://www.macleans.ca/news/canada/the-teachers-taking-on-quebecs-bill-21.

Multicultural Churches as Counter-Narrative in Pluralist Canada

Our Role as Sign and Foretaste of an Alternative People/Nation

Dan Sheffield

Our society is asking for *something more* on a massive scale, and we as Christians are cowering. Our collective Christian guilt about how organized religion got so much, so wrong, has led either to paralyzing inertia on social concerns, or defensive retreat into self-justification. At this particular *kairos* moment of reckoning, however, we need to do better. Forty years ago, Parker Palmer identified that "public life has withered, and private life has become anxious and obsessive."[1] He goes on to say, "the church could become a kind of halfway house between the comforts of private life and the challenges of diversity—but only if it can stay open to strangeness and help us experience our differences within the context of a common faith."[2]

In our fractured and divisive society, can Christian congregations live out the truth of the gospel in such a way that these divisions are broken down via reconciled relationships? In our polarized, *woke*, virtue-signaling society, where are the *brave spaces* to actually enter into meaningful dialogue and reconciliation? When the wider society refuses to listen to our words any longer, can/do multicultural churches serve

---

1. Palmer, *Company of Strangers*, 35.
2. Palmer, *Company of Strangers*, 31.

as sign and foretaste (*arrabon*)—as an apologetic—for the truth of the reconciling gospel?

OUR SOUTH AFRICA STORY

In the fall of 1989, my wife and I moved to South Africa to spend a year teaching at a Bible college. It was a unique, unexpected opportunity. I had spent years studying and preparing for ministry in the Muslim Middle East. My only introduction to South Africa was James Michener's novel, *The Covenant*, and a few news articles here and there. As the Berlin Wall was being dismantled in Germany in the fall of 1989, F. W. de Klerk began to dismantle Apartheid, unbanning the ANC (African National Congress) and releasing Nelson Mandela in February 1990. Those were heady, jubilant days.

After several years pastoring in Canada, we returned to South Africa in 1994, on the heels of Mandela's election as president, to plant a multicultural congregation. We were invited by the black leadership of our denomination in South Africa to "try" this experiment, during those early, optimistic days of the *reconstruction* of civil society. Five years later, we left behind a congregation of 120 attendees, representing multiple cultures. At one point, the congregation's leadership team included people from seven different cultures and five languages. Urban mission engagement led to the development of an affordable housing company and women's shelter for domestic violence victims.[3]

We made mistakes, struggled together, laughed together, and had a clear sense of working hard at building a faith community that would pose as an alternative to the Apartheid churches—whites only, blacks only, coloreds only, or Indians only. In so doing, we experienced the very real possibility of Christians from multiple cultures intentionally breaking down barriers to be a sign of something different in a racially and culturally fractured society.

OUR ST. CATHARINES STORY

Fast forward twenty years, and I find myself pastoring a culturally diverse congregation again, but with very different players in a vastly different social context. Our seventy-ish sized congregation is made up of black

---

3. Sheffield and Sheffield, "Ubunye Church."

Africans recently arrived, black Caribbean backgrounds not so recently arrived, Indians, South Koreans, Laotians, Mandarin-speaking Chinese, and a few white Euro-Canadians around the edges. BIPOC (Black, Indigenous, and other People of Color) represent two-thirds of our congregation. One third of the adults, of all backgrounds, have a master's degree or higher. In a tier-3 city of 135,000, our congregation is unique in intentionally including diverse voices in our public worship and at the highest decision-making tables. Many of our people come from settings where "Christendom" is flourishing; so, they are struggling in godless, no-religious-affiliation, Canada. We do not have hipster-ish millennials asking us to renegotiate our belief spectrum "so I can persuade my friends to come back to church."

When asked why they have chosen to become part of this culturally diverse faith community, our people have several responses: "I came to Canada to study and learn. Yes, I can attend a church of my own people, our own language, but there I wouldn't be entering into this new place. It's challenging, but I wouldn't have it any other way"; "I think this is the way Jesus would want us to be—not separate but together"; "My kids are going to grow up here, I want them to experience the differences and make friends from different backgrounds"; "When I came here, I found people like myself leading worship, and I found people of other cultures who came up freely and talked to me. I don't find that in other places"; "I grew up here when this was a white church; there is something that God is doing here now and I want to be a part of it"; "I have lived in a number of places around the world, and so I'm not comfortable just being with people all like myself anymore."

And then, we find ourselves in this unique cultural moment, a combination of global pandemic that has Christian leaders and churches reimagining many things, alongside a social uprising around race, Black Lives Matter, and police brutality. As Christians, we have to recognize this as a *kairos* moment, a moment when God is calling us to step out of ourselves and engage. If we do not have a gospel-informed response to this moment, we are of all people, most to be pitied, I am afraid.

EKKLESIA AS SIGN AND FORETASTE

God has been calling out a people to live in an alternative way to the world's systems since Abraham was tapped on the shoulder. The people of God in the story of Israel struggled to realize God's intention. Jesus arrived with the answer to this struggle—the defeat of the evil one at the cross, proclamation of the emergence of the kingdom of God, and the ongoing, sustaining presence of the Holy Spirit. Once again, a people are called forth to live as a contrast to the patterns of the world—not called out to live as cloistered, separate, *holy huddles*, but as distinctive communities engaged in kingdom ministry.

For too long, we have sought the forms of earthly power (marketing, consumerism, management strategies, or political relevance) to achieve this kingdom reality and thereby lost our role as sign and foretaste of the coming kingdom. When the people of God follow the way of Jesus, however, "unmasking and challenging the powers of darkness and bearing in its own life the onslaught of those powers, then there are given to the Church signs of the kingdom, powers of healing and blessing which . . . are recognizable as true signs that Jesus reigns."[4] Thirty years ago, Lesslie Newbigin set a laser focus on the role of local congregations as the still point for Christian impact on public life. The only way that the good news of Jesus' victory on the cross is credible, "the only hermeneutic of the gospel, is a congregation of men and women who believe it and live by it."[5]

The Apostle Peter is just as clear: "Dear friends, I urge you, as foreigners and exiles, to abstain from sinful desires, which wage war against your soul. Live such good lives among the pagans that, though they accuse you of doing wrong, they may see your good deeds and glorify God on the day he visits us" (1 Pet 2:11–12, NIV).

Newbigin expands, "The business of the church is to tell and embody a story, the story of God's mighty acts in creation and redemption and of God's promises concerning what will be in the end. The church affirms the truth of this story by celebrating it, interpreting it, and embodying it in the life of the contemporary world."[6] Jayakumar Christian, former head of World Vision India, articulates the role of local churches in a challenging and stratified social context:

> The church's presence in the margins of our society is to be a jubilee community providing a counter narrative to the perspectives of the so-called mainstream—a narrative of the issues that

---

4. Newbigin, *Gospel*, 108.
5. Newbigin, *Gospel*, 227.
6. Newbigin, *Proper Confidence*, 76.

are critical for those on the margins. The local church's presence in the margins is a redemptive-disruptive prophetic presence—a signpost to the kingdom of God.[7]

MULTICULTURAL CHURCH AS COUNTER-NARRATIVE

Human relations are built on a common ground of shared beliefs, values, and behaviors, with people largely like ourselves. Our normal response to difference, to the stranger, is to respond defensively, seeing the world around us through the only lens we have. Again, Parker Palmer describes the challenge:

> No, we are most fundamentally threatened by changing human relationships. We are comfortable in neighborhoods populated by people of similar social background, but when strangers move in we feel somehow not at home . . . we feel at home when we can stay within an enclave, surrounded and protected by people of "our own kind"; we feel exiled when exposed to the larger society with all its pluralism and variety.[8]

For those who have been largely socialized in one cultural community, with little personal engagement with difference, "cultural differences are experienced as divisive and threatening. Cultural difference is seen as an obstacle to be overcome and this sense of superiority can lead to overconfidence and a view that 'our' way of doings things is the best way."[9] That is the normal narrative, adequately recorded in the Christian Scriptures, from Genesis to Revelation. The God of those same Scriptures, however, is constantly calling the people of God into a counter-narrative.

Over the years I have argued that the essential assumptions of multicultural social theory are compatible with a Christian worldview:[10] (1) recognition/acceptance of difference adds value and richness; (2) duality of interaction/adjustment is necessary; and (3) a confident sense of cultural identity and self-respect is required for engaging differences and maintaining equality and power balance.[11]

---

7. Christian, "Prophetic Presence," 54.
8. Palmer, *Company of Strangers*, 69.
9. Hammer, "Intercultural Development Inventory," 207.
10. Sheffield, "Can Multicultural Social Theory Help Us?"
11. Sheffield, *Multicultural Leader*, 14; Taylor, "Interculturalism or Multiculturalism?" 415.

Part One: For King or Country?

Charles Taylor indicates that this multicultural reality is framed by a range of policies that "have as common ultimate goal that they transform the culture of interaction so as to remove the inequalities and confer the status of normative citizen or member, on everyone."[12] In addition, he goes on, "We also need an articulated account of what we're doing—we need to articulate what the new culture of interaction will be, and the way it differs from the old . . . We need a narrative of the transition we're trying to bring about."[13]

It is here where the narrative of the early church provides an *articulated account* of how people of diverse cultures should interact in this one new humanity (Eph 2). Assuming a certain amount of biblical knowledge in our audience, let me briefly reference the profoundly disorienting dilemma that Peter was confronted with in his dream sequence in Joppa and subsequent interactions with Roman Cornelius (Acts 10–11). As his worldview was being reshaped, Peter had to be confronted again on this matter of cultural acceptance by Paul in Antioch (Gal 2). Years later, as Peter is clarifying what sign and foretaste looks like among the Christians to whom he is writing, he exhorts, "show proper respect to everyone" (1 Pet 2:17).

In Paul's letter addressing theological and cultural challenges in the Roman church, he articulates a "new culture of interaction" among these diverse followers of Jesus: "do not think of yourself more highly than you ought, but rather think of yourself with sober judgment . . . so in Christ we, though many, form one body, and each member belongs to all the others" (Rom 12:3–5, NIV). Again, Paul urges, "Accept one another, then, just as Christ accepted you, in order to bring praise to God" (Rom 15:7, NIV).

As Christians, we have been given a counter-narrative on these matters of culture and race. In this moment, it is apparent that this counter-narrative has not been articulated and practiced in many of our congregations. We have not taught and discipled our people in this area and Miroslav Volf suggests, "it may not be too much to claim that the future of our world will depend on how we deal with identity and difference."[14] Made in the context of the ethnic clashes of the Balkan War

---

12. Taylor, "Interculturalism or Multiculturalism?" 416.
13. Taylor, "Interculturalism or Multiculturalism?" 416.
14. Volf, *Exclusion and Embrace*, 20.

and the Rwandan Genocide, twenty-five years ago, his claim, obviously, still stands.

From culturally complex India, Christian observes, "many of the root causes of marginalization, fragility, and conflicts are rooted in issues of truth, perception, beliefs, ideology, and worldview. The god complexes, broken relationships, and marred identities are rooted in lies that parade as 'ideologies.'"[15] And so, "the church is called to be in the margins to articulate the mind of God on these issues and to offer a counter narrative to the dominant culture that birthed these margins."[16]

CREATING A BRAVE SPACE

And so, this is our assignment and mission. Make disciples via forming a community of Jesus followers who believe, articulate, and practice an alternative kingdom reality: *As the Father sent me, so I am sending you.*

Intercultural, social science observation, research, and practice have produced a rich and *thick* understanding and experience around building social cohesion and integration. Influential vectors include the role of diverse agents (family, friends, media, and institutions); recognition and acceptance of cultural attributes (dress, food, celebrations, and norms of conduct); common interpersonal mechanisms (discovery observations, word of mouth, trust, facilitated conversation, social participation, or social media) as well as issues of legal status and employment.[17]

A good example is the introduction of intercultural understanding as a pedagogic competency in the Australian school curriculum, with its emphasis on key personal, interpersonal, and social skills and cross-cultural capability. Research found that the students with the most developed intercultural competencies were those who attended schools with "*a strong, explicit and well-established culture* of racial, religious and cultural equality in all areas of its operations."[18] They found a demonstrated connection between the desire for notions of justice and the actual capacity to develop interpersonal and intercultural affinity. The key was *the*

---

15. Christian, "Prophetic Presence," 56.
16. Christian, "Prophetic Presence," 53.
17. Ares and Fernandez, "Toward a Mixed Integration Model," 638–39.
18. Halse et al, "Doing Diversity," 3 (italics mine).

power of positive narratives about the everyday workings of diversity and intercultural relations.[19]

If this issue is a top-of-shelf concern in Canadian society, what are our churches doing to tell a different story, a counter-narrative, to develop a strong, explicit and well-established culture in all of our operations? How does one do this work?

We need to articulate a different story. I have a feeling that many Evangelical Christian leaders in Canada are not competent to articulate a counter-narrative because they have not done the biblical, theological, and sociological work required to do so.

We need to listen to the voices of others; Newbigin says, "The only way in which the gospel can challenge our culturally conditioned interpretations of it is through the witness of those who read the Bible with minds shaped by other cultures. We have to listen to others. This mutual correction is sometimes unwelcome, but it is necessary and it is fruitful."[20]

We need to develop alternative practices. The practices of Evangelical discipleship that presently shape our congregational cultures are not sufficient but deficient. The discipleship tools to create more robust engagement with our social context are available but will require work on the first two initiatives to become normative in our practice.

We need to hold one another accountable. Like Paul with Peter, this will include challenging, interpersonal confrontations, if the subtle, prompting work of the Spirit is not responded to consistently.

We need to normalize the counter-narrative in our congregations. Will we exegete the counter-narrative of Scripture? Will we challenge our people to transform their practices toward *the stranger* in a manner consistent with the character called out by Jesus' loving sacrifice for us, the unlovely? Will this work create alternative communities that serve as sign and foretaste, here, today, of the kingdom coming on earth as it is in heaven?

In our present climate, this kind of work takes courage on all sides. "There is no such thing as 'safe space'—we exist in the real world."[21] But we have a counter-narrative regarding how to engage in this space; the story of a kingdom that seeks to live out an alternative reality in the midst of this real world.

---

19. Mansouri and Modood, "Complementarity," 12–13.
20. Newbigin, *Gospel*, 196–97.
21. Strano, "Untitled Poem."

BIBLIOGRAPHY

Ares, Alberto, and Mercedes Fernandez. "Toward a Mixed Integration Model Based on Migrants' Self-Perception." *Studi Emigrazione* 212 (2018) 633–52.

Christian, Jayakumar. "A Prophetic Presence in the Margins." *Transformation* 36 (2019) 53–57.

Halse, Christine, et al. "Doing Diversity: Intercultural Understanding in Primary and Secondary Schools." DRO: Deakin University's Research Repository, 1–52. Melbourne: Deakin University, 2015.

Hammer, Mitchell R. "The Intercultural Development Inventory: An Approach for Assessing and Building Intercultural Competence." In *Contemporary Leadership and Intercultural Competence: Exploring the Cross-Cultural Dynamics Within Organizations*, edited by Michael A. Moodian, 203–17. Thousand Oaks, CA: Sage, 2008.

Mansouri, Fethi, and Tariq Modood. "The Complementarity of Multiculturalism and Interculturalism: Theory Backed by Australian Evidence." *Ethnic and Racial Studies* 44 (2021) 1–21.

Newbigin, Lesslie. *The Gospel in a Pluralist Society*. Grand Rapids: Eerdmans, 1989.

———. *Proper Confidence: Faith, Doubt, and Certainty in Christian Discipleship*. Grand Rapids: Eerdmans, 1995.

Palmer, Parker. *The Company of Strangers: Christians and the Renewal of America's Public Life*. New York: Crossroad, 1981.

Sheffield, Dan. "Can Multicultural Social Theory Help Us in Leading Multicultural Faith Communities?" In *Reflecting God's Glory Together: Diversity in Evangelical Mission*, edited by Scott Moreau and Beth Snodderly, 3–20. Pasadena: William Carey, 2011.

———. *The Multicultural Leader: Developing a Catholic Personality*. 2nd ed. Toronto: Clement, 2015.

Sheffield, Dan, and Kathleen Sheffield. "Ubunye Church and Community Ministries." In *Serving with the Urban Poor*, edited by Tetsunao Yamamori et al., 34–47. Monrovia: MARC, 1998.

Strano, Beth. "Untitled Poem." *Facing History & Ourselves*. No pages. Online: https://www.facinghistory.org/resource-library/untitled-poem-beth-strano.

Taylor, Charles. "Interculturalism or Multiculturalism?" *Philosophy and Social Criticism* 38 (2012) 413–23.

Volf, Miroslav. *Exclusion and Embrace: A Theological Exploration of Identity, Otherness, and Reconciliation*. Nashville: Abingdon, 1996.

Changing World, Changing Church

Amanda Ross

It is clear this world is changing. Increasing globalization and hybridization of cultures call for Christian churches to mobilize and equip themselves in new ways to serve well in this increasingly diverse world. One need only observe passersby on the sidewalk of any major Canadian city to see that ours is a country of great diversity, a cultural kaleidoscope whose multi-colored patterns are ever-changing.[1] And with 59 percent of new immigrants identifying as Christians, Canadian churches, too, are becoming increasingly diverse.[2] To answer this great need of ministry to and with an ever-changing milieu of social patterns, we must enter into open and honest dialog with these new perspectives. In such conversations we will find new areas of connection and allow opportunity for broadened patterns of thinking and see doors open for hearing God in fresh ways. This chapter will enter that widening, and needed, conversation, to consider how Canadian churches, who engage in the mission of God to share good news with all the world, might welcome and respond to the changes being introduced by this changing world.

CHALLENGES OF LOVING THE *OTHER*

With its frequent instructions to love neighbour, stranger, and enemy, the Christian Scriptures speak a message of care for all people. However, our human propensity has been to love only those who are like us, those

---

1. Watson, "Mapping our Community," 101.
2. Watson, "Mapping our Community," 100.

whom it is easier to love. Even more, we live in a world which demonstrates daily the extremes to which human hatred can turn. These acts of hatred only add to a growing fear of *the other*, and fear, too, is a hindrance to love, for it urges protection of oneself and one's own. Yet, Christians need not look only to themselves for an answer but to their God; God, who is both three and one, models both otherness and intimate community. The Christian call to fearless love of the other is built on the character of the God of love. Zizioulas describes:

> In our culture, protection from the other is a fundamental necessity. We feel more and more threatened by the presence of the other. We are forced and even encouraged to consider the other as our enemy before we can treat him or her as our friend. Communion with the other is not spontaneous; it is built upon fences which protect us from the dangers implicit in the other's presence. We accept the other only in so far as he or she does not threaten our privacy or in so far as he or she is useful for our individual happiness.[3]

Zizioulas continues in his writing to direct Christians to look not to themselves for an answer but to God; God, who is both three and one, models both otherness and intimate community. This chapter, too, will follow that line on which the Christian call to fearless love of the Other is built on the character of the God of love.

THEOLOGICAL FOUNDATIONS OF LOVE

Perhaps the most remarkable revelation of the divine in Scripture is that God is one who willingly seeks and enters into relationship with humanity. The God who calls to a guilty and hiding Adam, "Where are you?" is also the God who calls Abraham to leave his home and be made into a new family; God says, "in you all the families of the earth shall be blessed" (Gen 12:3, NRSV). From the beginning, God, who is wholly other, demonstrates a willingness to embrace otherness.[4] This pattern seen in Eden and Abraham is seen over again throughout the biblical narratives of God's interactions with humanity. The creation mandate to

---

3. Zizioulas, *Communion and Otherness*, 1.

4. Woods ("God, Israel," 138) notes that in initiating relationship with and calling Abraham, God "takes the sovereign decision not to see otherness as toxic and negative but makes space for and comes to us."

the first humans required them to go out and fill the world; however, diverted through disobedience into a harsh exile, humans began to turn against each other. But redemption comes, even in God's call to Abraham to become a blessing to all.[5] This is not only a call to relationship with the true God but also a call to missions—to become a blessing to all the families of the earth. It is striking, when considering the missional aspects of God's call to Abraham, that this call included the instructions for Abraham to leave home and become a migrant. It is this wanderer whose family was to become a blessing to all. It is perhaps not surprising then that the spreading of God's blessing to all is still communicated through a scattering of God's people across the world.

This idea of God's calling of the migrant is seen again in the one about whom it is written: "the word became flesh and lived among us" (John 1:14, NRSV). Jesus, who journeys from heaven to earth to clear the way for humanity to reach for heaven in turn, was also in many ways an exile and outcast. Scorned by the established religious leaders and condemned by the state, Jesus yet humbled himself to welcome and love even those esteemed as the lowest members of his society. In this way, Jesus first transcends the "widest gulf of differences conceivable"[6] by becoming human and then gives himself as an example of the greatest human to human service *in* his life and ultimately *with* his life. In this great exchange, Jesus stands as the consummate model of love, a love which gives itself for the other. Those who choose to become followers of Jesus and be called by his name are entreated to imitate this way of love and "ministry of reconciliation" (2 Cor 5:18–19, NRSV).

The apostle Paul, when writing to the divisive and disgruntled believers in Corinth, provides further implications of what it means to be a follower of Christ; that is, to have been baptized into Christ, means being baptized into one body: "Jews or Greeks, slaves or free" all are baptized by one Spirit into one body (1 Cor 12:13). 1 Corinthians 12 describes in detail this body with its many parts, all with different abilities and responsibilities. Yet, in Christ, all are one and move together in a common bond of love, which Paul describes in length in the thirteenth chapter. This unity is intercultural and transcends societal hierarchies, and it is the kind of unity with diversity to which all Christians are called.

---

5. On creation, fall, and redemption as a call of the marginalized to missions, see Harvey, "Pilgrims," 149.

6. Baker et al., "Mission," 355.

When considering the depth and difficulty of this call toward unity and love, it is comforting and empowering to know that we are not left to walk out this calling alone. In John's gospel, when Jesus enjoins his disciples to obey his command to love, he speaks also of an "Advocate" which he will send from the Father to be with them forever (John 14:16–17), who will teach them and remind them of the things which Jesus had spoken to them (John 14:26) and guide them into truth (John 16:13). In the book of Acts, we find that the Holy Spirit is also one who directs and empowers missions. It is the Spirit who directs Philip to speak with the Ethiopian eunuch (Acts 8:29) and the Spirit who instructs Peter to go to share the good news with the Roman Cornelius (Acts 10:17–23). The work of the Holy Spirit in the life of the believer is critical for the service of the believer in the life of missions.

THE CHURCH'S OPPORTUNITY TO CHANGE

In this changing world, churches are faced with the need and the opportunity to respond to and serve in increasingly diverse communities of Canadians from all nations. Yet this need stands in continuity with the character of the Christian God. This God is one who calls people to be a blessing to all nations and urges them to follow Christ's example of self-sacrificial love for all, and whose Spirit works to empower and enable Christian mission. Now is the time for God's church to respond, once again, to a changing world by learning a new way of being and new ways of serving as we are moving from monocultural to intercultural communities.

Learning new ways can be intimidating and change is seldom easy. Yet, all life must adapt to survive, and so must the life of the church. We need not be afraid of change, for disruption is "God's way of transforming the church."[7] A helpful example of the willingness to adapt oneself for the sake of the gospel is seen in the apostle Paul. Though declaring himself free, Paul also claims, "I have made myself a servant to all, that I might win more of them" (1 Cor 9:19, ESV) and "I have become all things to all people, that by all means I might save some" (1 Cor 9:22, ESV). While this pattern of "self-contextualization"[8] has been frequently

---

7. Pullenayegem ("Surviving or Thriving?" 183) offers a helpful strategy for managing both "survival anxiety" and "learning anxiety."
8. Newall, *Crossing Cultures in Scripture*, 250.

addressed to, usually international, cross-cultural missions, the application for Canadian intercultural ministry is clear: the nations who come to Canada and enter our communities are not merely guests here for a visit; they are family, here to belong. As every family knows, the addition of new members brings change and opportunity for growth to all as each member contributes meaningfully to the character of the whole. One need not see the nations flocking to Canada as a disruption of the "Canadian way" but should see it as an opportunity for creativity, learning, and growth for all. Instead of fear, we are called to embrace in love—which in turn will increase curiosity and the desire to learn, even from our mistakes. The learning called for by this changing world must begin with humility and a willingness to hear new and previously unfamiliar voices. We who have lived in this good country for generations are called now to move past the single, predominantly Western-European perspective we have grown accustomed to and welcome God's message spoken to us from voices from all over the world. Truly, "the time of European and Western monologue is over."[9] And this wider conversation with voices from around the world and within our own communities brings great opportunity to sharpen old patterns of thinking—if we are willing to hear them.[10]

Many well-intentioned Christians interact with and even attempt to serve other cultures with openness and generosity. But of course, good intentions do not necessarily equal good results. Intercultural ministry can be steeply challenging because we do not always know what others need nor even want. Thus, we must first become willing to learn. Loving others as Jesus would does not mean "a facile enthusiasm for the exotic, or a patronizing pity, but a genuine attentiveness that is willing to learn *from* as well as learn *about*."[11] Yet, as we are learning from others, we must also take care to learn about ourselves as well. We must come to recognize our own basic values and assumptions into order to truly understand why another may differ. If we do not learn to hold our own assumptions up to careful scrutiny, we may find ourselves trapped in a

---

9. Escobar, *New Global Mission*, 136.

10. Quoting William Dyrness, an American Missionary serving in the Philippines, Escobar goes on to affirm, "The day is surely past when we simply allow third world believers to 'have their say' while we Western theologians prepare the definite answers to their questions. For now, we recognize that if we listen carefully we find our own assumptions challenged and our thinking sharpened" (*New Global Mission*, 137).

11. Smith (*Learning*, 77) identifies fear, struggles for power, incomplete knowledge, and limited perspective as hindrances to faithful Christian living in a multicultural world and instead urges hospitality, humility, and a willingness to hear the other.

narrow "cultural prison" of our own making.[12] Instead, as we work to expand our own cultural intelligence, we may find ourselves more able to reach across cultural divisions effectively and respectfully.[13] Finally, though not exhaustively, we may be encouraged to remember that change rarely happens in a straight line. Rather, when working with humans, messy and often muddled as we are, we can know that the process of change, too, will not be neat and orderly. Yet, through patience, willingness to learn, and the determination to bear even the disorderliness of effective change, we may indeed see needed and lasting change.[14]

CONCLUSION: LIFE AFTER CHANGE

Clearly, in this changing world, Canadian churches who wish to engage well in ministry to and with this culturally diverse landscape must be willing to change themselves. It is no longer sufficient to remain pocketed in our own groupings of *people like us*. Rather, we are called to be one nation, one diverse but unified family. And despite our fears and the challenges inherent in loving those who appear different from oneself, Christians can look to their God for both example and support. God, who initiates relationship with humans has already bridged the furthest extreme of loving the other. Jesus, who gave even his own life for those he loves, calls on his church, his body, to continue to do the same, and the Holy Spirit enables and empowers this self-giving love. The church is invited, then, to welcome this opportunity to change by replacing fear with love and embracing humility and the willingness to learn from and be sharpened by the other. These new voices speaking from new perspectives will challenge and sharpen old patterns of thinking, and this is a blessing. By becoming learners—carefully understanding oneself in order to truly understand the Other, working to improve cultural intelligence, and intentionally pursuing real relationship with people of different cultures—churches today will, we pray, be able to adapt and learn to love well the multitude of nations living in this dear country we all call "home."

---

12. Lingenfelter and Mayers, *Ministering Cross-Culturally*, 108.

13. Livermore (*Cultural Intelligence*, 12) urges, "we must actually become more multicultural people so that we might better express love cross-culturally."

14. Dan Sheffield offers a helpful description of various cycles involved in a congregations' transition into true multiculturalism (see "Adjustment Required," 194).

Part One: For King or Country?

BIBLIOGRAPHY

Baker, Ken, et al. "The Mission of the Church through Understanding and Pursuing Intercultural Unit." In *Scattered and Gathered: A Global Compendium of Diaspora Missiology*, edited by Sadiri Joy Tira and Tetsunao Yamamori, 353–59. Oxford, UK: Regnum, 2016.

Escobar, Samuel. *The New Global Mission: The Gospel from Everywhere to Everyone*. Downers Grove, IL: InterVarsity, 2003.

Harvey, Thomas. "Pilgrims on a Journey: Diaspora and Mission." In *Scattered and Gathered: A Global Compendium of Diaspora Missiology*, edited by Sadiri Joy Tira and Tetsunao Yamamori, 147–60. Oxford, UK: Regnum, 2016.

Lingenfelter, Sherwood, and Marvin Mayers. *Ministering Cross-Culturally: A Model for Effective Personal Relationships*. 3rd ed. Grand Rapids: Baker Academic, 2016.

Livermore, David. *Cultural Intelligence: Improving your CQ to Engage our Multicultural World*. Grand Rapids: Baker Academic, 2009.

Newall, Marvin. *Crossing Cultures in Scripture: Biblical Principles for Mission Practice*. Downers Grove, IL: InterVarsity, 2016.

Pullenayegem, Chris. "Surviving or Thriving? Principles for a Church That Is Becoming." In *From the Margins to the Centre: The Diaspora Effect*, edited by Michael Krause et al., 181–90. Toronto: Tyndale University Press, 2018.

Sheffield, Dan. "Adjustment Required—Transitioning to a Multicultural Congregation." In *From the Margins to the Centre: The Diaspora Effect*, edited by Michael Krause et al., 191–99. Toronto: Tyndale Academic, 2018.

Smith, David. *Learning from the Stranger: Christian Faith and Cultural Diversity*. Grand Rapids: Eerdmans, 2009.

Watson, James W. "Mapping our Community: Understanding Diversity, Change, and Neighbourliness." In *From the Margins to the Centre: The Diaspora Effect*, edited by Michael Krause et al., 98–109. Toronto: Tyndale Academic, 2018.

Woods, Paul. "God, Israel, the Church and the Other: Otherness as a Theological Motif in Diaspora Mission." In *Scattered and Gathered: A Global Compendium of Diaspora Missiology*, edited by Sadiri Joy Tira and Tetsunao Yamamori, 134–46. Oxford, UK: Regnum, 2016.

Zizioulas, John. *Communion and Otherness: Further Studies in Personhood and the Church*, edited by Paul McPartlan. London: T. & T. Clark, 2006.

Part Two

Towards Kingdom Cultures

WHAT PEOPLE LONG FOR as individuals and as a community of believers is beyond a state of hospice or shelter. What is longed for is *home* in its fullest sense—more than a social space, it is a state of belonging and flourishing. Theologian Miroslav Volf suggests that what we long for is a home with God, and it is a home that Christ-followers work together, with God, to build. This kind of a community of faith offers an uncommon hope centred around King Jesus which provides a strong sense of identity and belonging, finding expression through concrete acts of love and service to the other. It is this essence of home that permeates Jesus' kingdom culture, in which humility, compassion, and self-giving love are valued over superiority, domination, and aggression.

In this second part, you will hear the voices of authors who describe kingdom cultures in their communities, highlighting the integral roles of mutuality and multivocality. Although their ministry contexts may look very different than yours, what concepts could be applied to your community?

What the Peoples of St. Barnabas Church Have Taught Me about Intercultural Preaching

Interruptions, Incarnations, and Invocations

Jennifer A. Singh

WHAT IS THE GOOD *news of Jesus Christ to the people of St. Barnabas Church Tsuut'ina this week?* This is the top exegetical question I ask myself in my weekly sermon preparation. It is a question I ponder as I study a biblical passage, go for my daily walk, visit with people from my congregation, and carry out my mundane tasks. I have come to call it my WOQ (Weekly Obsessive Question), frustrating me at times, consuming me most of the time: it is *the* question that has made me *sidzanaghazud* [1] for the past few years.[2]

CULTIVATING A HUNGRY HEART: SEQUENCING THE QUESTIONS

Having a hungry heart is nothing unique—didn't Bruce Springsteen croon, "everybody's got a hungry heart?" Thomas G. Long emphasizes

---

1. The word for hungry in the *Tsuut'ina* language which also carries connotations of "my heart is hungry," as explained in a *Tsuut'ina* language course I took, led by the *Tsuut'ina* Gunaha Institute (May 2021).

2. I started volunteering as the Minister of St. Barnabas Church *Tsuut'ina* at this time after the church had experienced a six-month hiatus in leadership as a result of the passing of their former Minister.

PART TWO: TOWARDS KINGDOM CULTURES

this point in his classic work *The Witness of Preaching*.[3] Long proposes a nomenclature for the types of preachers that exist: the herald, the pastor, the storyteller/narrator, and the witness.[4] Though Long prefers the witness, he underscores that one of the main tasks of the-preacher-as-pastor is to listen for the felt needs of the people of God, and to then respond by "intervening with the Gospel, by speaking a word that clarifies and restores."[5] This seems like a simple enough formula: listen to your community and then respond appropriately with a message that will assuage their hunger. But what does it mean to listen to and understand the deep needs of the people? Long advises that in order for the preacher-as-pastor to answer this question, they must *"know people and know how they listen."*[6]

In the process of trying to heed Long's wise counsel, I have realized the deeper hunger in my own heart to understand who Jesus Christ is in the eyes of the people of *Tsuut'ina*.[7] Without an understanding of how the people of St. Barnabas Church see, hear, feel, smell, taste, and experience the touch of God, I will continue to perpetuate the dehumanizing harms that have been caused by colonization.[8] The context[9] of the people I serve is a vital hermeneutical key[10] to answering my WOQ.

---

3. Long, *Witness of Preaching*, 29.

4. Long, *Witness of Preaching*, 19–51.

5. Long, *Witness of Preaching*, 29.

6. Long, *Witness of Preaching*, 29 (italics mine).

7. This yearning was spurred by my PhD research that sought to understand how women in prostitution theologically made sense of their life experiences. I spent over a year participating in weekly inductive Bible studies with my research participants in Addis Ababa, Ethiopia, who provided me with new ways of seeing, hearing, and experiencing the God that we all served. In my weekly quest to answer the question "What is the good news of Jesus Christ for the people of *Tsuut'ina*?" I have had to come back to what the women in Ethiopia taught me, that is, how to understand Jesus Christ through the eyes of prostituted woman in Addis Ababa (see Singh, "Toward a Theological Response to Prostitution").

8. The Truth and Reconciliation Commission of Canada, *Honouring the Truth*. 43–51.

9. Travis, *Decolonizing Preaching*, 32.

10. Travis, *Decolonizing Preaching*, 33. My WOQ has exposed many things, including my ignorance of the history and culture of the people I serve, my blind-spots and biases that are a product of my immigrant settler-privilege I inhabit, and my sparse library of Indigenous authors. These are three areas that I have sought to rectify through: listening to and learning from the people of *Tsuut'ina* and by reading and studying various Indigenous scholars from a variety of academic disciplines.

SINGH *What the Peoples of St. Barnabas Church Have Taught Me*

The hunger in my heart to understand the Jesus of the *Tsuut'ina* First Nation has spurred three vital questions: (1) How can I *know* the people of *Tsuut'ina*?; (2) How do I *listen well* to the people of *Tsuut'ina*?; (3) How do the people of *Tsuut'ina experience the presence* of the risen Lord? Before answering my WOQ, I give priority to these three questions. And I do that by paying attention to the moments of interruption, incarnation, and invocation in our community, and by allowing these moments to inform the way that I preach.

HOW CAN I KNOW THE PEOPLE OF *TSUUT'INA*?

Interruptions (and Ingestions)

When entering a culture, it is essential to quickly learn the beliefs, values, norms, and social practices of the people you are among so that meaningful relationships can be formed.[11] Indigenous theologian Cheryl Bear points out, "Indigenous people value relationships over time," underscoring that, when people gather together, promptness is not a priority because the relationship takes precedence.[12] This does not mean that all of the people in our church arrive after our service begins at 11:00 am. What it does mean, is that while most people arrive before 11:00 am, our service only starts when the vast majority of folks have fixed themselves a warm cup of coffee, caught up with those that have arrived, and are seated comfortably in their pew.

Indigenous theologian Richard Twiss uses the word "appropriateness" to describe an Indigenous understanding of time and says, "an event begins when it is appropriate."[13] If someone arrives half-way through the service, it is not *inappropriate* for me to greet that person and ensure they have received an order of service. It is *appropriate* for folks, whenever they show up, to be acknowledged as an integral part of the gathering—the event has been enriched by their presence, not by their timeliness. Greeting someone in the middle of giving a sermon or celebrating the Lord's Supper can seem like an interruption, but I have learned that taking a brief moment to welcome a person entering the room mid-service is a way of extending the holy embrace that Christ welcomes each of us

---

11. Lustig and Koester, *Intercultural Competence*, 26.
12. Bear, *Introduction*, 11.
13. Twiss, *One Church, Many Tribes*, 98.

with. Being seen and named in the Sunday gathering is not viewed as an act of shaming; rather, it is seen as wholly *appropriate*. It confers Jesus' desire to be known more deeply as Immanuel, God with us.

Our service ends with a final benediction, but only after everyone has been offered what is being served up that week in our St. Barnabas crockpot, after people have had time to connect with one another.[14] One of the most significant ways that I have been able to get to know the people of St. Barnabas has been through sharing this family meal together. Preaching always happens in a context, and in most cultures of the world, sharing a meal is extremely important. Often, the most impactful time of our service is not the liturgy, sermon, or even the Lord's Supper; it is our family meal where people, quite literally, digest together how their hearts have been stirred through the service, lament with one another about the struggles and challenges of the past week, and find nourishment for the week ahead.

While our family meal signals the conclusion of our formal service, people often linger afterwards to ask for personal prayer or to seek out a conversation about a family situation that is weighing heavily on them. This is where I believe our church stops running on *chronos* and pivots to *kairos*[15]—some of the most profound experiences of getting to know our people has happened here. Postcolonial feminist theologian Musa Dube Shomanah identifies these moments as the axis of faith.[16] She notes this in Mark 5 where the bleeding woman interrupts the linear trajectory of the story by stopping Jesus on his emergency call to Jairus's dying daughter.[17] This woman slows down the fast-forward pace of the story; the reader is moved "from the space of human possibilities where we rush to beat time, to an exceptional space of faith, where not only is time no more, but where the human impossible becomes possible."[18] I believe that our weekly meal creates such an environment. Week after week, people feel safe enough to tell me their stories—maybe not their whole story, as

---

14. Without a kitchen, washroom, or any running water in a building that is more than 100 years old, serving a warm meal in hygienic ways has definitely been a challenge requiring a certain degree of creativity, but so far, we have managed to prevent any sort of food borne illness, even in the midst of a pandemic.

15. In Greek, *chronos* is chronological or sequential time; *kairos* is considered divinely appointed time.

16. Dube Shomanah, *HIV & AIDS Bible*, 83.

17. Dube Shomanah, *HIV & AIDS Bible*, 80.

18. Dube Shomanah, *HIV & AIDS Bible*, 83.

the bleeding woman did to Jesus, but certainly more of their story. I often witness the human impossibility of trust becoming possible.

This meal has also served as a gateway into people's homes. Trust has been established through the simple act of eating together, especially through our congregants' very honest evaluation of my cooking.[19] These conversations and candour have emboldened me to invite myself over to people's homes, sometimes on very short notice. My elders do not seem to mind the interruption.

HOW DO I LISTEN WELL TO THE PEOPLE OF *TSUUT'INA*?

Incarnations

Silence is a strong value of Indigenous people.[20] Often a non-Indigenous person will encounter long pauses while conversing with an Indigenous person. Cheryl Bear explains that these pauses are deliberate; the speaker is clearly demonstrating that they are listening carefully to the other person's words and that they value them.[21] Bear stresses that Indigenous people "choose their words wisely and speak slowly so that every word is heard and understood."[22]

When I listen to the people in my church, I pay attention to the cadence of their speech, their thoughtful pauses, and their witty humour. It has given me a new appreciation for both words and silence. When my elders tell me stories about their lives, especially what life used to be like on the Nation when they were growing up, I find myself captivated by a narrative that I never heard when I was growing up. For example, our church is located on Old Agency Road on the *Tsuut'ina* Nation, named after where the Indian agent[23] once lived and where the former residential school—then day school—were located. People in our community believe that this part of the reserve still possesses the spirits of the children who died during the eras of the residential and day schools.

---

19. Apparently, I cook with too much garlic for the palate of some of the folks in our church.
20. Bear, *Introduction*, 11.
21. Bear, *Introduction*, 11.
22. Bear, *Introduction*, 11.
23. Joseph, *21 Things*, 50.

Part Two: Towards Kingdom Cultures

Often people will say that they hear, when no one else is around, children laughing or crying around our church building.[24]

Instead of dismissing these stories as folklore, I have learned to listen to how these stories shape the identity of the Tsuut'ina Nation and echo the people's resounding lament. These stories help to map their geography and history. Showing up weekly to this complicated space where our church is located, and there incarnating the good news of Jesus Christ, is one way to acknowledge the harms of the past while seeking a just future. These stories are the primary vehicle through which the people I serve convey their joy and pain, and being present to these stories, both past and present, is essential to preaching with relevance about God's inbreaking kingdom.

As a part of the Truth and Reconciliation Commission's 94 Calls to Action, postsecondary educators and church leaders have been tasked with developing education strategies that teach about the history and spirituality of Indigenous people, and particularly the church's role in perpetuating the erasure of Indigenous identity and spirituality.[25] To this end, I seek out Indigenous exemplars, both past and present, as my go-to resources for sermon illustrations. For example, when preaching on the story of Stephen in Acts 7, I leaned on the First Nation's version of the Bible which names Stephen as "Many Feathers,"[26] drawing attention to God's favour and presence on Stephen. In addition, I told the story of Chief Spokane Garry as an Indigenous example of faith under fire.[27] As well, I do not shy away from speaking about the colonial context in which large portions of our biblical narrative were written, and I speak openly about ways in which North American colonization has undermined Jesus being incarnated into Indigenous cultures[28] and worldviews.[29] For sermon preparation, I rely on Indigenous theologians, biblical scholars from

---

24. This is a story recounted by several *Tsuut'ina* elders to me over the course of my time in the community.

25. The Truth and Reconciliation Commission of Canada, *Honouring the Truth*. 330 (esp. articles 59 and 60). Also, I have sought to teach my students at Ambrose University about indigenous spirituality, on its own terms, through various courses I teach and some of these students have come out to the *Tsuut'ina* Nation in order to listen to and learn from the people of St. Barnabas church.

26. Wildman, *Walking the Good Road*, 273–78.

27. See Richard Twiss's exposition of Chief Spokane Garry's story in *One Church, Many Tribes*, 138–57.

28. Bear, *Introduction*, 9.

29. Bear, *Introduction*, 70.

the Majority World, and commentaries that focus on the socio-political factors that were present in biblical times .[30] These sources help me to build bridges between the world of the text and the world that the people in my congregation inhabit.

Lastly, I have learned how to listen well to the people of *Tsuut'ina* by showing-up at all sorts of community events and accepting invitations to ceremonies.[31] Being present in community to people's deep gladness and profound pain has changed how I speak from the pulpit. It has tuned my heart to sing of God's incredible kindness and tuned it to lament God's seeming inability at times to prevent tragedy. A sound that has formed me deeply over the past year is the weeping of mothers, grandmothers, and aunties who have lost a child or one who was like a child to them. Few things in this world are more haunting than that sound. It is harrowing. It is reminiscent of Christ's cry of dereliction from the cross: "My God, my God, why have you forsaken me?" (Mark 15:34, ESV).

The heartbreak of inexplicable loss has often rendered me silent. In times like this, showing up with a Tim Horton's "Take 20" or a bucket of Kentucky Fried Chicken and sitting for hours in a hard-back chair, not saying a word, matters the most. Allowing my own tears to well up as I watch people I love try to cope with unspeakable loss—such small acts give comfort to those who suffer the loss, and they speak volumes to the community at large.

I have returned again and again to the story of the widow of Nain in Luke 7. Before raising the widow's son from the dead, Jesus *saw* her weeping, *heard* her wailing, and *witnessed* the crowd of mourners behind her. His heart was deeply moved by her pain, and instead of continuing his journey, with a large crowd following him, he stopped. He listened. He then responded, "Don't cry" (Luke 7:13, NIV). Jesus could say that because he knew what he was about to do. This story, however, is a good reminder to me that even as the pastor, I am just one of the people in the funeral procession. My role is to follow those who are grieving, to be a physical presence of comfort, and to make space for Jesus to incarnate *his*

---

30. Carter, *Matthew and the Margins*, for example, is an excellent biblical commentary that gives attention to the deep marginalization that followers of Jesus faced under Roman occupation.

31. During my time in *Tsuut'ina*, I have attended a number of birthday feasts, commemoration feasts, community-wide prayer meetings and had the privilege of being invited to a pipe ceremony with traditional elders of the Nation where we spent several days praying for the Nation.

presence among them. It is never my role to say, "Don't cry," but rather to weep, to walk, and to wait with those who are grieving for God's grace to manifest itself.

HOW DO THE PEOPLE OF *TSUUT'INA* EXPERIENCE THE PRESENCE OF THE RISEN LORD?

Invocations

Postcolonial preaching scholar HyeRan Kim-Cragg describes sermon preparation as a process that involves anticipation and expectation characterized by both active and passive actions.[32] Kim-Cragg says that a preacher, as they ruminate on a text and wait for a sermon to reach its *kairos* moment, will sometimes experience "a process of active waiting akin to waiting for an anticipated event like a graduation or job interview."[33] For me, this process of active waiting often happens on the phone with, or in the homes of, my parishioners between Sunday services. This is when I have the privilege of praying with them for God to answer the deep desires of their hearts.

Listening to how people make their invocations to God gives you a glimpse into how they see and know Jesus. One of our dear elders who recently passed away would lead our services by praying with sweetgrass in the *Tsuut'ina* language. I loved watching and listening to elder RB pray for our community, his head slightly bowed, a deep reverence reverberating from his voice, and the fragrant smoke from the sweetgrass encircling him. While I may not have understood the words he uttered, I had no doubt that when elder RB prayed, our prayers had ascended to the very heart of our creator and that the presence of the Holy One had descended on our little church.

As he became frailer and was unable to attend our services, I would visit him at his home and was always struck by the deep thankfulness he expressed to *Nat'o*,[34] his caregivers, and to all those that would come to visit, even when his speech was failing. I loved holding hands with him, bowing our heads, and praying in *Tsuut'ina* and English. The countenance of God was all over elder RB, and as his time drew near to leave

---

32. Kim-Cragg, *Postcolonial Preaching*, 17.
33. Kim-Cragg, *Postcolonial Preaching*, 17.
34. The word for God in the *Tsuut'ina* language.

us, the weightiness of God's glory became even more powerful. The day before he passed away, elder RB joined us at church via Zoom and intently prayed and sang throughout the entire service. Our last hymn that day was a favourite of our congregation, the old country gospel song "I'll Fly Away." Little did any of us know that we would be singing our dear elder RB into the very presence of God, anticipating his journey from this life into the life to come. Watching elder RB make his final invocations that Sunday was a holy privilege and showed me what it looked like for a godly man to anticipate meeting the risen Jesus.

Another way that I have learned how the people of *Tsuut'ina* experience the risen Lord is through the spiritual metaphor of the "Good Red Road." One day, sitting at the kitchen table of elder AB, he shared with me this common metaphor used by many Indigenous people to describe the balance and harmony sought in the spiritual life.[35] My elder explained to me that this metaphor acknowledges that all those walking on the "Good Red Road" are human. He said that humans make mistakes, but that making mistakes is not always bad because we can learn from them. The "Good Red Road" reminds us that we can never take the place of God, that we all have a place in his good creation, and that we need one another to keep putting one foot in front of the other and to pull each other out of the ditches we may fall into.[36] Elder AB's exposition of the "Good Red Road" is a theme that I have incorporated into a number of sermons. It has helped me to understand that discipleship for my friends is being supported on their walk down the "Good Red Road" to the heart of creator—where we will meet God face-to-face.

Including this metaphor in our pastoral prayers during our services has enabled me to hear what the gospel sounds like in the ears of the people I seek to serve, and to join my heart in prayer with theirs for things such as freedom from all that enslaves, courage and strength to keep walking in times of devastating grief, and wisdom for how to make good decisions that will keep all of our feet firmly planted on this "Good Red Road." Praying together has opened my eyes to see how Jesus is profoundly at work in the lives of his people at St. Barnabas Church.

---

35. Woodley, *Shalom*, 73. According to Woodley, some Indigenous people refer to the Good Red Road as Walking in a Good Way, a Good Path, or the Beauty Path.

36. Conversation with elder AB, Dawson Hill, *Tsuut'ina* Nation, January 2021.

PART TWO: TOWARDS KINGDOM CULTURES

CONCLUSION

Paying attention to moments of interruption, incarnation, and invocation within the community of St. Barnabas *Tsuut'ina* has helped to feed my *sidzanaghazud* ("hungry heart") and its desire to see, know, and understand who Jesus is in the eyes of these brothers and sisters in Christ. I would have no WOQ if it were not for the people of St. Barnabas. They have given me the privilege of bearing witness to the good news of Jesus Christ among the people of the *Tsuut'ina* Nation, and in turn, the privilege of witnessing how the people of the *Tsuut'ina* Nation proclaim the good news of Jesus Christ to all the world.

Each of ministers in a different context where our communities have unique cultures which shape the day to day of the people. I encourage you to be intentional and pay attention to those moments within your own community; develop your own WOQ. By cultivating a hungry heart, what can you learn from the cultures around you?

BIBLIOGRAPHY

Bear, Cheryl. *Introduction to First Nations Ministry*. Cleveland, TN: Cherohala, 2013.
Carter, Warren. *Matthew and the Margins: A Sociopolitical and Religious Reading*. Maryknoll, NY: Orbis, 2000.
Dube Shomanah, Musa W. *The HIV & AIDS Bible: Selected Essays*. Scranton, PA: University of Scranton Press, 2008.
Joseph, Bob. *21 Things You May Not Know about The Indian Act: Helping Canadians Make Reconciliation with Indigenous People a Reality*. Port Coquitlam, BC: Indigenous Relations, 2018.
Kim-Cragg, HyeRan. *Postcolonial Preaching: Creating a Ripple Effect*. London: Lexington, 2021.
Long, Thomas G. *The Witness of Preaching: Second Edition*. Louisville: Westminster John Knox, 2005.
Lustig, Myron W., and Jolene Koester. *Intercultural Competence: Interpersonal Communication Across Cultures*. 7th ed. Boston: Pearson Education, 2013.
Singh, Jennifer. "Toward a Theological Response to Prostitution: Listening to the Voices of Women Affected by Prostitution and of Selected Church Leaders in Addis Ababa, Ethiopia." PhD diss., Oxford Centre for Mission Studies, 2018.
Travis, Sarah. *Decolonizing Preaching: The Pulpit as Postcolonial Space*. Eugene, OR: Cascade, 2014.
The Truth and Reconciliation Commission of Canada. *Honouring the Truth, Reconciling for the Future: Summary of the Final Report of the Truth and Reconciliation Commission of Canada*. Winnipeg, MB: Truth and Reconciliation Commission of Canada, 2015.
Twiss, Richard. *One Church, Many Tribes: Following Jesus the Way God Made You*. Bloomington: Chosen, 2000.

Wildman, Terry M. *Walking the Good Road: The Gospels and Acts with Ephesians— First Nations Version*. Maricopa, AZ: Great Thunder, 2017.

Woodley, Randy S. *Shalom and the Community of Creation: An Indigenous Vision*. Grand Rapids: Eerdmans, 2012.

Towards a More Intercultural Church
Lessons Learned from the Royal Canadian Chaplain Service

THICH TRUONG

OUR INCREASINGLY DIVERSE SOCIETY is experiencing complicated and dynamic shifts due to social, economic, and political changes and pressures. These changes and pressures have been particularly evident over the past number of years as the world has witnessed prolonged civil wars and conflict, an increase in migration and refugeeism, economic uncertainty, the rise of authoritarian regimes, and the resurgence of populism and ethnic and racial strife across the world. To compound matters, our world is navigating the complex and painful reality of social and physical isolation due to a global pandemic. There is a *convergence of* and a *conflict between* generations, cultures, traditions, races, and ethnicities that is at the heart of some of these issues. We are witnessing problems arising from a world wrestling with intercultural issues.

THE CANADIAN CONTEXT

In Canada, we have not escaped these complexities. Amidst the political, economic, and social turmoil, people are looking for peace and stability. For many, they are looking for answers that only faith, spirituality, and religion can address. Despite this need, the church has yet to present a meaningful response.[1] Perhaps the reason why the church has yet to

---

1. At the writing of this chapter, racial tensions and conflict are high in Canada as

speak to these matters is because we have isolated and sterilized ourselves from the pain and suffering that others are experiencing. The church cannot speak to these problems from a homogenized and monocultural perspective.[2] Our world has changed; our society is more diverse—culture can no longer be understood as a static and monolithic construct. The modern research and definitions of culture no longer address the complexities of a post-postmodern culture that is intercultural and experiencing hybridization.[3] Only a diverse church can speak to the challenges of a diverse world—the church must become more intercultural and create a space that Volker Küster describes as "in-between cultures" where two or more cultures can learn to relate and thrive, and perhaps even co-create.[4]

---

issues of police brutality against black, indigenous, and people of color continue to be at the forefront of news reports and articles. In the Maritimes, lobster harvesters who are predominantly from a white heritage in Nova Scotia continue to assault, vandalize, and destroy property and harvests owned by indigenous Mi'kmaq peoples over the legal definitions of what it means for the Mi'kmaq people to exercise their treaty rights to fish for a moderate livelihood. In Western Canada, oil and gas producers face organized protests by indigenous communities who refuse to allow pipelines to run through their traditional territories. Despite the prominence of these racial and ethnic issues, churches and denominations appear to have provided little in response to these community issues and have not actively engaged in the process of peacemaking and reconciliation.

2. It is outside the scope of this chapter to address this assertion that the church in North America, and particularly in Canada, is predominantly homogenous. There is broad scholarship available speaking to the realities of a largely Western (and white) church in North America that emerged from church growth movements, such as Donald McGavran's HUP (Homogenous Unit Principle) of the 1970s and 1980s, and more recent church planting models that focus on numerical growth of congregations in cities across North America. A homogenous church, or a church with a single dominant culture, will struggle to see and hear the pain of Christians and non-Christians who exist outside of their cultural periphery.

3. Weerakoon, "Evangelical Intercultural Identity," 57, who says that hybridization is "the variegated personal identity and way of life that characterizes people who have been formed by multiple, potentially contradictory, cultural influences, such as members of a global diaspora." Hybridization is an important factor in the conversation regarding globalization and intercultural studies. While it is outside of the scope of this chapter to discuss hybridization in detail, it is important for ministry practitioners to be aware that a people group can no longer be described by a singular definition of culture or a monolithic interpretation of culture. We are seeing that cultures are becoming increasingly hybridized due to their exposure and proximity to people and the symbols (music, language, art, and history) of other cultures.

4. Küster, "Project," 417.

Part Two: Towards Kingdom Cultures

As a military chaplain, I share my perspective on what would need to change for the church to be more intercultural.[5] Though I am writing from my perspective as a chaplain of the Canadian Armed Forces (CAF), my views are my own. I write from the lens of a Canadian Evangelical Christian who is an immigrant, a former refugee, and a member of a visible minority group. My views regarding intercultural church ministries are influenced by these facets of my identity.

THE ROYAL CANADIAN CHAPLAIN SERVICE

The Royal Canadian Chaplain Service (RCChS), also commonly referred to as "the Chaplaincy," is a diverse organization comprised of ordained and/or appointed men and women from several different religious faith traditions.[6] The mandate of the military chaplain is to "care for all" members and their families within the CAF.[7] Chaplains are mandated to represent their commanding officer in facilitating the provision of spiritual care and support for members and their families.[8] Chaplains engage in a holistic ministry of presence, helping CAF members to

---

5. The aim of the church to become more intercultural is not simply a move towards diversifying its demographics. It is the pursuit of an ecclesiology that is representative of the global church envisioned in Eph 2 and Rev 7:9–10, a new humanity that is comprised of every tribe and tongue. A church that is intercultural is missiological and eschatological in trajectory; it is a faith community that recognizes that an intercultural worldview and practice can address and meet the complex needs of an intercultural world. Such a community bears witness to the picture of God's reconciled people. It is a church that is an inclusive community of worship as well as a social reality of reconciliation and communion. Leaning on the work of missiologists, such as Catholic theologian Robert J. Schreiter, intercultural ministry and theology has a trajectory towards reconciliation and healing, a model that can be employed both in global missions and for local church ministries (see Schreiter, "Reconciliation").

6. The RCChS is currently comprised of chaplains from several faith traditions. Many of the chaplains are from Christian traditions (Roman Catholic, Protestant, and Orthodox), serving alongside several Jewish rabbis and Muslim chaplains. To further diversify the chaplaincy, in 2020, a Sikh, a Buddhist, and a Unitarian chaplain have been welcomed into the organization.

7. CAF chaplains are expected to be able to provide all levels of spiritual care to members and their families, regardless of the member's adherence to a religion or spirituality or no spirituality at all. The full mandate stipulates that the calling of military chaplains is "to care for all, to facilitate the worship of others, and to minister to their own across the full spectrum of environments and operations" ("Chaplain Services," 12).

8. "33.04: Mandate."

navigate problems at work, mental health issues, domestic challenges, and loss and grief. The chaplaincy has also taken on a role in advocating for a diverse and inclusive military in support of the Chief of Defence Staff's defence policy.[9] The RCChS supports diversity initiatives and programs, such as Operation HONOUR, Gender-Based Analysis (GBA+) and intersectionality training,[10] and conducting Religious Leader Engagements and Religious Area Assessments.[11]

CARING FOR ALL AND LOVING OUR NEIGHBOURS

I suggest that the RCChS exists precisely because it is the only institution in the CAF that is organized to care for all members on a holistic level (physical, mental, emotional, vocational, familial, and spiritual). The work of a *Christian* chaplain in this context is to be the hands and feet of Jesus Christ to a people who are hurting and need help, to be present with them in their pain, and to lead them to a place of health and wholeness. Many commanding officers recognize the necessity of having their chaplains "walk the lines" in their units (incarnational ministry)[12] and having

---

9. The policy states, "Canada's unique, diverse and multicultural population is one of its greatest strengths. While positive steps have been made towards greater diversity, inclusion and gender equality, we can do much more to reflect and harness the strength and diversity of the people we serve, in both military and civilian ranks" (Minister of National Defence, "Strong, Secure, Engaged," 23).

10. Both Operation HONOUR and GBA+ training are initiatives stemmed from the CAF's direction to develop an inclusive and safe workplace. The experiences of CAF members around sexual misconduct as well as LGBTQ2+ inclusion have moved the organization towards policies that maintain respect and professionalism for all members regardless of their sex, gender, and orientation. More recently, the policy on hateful conduct was released in 2020 to address occurrences of discrimination in the CAF. The Chaplain School at Canadian Forces Base Borden has hosted two virtual sessions on discussions about the issues of racism and diversity within the CAF.

11. Religious Leader Engagements and Religious Area Assessments are practices and tools that were developed by chaplains during deployed operations. They are designed to assist chaplains to engage in peacemaking initiatives with other religious leaders and to help chaplains, their chains of commands, and CAF members to understand how to navigate the religious and cultural complexities of their area of operations during Exercises and Operations.

12. Slater ("Living Church," 312) suggests that "a key characteristic of chaplaincy is that its primary context is the world rather than the institutional church and that a defining characteristic of chaplains is that they are 'embedded' in social structures." Chaplaincy is incarnational—spiritual caregivers who are embedded into communities, societies, and organizational structures. Chaplains, from a missiological view, are

PART TWO: TOWARDS KINGDOM CULTURES

the chaplain available and accessible to provide support to troops during times of duress or injury (pastoral/spiritual care ministry).[13]

We "care for all" is the mission that military chaplains have been entrusted with. I believe the church has received a similar mission: to love our neighbours as we love ourselves (Matt 22:34–40). It is said that people often feel that they need to *belong* before they can *believe*. The experience of the chaplaincy suggests that there is an alternate perspective to this idiom: people need to feel *beloved*, and when they feel safe enough to *belong*, they are free to receive opportunities to *believe*. While the chaplaincy does not engage in proselytization, chaplains, by expressing God's love to the soldiers we serve through our presence, actions, and timely words, become "visible reminders of the eternal, and symbols of the sacred. [Chaplains] are a source of vision and a sign of hope."[14]

The church is called to love God and to love our neighbours. In loving our neighbours freely, we create pathways for our neighbours to belong and believe. A diverse society that is foreign to the Christian worldview needs to not only know that God loves them but also to know God's *people* love them. An intercultural church is precisely interested in creating a space for people to be loved and to belong so that they can believe. Intercultural work is grounded in incarnational ministry and the pastoral/spiritual care of *all peoples*. The church that desires to become more intercultural must engage in a ministry of presence to respond to the needs of an intercultural world. Like chaplaincy, the church is mandated to *care for all peoples*.

APPLYING LESSONS LEARNED

In the military, after an exercise or an operation, insights and observations are gathered from the participants to compile what is known as "Lessons Learned"—a set of recommendations that are sent up for the chain of command to review and adapt for future operations and activities.

I recognize that the church does not share the same vision or organizational goals as the RCChS or the CAF. However, there are valuable

a *sent* people who live out the *missio Dei*.

13. Chaplaincy is deeply involved in the work of spiritual care which is "to facilitate healing and wholeness rigorously, of the mind first, and then of the human spirit so as to equip people to face the existential struggles of the human condition with greater resourcefulness and courage" (Thorstenson, "Emergence," 5).

14. "Chaplain Services," 14.

lessons learned—insights and practices—that the church could adopt from the chaplaincy to help it become more intercultural. To move forward, the church must assess and change its current organizational structure, spiritual practices, and social response.

ORGANIZATIONAL STRUCTURE: LEADERSHIP DEVELOPMENT IN THE CANADIAN CHURCH

Despite participating in annual leadership symposiums and conferences, many churches have church boards and staff that demographically (economically, politically, racially, and ethnically) look the same—there is little diversity in Canada's church leadership. The current hiring and staffing practices of Canadian churches need to be assessed for diversity to avoid echo chambers, groupthink, and to prevent theological and missiological blindness to intercultural realities.

The RCChS has recognized the need for diversity as an organizational advantage and actively seeks out new chaplains from different ethnicities, cultures, and faith traditions to further strengthen its ability to respond to the spiritual and operational needs of the CAF. The church would benefit in diversifying its staffing practices by hiring women leaders and leaders from different cultural and ethnic backgrounds to respond to the spiritual needs of their communities and the world. Diversity in leadership is a matter of representation, and it is also a matter of theology.[15] The apostle Paul wrestled with the same issues of power

---

15. The theologian Jürgen Moltmann (*Way of Jesus Christ*, 2) has said, "Community in contradiction is often stronger than community in agreement." Too often, the argument against diversifying leadership is that bringing in different people will slow down the work of the local church because there will be differing views. However, the problem is not *differing views*, the problem is *the metric* by which a healthy church is defined and assessed—too often, that metric is based on numerical growth rather than dynamic, complex, and vibrant community—the kind of faithful growth that the late Eugene Peterson described as the "long obedience in the same direction." When practised with mutual submission, differentiation within leadership leads to different insights and perspectives towards problem-solving and organizational growth. It is a necessity for diversity and differentiation to exist in the Church. We cannot be content to foster a community of sameness. From a theological lens, the church is to reflect the life of the Trinity: there is an interaction of Otherness between the Father, the Son, and the Spirit that can be mirrored in how diverse leaders and congregations interact with, submit to, and complement one another. Lastly, an intercultural congregation must be able to see itself in the diversity of its leadership. Representation matters in leadership because in seeing otherness celebrated in the space where decision-making

imbalance and ethnic representation in church communities in his letters to the Galatians and to the church in Ephesus—this is an age-old problem that the church must correct. A diverse church leadership creates spaces for innovation and insight to address social and spiritual issues.

Churches would also benefit from their leadership and laity receiving professional and theological development in intercultural training, understanding bias, women's issues, and gender sensitivity training. Such training can create a culture within local church congregations that can welcome differentiation and diversity within their boardrooms and their sanctuaries and create opportunities for churches to "care for all" inside and outside their communities. The organizational structure of the church and its leaders need to look, learn, and lead interculturally.

SPIRITUAL PRACTICES: EMBRACING LAMENT AS A LANGUAGE OF FAITH

Lament has been the spiritual language that Canadian military chaplains have had to embody and teach soldiers to speak since the First World War and, more recently, the Afghanistan War. The loss of brothers and sisters-in-arms during combat missions, friendly-fire incidents, training accidents, or to suicide have placed a mental, emotional, and spiritual toll on many soldiers in the CAF. From conducting ramp ceremonies in Afghanistan to receiving fallen soldiers at Canadian Forces Base Trenton and their subsequent departure on the Highway of Heroes, chaplains have had to learn the delicate but necessary task of leading soldiers through their grief and suffering.

In addition, I write this chapter amidst a global pandemic that has seen an intensified level of grief amongst soldiers and their families due to the separation from or loss of their families and friends due to the COVID-19 pandemic.[16] The chaplain's task has been and continues to

happens, there is a dispersion of power that welcomes the marginalized and promotes reconciliation.

16. While many Canadians experienced similar constraints due to working from home, physical distancing guidelines, and traveling restrictions, soldiers have experienced a unique level of stress and grief due to their commitment to "Unlimited Liability"—the expectation that "all members accept and understand that they are lawfully ordered into harm's ways under conditions that could lead to the loss of their lives." The expectation that soldiers have committed themselves to a vocation where they may end up sacrificing their lives for their country is a reasonable one that all soldiers understand when they volunteered to enlist. However, there has never been

be to help soldiers and their families to manage their grief, live with their pain, and learn to lament.

The church has enjoyed decades of numerical and spiritual growth which has unfortunately produced a culture of triumphalism that has avoided suffering, pain, loss, and grief.[17] Many Christians cannot competently address issues such as poverty, suffering, and even suicide because our churches have been insulated through worship services and church programs that shield us from our own suffering and from the suffering of society at large. The lack of familiarity with lament, suffering, and trauma in our worship practices is a key reason why churches in Canada have not been able to speak to the issue of racism and racial violence against Canadians who are black, Indigenous, and people of colour. Our songs of worship and praise could benefit by reflecting on the experiences of disappointment, anger, grief, loss, suffering, trauma, and injustice to allow faith communities to share in one another's pain. An intercultural church suffers and grieves together so that it can learn to *heal together*.[18] The church needs to recover the language and practices of lament to speak compassionately to the pain experienced by an intercultural society.

SOCIAL RESPONSE: CHURCH PLANTING, JUSTICE, AND COMPASSION

Many denominations are engaged in church planting, and justice and compassion initiatives. Churches and denominations employ community needs assessments and marketplace research methods to identify

---

a time in Canadian history where soldiers have risked exposing their families to the same unlimited liability; placing the health and well-being of their families at risk has caused an incredible amount of stress and burden on soldiers and their families (see Minister of National Defence, "Duty with Honour," 27).

17. Peter C. Phan, a Catholic theologian, writes about Christian triumphalism as an impediment to developing healthy intercultural churches. Triumphalism situates local congregations into rhythms of comfort. To seek differentiation and diversity will naturally push local churches into spaces of discomfort. The church must be willing to dialogue with the experience of pain and suffering and hold it in tension with our belief that God's salvation has come but the full culmination of our salvation has not yet been fully realized. In being theologically honest about the reality of suffering and by creating a language of lament in our worship, we can affirm that sin is pervasive in our society and deeply and negatively impacts many who come from disadvantaged and marginalized backgrounds (see Phan, *Christianity*).

18. Deusen Hunsinger, *Bearing the Unbearable*, 16.

where to best plant churches and engage in localized ministries. What has often resulted is that churches are being planted in suburban and affluent areas or into gentrified neighbourhoods,[19] sometimes contributing to the forced migration of the urban poor.[20]

An intercultural church does not engage in the displacement of marginalized peoples—the church must learn to situate itself amongst those who are suffering to provide care and community support. Chaplains are not involved in the work of planting churches, but they are planted into units, bases, and wings to advocate for and give agency to soldiers and families who experience challenges. There is a role for suburban and urban church communities to minister amidst the context of suffering and injustice often experienced by intercultural communities. One author suggests that "[church] planting can be seen as a type of specific missional activity that promotes human flourishing."[21] Church planting initiatives must bring healing and well-being into the neighbourhoods where new faith communities are being cultivated.

The church's role as an incarnational presence in marginalized communities is also that of advocacy and giving agency to those who are marginalized and suffering. Chaplains are required to be well-versed in military policies to promote the financial, vocational, familial, mental,

---

19. The church planting movement's use of community needs assessments identifies key neighbourhoods where there are fewer churches and large numbers of "unchurched" or "unreached" peoples. Suburban neighbourhoods and new community developments continue to be areas of church planting focus. As individuals and families experience a lift in their economic situation, many move away from poverty and crime into "safer" neighbourhoods. Often these suburban areas do not have many established church congregations. Some urban centers are seeing a re-urbanization with new businesses and shopping moving into "trendy" or "boutique" neighbourhoods. Often it is the suburbanites who long for an active and entertainment lifestyle who move into these "gentrified" urban centres. Church planting in gentrified neighbourhoods is focused on reaching the unchurched peoples who live in "revitalized" urban neighbourhoods.

20. Church planting has been predominantly seen through a positive lens due to the development of local faith communities that are creating a positive impact in their neighbourhoods. However, there is little to no research on how church planting has been involved in or has impacted the re-urbanization/gentrification of urban centers across North America. While the empirical research remains to be conducted, there are church planting practitioners who are exploring the practical and theological ramifications of church planting practices that may be causing harm to local urban communities (see Cross and Riedel, "When Church Planting Harms the City"; see also Mayfield, "Church Planting"; Bergquist, "Church Planting").

21. Niebauer, "Virtue Ethics and Church Planting," 317.

and spiritual well-being of their members. Churches can assume a similar role in advocating for programs, policies, and laws that improve the livelihood of their neighbours. Such advocacy can include providing crime prevention strategies, anti-racism awareness, vocational, and healthcare programs.

To become more intercultural, the church needs to reframe its incarnational activities in its church planting and justice and compassion initiatives to resemble the chaplain's ministry of presence—an intercultural church must be present with and minister to those who are suffering and provide pathways for human flourishing that includes their physical and spiritual well-being.

CONCLUSION

It will not be an easy task for the church in Canada to move towards becoming a more intercultural community of faith. The church can leverage the experience and practices of other Christian practitioners, like chaplains and other ministry organizations, to help cultivate an intercultural ethos and mission. Churches will need to prayerfully consider how their leadership and congregations can reflect and foster the intercultural reality of Canada; changes are needed regarding hiring and staffing practices. A realignment of leadership training and development must involve diversity and intercultural awareness. The church's culture and language of worship and spirituality requires the inclusion of lament to bring healing to those who suffer in our society as well as in our congregations. Worship can tune the church's heart to the pain experienced by an intercultural society. Lastly, denominations and organizations should alter church planting initiatives for the church to interrupt its suburban status quo and its pursuit of urban relevancy to advocate for and create agency for marginalized peoples. For the church to become more intercultural, it will require both courage, conviction, and commitment to do hard introspective work to be a source of light and life to a diverse, complex, and intercultural world.

BIBLIOGRAPHY

Bergquist, Linda. "Church Planting and the Urbanization of the Rich." *Church Planting* (August 17, 2011). No pages. Online: https://www.churchplanting.com/church-planting-and-the-urbanization-of-the-rich.

Part Two: Towards Kingdom Cultures

Cross, Shaun, and Bill Riedel, "When Church Planting Harms the City." *The Gospel Coalition* (January 22, 2019). No pages. Online: https://www.thegospelcoalition.org/article/church-planting-harms-city

Deusen Hunsinger, Deborah van. *Bearing the Unbearable: Trauma, Gospel, and Pastoral Care*. Grand Rapids: Eerdmans, 2015.

Küster, Volker. "The Project of an Intercultural Theology." *Svensk Missionstidskrift* 93 (2005) 417–32.

Mayfield, D. L. "Church Planting and the Gospel of Gentrification." *Sojourners Magazine* (July 2017). No pages. Online: https://sojo.net/magazine/july-2017/church-planting-and-gospel-gentrification.

Minister of National Defence. "Duty with Honour: The Profession of Arms in Canada 2009," 2009. Online: https://www.canada.ca/content/dam/dnd-mdn/documents/reports/2019/duty-with-honour-en.pdf.

Minister of National Defence. "Strong, Secure, Engaged: Canada's Defence Policy," 2017. Online: https://www.canada.ca/content/dam/dnd-mdn/documents/reports/2018/strong-secure-engaged/canada-defence-policy-report.pdf.

Moltmann, Jürgen. *The Way of Jesus Christ: Christology in Messianic Dimensions*. Translated by Margaret Kohl. New York: HarperCollins, 1990.

Niebauer, Michael. "Virtue Ethics and Church Planting: A Critical Assessment and Reevaluation of Church Planting Utilizing Alasdair MacIntyre's After Virtue." *Missiology* 44 (2016) 311–23.

Phan, Peter C. *Christianity with an Asian Face: Asian American Theology in the Making*. New York: Orbis, 2003.

"QR&O: Volume I—Chapter 33 Chaplain Services." *Government of Canada*. No pages. Online: https://www.canada.ca/en/department-national-defence/corporate/policies-standards/queens-regulations-orders/vol-1-administration/ch-33-chaplain-services.html.

Schreiter, Robert J. "Reconciliation and Healing as a Paradigm for Mission." *International Review of Mission* 94 (2005) 74–83.

Slater, Victoria. "Living Church in the World: Chaplaincy and the Mission of the Church." *Practical Theology* 5 (2012) 307–20.

"33.04: Mandate to Provide Chaplain Services." *Government of Canada*. No pages. Online: https://www.canada.ca/en/department-national-defence/corporate/policies-standards/queens-regulations-orders/vol-1-administration/ch-33-chaplain-services.html#cha-033-4.

Thorstenson, Timothy A. "The Emergence of the Chaplaincy: Re-Defining Pastoral Care for the Postmodern Age." *The Journal of Pastoral Care & Counseling* 66 (2012) 1–7.

Weerakoon, Kamal. "Evangelical Intercultural Identity: A New Resource for Twenty-First Century Mission?" *Colloquium* 47 (2015) 45–61.

The Means of Grace and the Mission of the Church

Justin Bradbury

Daniel Treier asserts that theology involves "communicative praxis," or the way in which Christian practices, directly and indirectly, constitute a drama— the drama of God's redemptive work in salvation.[1] According to Stuart Murray and James Krabill, the church enacts this drama through a range of Christian habits that illustrate God's eschatological design.[2] This chapter seeks to offer a missiological perspective on those habits, called the "means of grace" by John Wesley, and how these universal Christian practices contribute to our vision for intentionally intercultural churches in Canada's globalizing and hybridizing context.[3] Wesley asserted that the world had yet to see "a Christian country upon earth," but that such would be filled with those whose lives displayed genuine scriptural Christianity enacted by universal love of God and neighbour.[4] Wesley viewed both the means of grace and the holy dispositions required to exercise them as the "interconnected system of Christianity" that equips Christians to practise mission communally.[5]

---

1. Treier, *Introducing Evangelical Theology*, 32–33.

2. Krabill and Murray, eds., *Forming Christian Habits*, 25.

3. Rack, "Using John Wesley Today," 8; Semple, *Lord's Dominion*, 300–305. Wesley's missiological influence on early Canadian missions to diaspora peoples is a warrant to consider the relevance of his "voice" for today.

4. Wesley, "Scriptural Christianity," 173.

5. Wesley, "New Creation," 510; Wesley, "General Spread of the Gospel," 494; Bradbury, "Rehearsing the New Creation," 2.

PART TWO: TOWARDS KINGDOM CULTURES

This is germane to missional ecclesiology as Christians rehearse together the drama of the new creation in these Canadian "suburbs of heaven."[6]

WESLEY'S VIEW OF THE NATURE OF GRACE

Wesley's interpretation of the means of grace emerges from his view of the nature and *telos* of God's grace. He affirmed that all human life is within the scope of the Triune God's reconciling interest. His theology focused on the renewal of the *imago Dei* in human lives and the conjoining of scriptural holiness to mission.[7] God, the author of grace, offers himself freely to all people.[8] God's awakening and empowering grace elicits human response to desire and do what pleases God.[9] Wesley depicted prevenient grace as "the drawings of the Father, the desires after God which, if yielded to, increase more and more as Christ sheds light upon the soul."[10] By this, people are enlightened to God's providence and attributes; to their unrighteousness before and alienation from God, and to their need for his salvation.[11] People are reconciled to God by his justifying grace, through faith in Christ's righteousness alone. Christ's reconciling power breaks the guilt and power of sin and makes us God's children.[12] By the new birth, believers are launched into a life of holiness and reinvigorated spiritual health that enables them to love God supremely and extend kenotic service to the temporal and spiritual needs of others.[13] The methodology to nurture the church's holy mission is found in the interconnected practice of the means of grace.[14] Through their use, people are enabled to discern and respond to God's gracious and reconciling intentions.

---

6. Ruth, *A Little Heaven Below*, 146–47.

7. Campbell and Burns, *Wesleyan Essentials*, 98–106.

8. Wesley, "Free Grace," 544; Wesley, "Letter to the Rev. Mr. Downes," 360.

9. Wesley, "Means of Grace," 383.

10. Faith for salvation is not self-generated, but by God's grace alone (see Wesley, "Salvation by Faith," 126; Wesley, "Scripture Way of Salvation," 156–57; Wesley, "The End of Christ's Coming," 480).

11. Wesley, "Witness of the Spirit," 267; Wesley, "Awake, Thou That Sleepest," 147, 152; Wesley, "On Working Out our Own Salvation," 200, 209.

12. Wesley, "Almost Christian," 139, 141.

13. Wesley, "New Birth," 187; Wesley, "One Thing Needful," 356.

14. Wesley, "On Zeal," 314. The terminology reflects Wesley's Anglican heritage.

WESLEY'S CONCEPTION AND USE OF THE MEANS OF GRACE

Wesley used the term "means of grace" broadly to encompass those activities that facilitated the reception of prevenient, justifying, or sanctifying grace.[15] These included the "works of piety," which serve to renew the believer's love for God; the "works of mercy," which stimulate joyful service to neighbours, strangers, friends, and enemies; and the cultivation of holy dispositions.[16] By their interconnected practice, believers grow in holiness and are formed for participation in God's mission in the world.[17] Wesley broadened the sacramental theology of the Church of England beyond the traditional sacraments, prayer, fasting, searching the Scriptures, and Christian conference, to incorporate works of mercy as "real means of grace" and essential to scriptural holiness.[18] The works of mercy are not merely "good deeds" or methods of outreach but are channels of God's grace. They change and reshape both those who benefit from and those who practise them.[19] This was a missional innovation on Wesley's part. Wesley included them as such to integrate our love for God and neighbour holistically. The works of piety help guide works of mercy in the search for those contexts where God's saving presence is most needed today.[20] The means of grace encompass an array of practices that draw people into the drama of their renewal in the *imago Dei*, equipping them for vital participation in the *missio Dei*.[21] He deployed this methodology in his cross-cultural and cross-class mission in America and England, as did early Canadian Methodists in Nova Scotia, Toronto, Winnipeg, and Vancouver.[22]

---

15. Wesley, "Means of Grace," 378, 380–81.
16. Wesley, "Character of a Methodist," 41; Campbell, "Means of Grace."
17. Knight, III, "Means of Grace."
18. Wesley, "On Zeal," 313; Wesley, "Principles of a Methodist," 54.
19. Rieger, "Between God and the Poor," 87.
20. Rieger, "Margins," 25.
21. Wesley, "Duty of Constant Communion," 429.
22. Airhart, *Serving the Present Age*, 75–76; Sutherland, *Methodist Church*, 220.

Part Two: Towards Kingdom Cultures
Works of Piety

Wesley taught that, through baptism, believers are inaugurated into the way of becoming scriptural Christians through the support of a community intent upon mutual discipleship.[23] Baptism implies a missionary orientation in word and deed toward neighbours, strangers, and the community at large.[24] Wesley upheld that the Lord's Supper displayed before people the continual remembrance of Christ's atonement and that it may occasion a person's conversion to Christ. He linked its practice to the evangelical mission of the church because it communicated God's reconciling intentions toward all people.[25] By its frequent use, the Lord's Supper fortifies believers in holiness, equipping them to extend scriptural Christianity outwardly through communal mission in the power of the Spirit.

Wesley stipulated that prayer is indispensable to the reception of grace; vital to effective ministry and harmonious relationships with Christians from divergent theological perspectives; and inseparable from the spiritual awakening of unbelievers.[26] Prayer is more than the exercise of personal or corporate spirituality but a vital means to mission in the community. When enjoined with fasting, believers focus more intently upon fellowship with God, growth in holiness, and preparation for missionary work by the Holy Spirit.[27] Fasting combined with works of mercy benefits one's neighbour in body and spirit and quickens believers to discern God's blessing upon methods to spread the gospel, and to drive out the work of devils.[28]

The reading, study, and preaching of the divinely inspired Scriptures is profitable for doctrine, Christian conversion, and discipleship.[29] Through them, the Holy Spirit reveals God's redemptive purposes to

---

23. Johnson, "John Wesley's Liturgical Theology," 135–78; Cragg, "Introduction," 250.

24. Meadows, *Remembering our Baptism*, 67.

25. Wesley, "Journal, November 7, 1739," 121; Rainey, "Future of Wesleyan Missional Ecclesiology," 69–70.

26. Wesley, "Character of a Methodist," 37; Wesley, "Father Thoughts," 127.

27. Wesley, "Upon our Lord's Sermon on the Mount," 594, 600; Hammond, *John Wesley in America*, 42.

28. Wesley, "'Large' Minutes," 845, 889, 923.

29. Wesley, *Explanatory Notes*, 7; Wesley, "Means of Grace," 388.

humanity, shines the light of Christ to elicit faith in him; they are vital to the believer's growth in holiness and preparedness for communal mission.[30]

Christian conference was the genus of Wesley's small group system to structure holiness of heart and life.[31] It fused evangelical preaching to the formation of trans-denominational groups to nurture growth in scriptural holiness and to practise the works of mercy together.[32] The groups welcomed seekers after Christ and offered mutual support and spiritual accountability.[33] It was essential to sustain Christian mission.

Works of Mercy

Wesley insisted that the fellowship of the church is the appropriate context for believers to mutually evoke works of mercy with zeal for the holy love of God and neighbour.[34] Such love is "the medicine of life, the never-failing remedy, for all the evils of a disordered world, for all the miseries and vices of men."[35] He classified any loving action to serve one's neighbour or share the gospel as a work of mercy because these reflect the missionary character of God.[36] Therefore, scriptural Christians do not hesitate to offer food to the hungry and vulnerable; to alleviate deplorable living conditions of fellow Christians and the poor around them;[37] to deliver general and religious education to children and those with limited access;[38] to offer medical care to alleviate human suffering;[39] to distribute personal surplus funds to the poor, whom God has appointed to receive it;[40] to admonish those who do what is evil, or morally wrong, and conversely, encourage those who do what is good in God's eyes, as

30. Wesley, *Explanatory Notes*, 534; Dayton, "Use of Scripture," 127–28.
31. Watson, *Class Meeting*, 19–27; Sheffield, "Making Disciples," 223–32.
32. Wesley, "Nature, Design, and General Rules," 69, 70, 73. Early Methodism was a trans-denominational renewal and evangelistic movement, not a separate denomination.
33. Wesley, "Nature, Design, and General Rules," 79.
34. Wesley, "Plain Account of the People Called Methodists," 259.
35. Wesley, "Earnest Appeal," 45.
36. Weslley, "Sermon 26: Upon our Lord's Sermon on the Mount," 573.
37. Wesley, *Thoughts*, 59; Heitzenrater, *Mirror and Memory*, 97.
38. Wesley, "On Visiting the Sick," 387, 389; Blevins, "To Be a Means of Grace."
39. Wesley, "A Plain Account of the People Called Methodists," 276–77.
40. Wesley, "Good Steward," 283, 295; Wesley, "Danger of Increasing Riches," 184.

expressions of concern and holy love for people's immediate and eternal well-being.[41]

The practice of entertaining or assisting strangers also exemplified the conviction that Christ calls believers to love and honour all people through the demonstration of justice, mercy, and truth.[42] Wesley exhorted Christians to extend hospitality to "saints . . . persecutors . . . friends, strangers, enemies—not only embracing those that offer, but seeking opportunities to exercise it."[43] He refused to categorize the poor as outsiders; rather, he broadened the concept of community to include them with equity.[44] He understood such acts of hospitality to be showing and receiving hospitality from Christ himself, as a vital means of grace to extend Christian mission.[45] Visiting the sick and imprisoned, and comforting the afflicted are real means of grace, and not to be done by proxy.[46] It may convey the grace of Christ and God's plan of redemption to the one being visited, but may also be a means whereby the grace of Christ is communicated to the visitor, a blessing not to be missed, no matter how unpleasant it may in some ways be.

Thus, Wesley sought to fortify the widespread nature of Christian mission through God's holy people.[47] Whilst zeal for the works of piety constituted the regular means to inculcate love for God and growth in holiness, zeal for works of mercy takes priority in the believer's life when human need is pressing, at love's "almighty call."[48] The works of mercy form Christians for holy mission because these are the outward expression of the works of piety. For Wesley, the means of grace assume a missiological priority, not only a devotional imperative.

---

41. His small group system expanded the traditional confessional by democratizing and enlarging its use through lay Christian leaders.

42. Wesley, "Sermon 30: Upon our Lord's Sermon on the Mount," 662.

43. Wesley, *Explanatory Notes*, 391–92.

44. Heitzenrater, ed., *The Poor*, 27, 35.

45. Wesley, *Explanatory Notes*, 87.

46. Wesley, "Nature, Design, and General Rules," 72.

47. Wesley, "Duty of Reproving Our Neighbour," 512–17.

48. Wesley, "On Zeal," 314–15, 319.

THE MISSION OF GRACE AND THE INTENTIONALLY INTERCULTURAL CHURCH

How might Wesley's methodology enhance participation in the *missio Dei* through intentionally intercultural churches? Twelve members of our congregation reflected on the role of the means of grace in the church planting process at the International Place of Friendship (IPF) in Winnipeg during a series of Focus Group meetings.[49] Five research participants were born in Canada, and seven migrated to the country since 2014. Diverse denominational backgrounds posed no barrier to their support of the IPF goal to bring Canadian and diaspora Christians together in mutuality and reciprocity of service and Christian witness among Winnipeg's immigrant communities. Friendships were forged and leaders identified to plan and lead a new congregation, New Horizons International Church (NHIC).

The participants gave feedback about the means of grace as practices that vitally connected their Christian formation and mission engagement in planting a church within the IPF. They discussed how the following components worked together in their Christian experience and the burgeoning mission of the church: prayer and exhortation; searching the Scriptures and instructing the uninformed; fasting and feeding the hungry; the Lord's Supper and entertaining or assisting strangers; and Christian conference and sharing one's testimony.

They concluded that the practices of "prayer and exhortation" become means of grace through the multi-voiced Sunday worship services, small groups, and various fellowship gatherings of the church.[50] First, the act of praying together within ethnic and linguistic diversity stimulates their faith and mitigates various dangers to robust Christian spirituality.[51] Secondly, answers to prayer encourage the whole congregation and stir the believers to continue praying, as this facilitates the experience of God's identity and presence working in the church.[52] Thirdly, praying

---

49. They examined the practice of the means of grace and their relationship to mission in a local Wesleyan church. Each meeting included food, the focus group exercise, data collection, de-briefing, and a short lesson. The methodology was called "Theological Action Research," as outlined by Cameron, et al., *Talking about God*, 17, 49–60.

50. Murray and Williams, *Multi-Voiced Church*, 36.

51. Knight, III, *Presence of God*, 8–9, 168.

52. Knight, III, *Presence of God*, 10–11.

together incites them to act upon identified needs within and beyond the congregation through the church's various settlement programs. In these ways, Christian affections evoke and order their response to God's identity and presence within the congregation and stimulate mission praxis as they serve God's new creation purpose.[53]

They identified the interconnected nature of "searching the Scriptures and instructing the uninformed" as a planting team. They compassionately responded to recent immigrants whose expressed primary need was for friendship and belonging, followed by English language proficiency, then to learn more about Christianity. This echoes the pattern of the early Wesleyan revival when Christians gathered to read the New Testament and became convinced that to be a scriptural Christian means to utilize the works of mercy to serve the temporal needs and spiritual awakening of others to Christ.[54] Wesley's example exhorts Christians to embrace an evangelistic lifestyle that does not detract people from faith in Christ by attitudes and actions that display indifference.[55] Searching the Scriptures together results in works of mercy when God's people are sensitive and responsive to the Holy Spirit's leadership.

Respondents recognized that fasting and feeding the hungry brings them closer to God and to people who are physically and spiritually depleted. Most identified fasting as a personal practice and felt that more corporate times of fasting would intensify the congregation's awareness of the needs of others. They resonated with Wesley's teaching that fasting is an obligation and benefit for overcoming any "feebleness and faintness of spirit" in the execution of their Christian duty.[56] They identified their participation in feeding the hungry through church organized food collections, cooking groups, and fundraising for local charities. Additionally, they connected these means of grace to teaching English to newcomers, widening their family tables to include newcomer friends, and inviting others to worship gatherings and events.

The participants confirmed that "the Lord's Supper and entertaining and assisting the stranger" work together as means of grace to display biblical hospitality. They maintained that the Lord's Supper is a visual stimulus for them to accept and serve the stranger because these practices

---

53. Knight, III, "Means of Grace," 143.
54. Wesley, "Character of a Methodist," 41.
55. Wesley, "Principles of a Methodist," 22.
56. Wesley, "'Large' Minutes," 917.

remind them that Jesus Christ first accepted them. They noted that the Lord's Supper is an impetus for outreach beyond the church because Christ cleanses and forgives them, thereby empowering them to serve others in his name.[57] They said that opening their homes is an appropriate way for them to express this means of grace, and that by doing so, they welcome Christ. The practice of biblical, mutual hospitality among immigrants must be intentional, to counteract the "loaded silence" some diaspora Christians have experienced in some Canadian churches.[58] The integrated use of these means of grace at NHIC illustrates how Canadian and diaspora Christians may grow together in scriptural holiness and orient its mission toward the eschatological vision of Rev 7 and 21.

Finally, the research participants concurred that "Christian conference" as a work of piety relates to "sharing one's testimony" as a work of mercy because Christian fellowship creates context for sharing their faith. One member from Nigeria commented that the practice of Christian conference "has strengthened our relationship with God and each other" within our diverse congregation. The Life Groups strengthened mutual spiritual edification, confession, forgiveness, love and a fuller social realisation of the Christian life.[59] Social holiness encourages biblical hospitality, friendship, healing, active partnership, and shared leadership of the congregation as a foretaste of the eschatological future believers share.[60]

A local respondent from Ecuador noted this has empowered their Life Group members to share their testimony in various languages at the IPF through conversations, classes, and special events. First generation non-Christian immigrants not only gain support in their settlement process but also often hear the message of the gospel in their own language from church members who serve in these programs. Personal testimony confirms the soteriological reality of the individual, while serving a missiological aim among those who hear it.[61]

When Canadian and diaspora Christians utilize the means of grace together with intentionality and consistency, trust in God's eschatological

---

57. Blevins, "John Wesley," 262; Rainey, "Future of Wesleyan Missional Ecclesiology," 72–73.

58. Janzen, ed., *Beyond the Welcome*, 13.

59. Rawlyk, *Canada Fire*, 55.

60. Wesley, "Great Assize," 374; Sheffield, *Multicultural Leader*, 23, 58. Social holiness means growth in scriptural holiness through small groups.

61. Blevins, "To Be a Means of Grace," 67; Runyon, *New Creation*, 102–40.

vision is undergirded; our growth in scriptural holiness is strengthened; and our engagement in the *missio Dei* empowers us to reconceive the drama of the church's priestly role in the Canadian "suburbs of heaven."

CONCLUSION

Wesley's missiological conception and use of the means of grace is a methodological groundwork for creating intentionally intercultural churches in Canada because these are universal Christian practices.[62] Enoch Wan also emphasised "the focus is on holistic missions and contextualization, integrating evangelism and social concern" in his pioneering missiological paradigm.[63] For Wesley, the means of grace as "the entire, connected system of Christianity" shapes Christians for participation in the *missio Dei* as they grow together in social holiness and reach out together in missions communally. Those who are awakened and justified are drawn into the formative process of Christian community and become new partners in faith and mission.[64] Ajith Fernando stresses that cognitive, affective, and evaluative transformation is the goal of discipleship.[65] Such mission-oriented discipleship is possible when Christians purposefully, and consistently, practise means of grace together in the power of the Holy Spirit through intentionally intercultural churches.

BIBLIOGRAPHY

Airhart, Phyllis. *Serving the Present Age: Revivalism, Progressivism, and the Methodist Tradition in Canada*. Montreal, QC: McGill-Queen's University Press, 1992.

Blevins, Dean. "John Wesley and the Means of Grace: An Approach to Christian Religious Education." PhD diss., Claremont School of Theology, 1999.

———. "To Be a Means of Grace: A Wesleyan Perspective on Christian Practices and the Lives of Children." *Wesleyan Theological Journal* 43 (2008) 47–67.

Bradbury, Justin. "Rehearsing the New Creation: Diaspora Missions and the Means of Grace in a Wesleyan Context in Canada." PhD diss., University of Manchester, 2021.

Cameron, Helen, et al. *Talking about God in Practise: Theological Action Research and Practical Theology*. London: SCM, 2010.

---

62. Hiebert and Meneses, *Incarnational Ministry*, 351–52.
63. Wan, ed., *Diaspora Missiology*, 98–99.
64. Chilcote, "Mission-Church Paradigm," 151–64.
65. Fernando, *Discipling in a Multicultural World*, 142–44.

Campbell, Ted A. "Means of Grace and Forms of Piety." In *The Oxford Handbook of Methodist Studies*, edited by William J. Abraham and James E. Kirby, 280–91. Oxford: Oxford University Press, 2009.

Campbell, Ted A., and Michael T. Burns. *Wesleyan Essentials in a Multi-Cultural Society*. Nashville: Abingdon, 2004.

Chilcote, Paul W. "The Mission-Church Paradigm of the Wesleyan Revival." In *World Mission in the Wesleyan Spirit*, edited by Darrell L. Whiteman and Gerald H. Anderson, 151–64. Franklin, TN: Providence House, 2009.

Cragg, Gerald R. "An Introduction to 'A Father Appeal to Men of Reason and Religion.'" In *The Works of John Wesley: Volume XI— The Appeals to Men of Reason and Religion and Certain Related Open Letters*, edited by Gerald R. Cragg, 203–71. Nashville: Abingdon, 1987.

Dayton, Donald. "The Use of Scripture in the Wesleyan Tradition." In *The Use of the Bible in Theology: Evangelical Options*, edited by Robert K. Johnson, 121–36. Atlanta: John Knox, 1985.

Fernando, Ajith. *Discipling in a Multicultural World*. Wheaton: Crossway, 2019.

Hammond, Geordan. *John Wesley in America: Restoring Primitive Christianity*. Oxford: Oxford University Press, 2014.

Heitzenrater, Richard P. *Mirror and Memory: Reflections on Early Methodism*. Nashville: Kingswood, 1989.

Heitzenrater, Richard P., ed. *The Poor and the People Called Methodists*. Nashville: Kingswood, 2002.

Hiebert, Paul G., and Eloise Hiebert Meneses. *Incarnational Ministry: Planting Churches in Band, Tribal, Peasant, and Urban Societies*. Grand Rapids: Baker, 1995.

Janzen, Rich, ed. *Beyond the Welcome: Churches Responding to the Immigrant Reality in Canada*. Kitchener, ON: Centre for Community Based Research, 2010.

Johnson, Steve. "John Wesley's Liturgical Theology." PhD diss., University of Manchester, 2016.

Knight, Henry H., III. "The Means of Grace and the Promise of New Life in the Evangelism of John Wesley." In *Considering the Great Commission: Evangelism and Mission in the Wesleyan Spirit*, edited by W. Stephen Gunter and Elaine Robinson, 135–44. Nashville: Abingdon, 2005.

———. The Presence of God in the Christian Life: John Wesley and the Means of Grace. Metuchen: Scarecrow, 1992.

Krabill, James R., and Stuart Murray, eds. *Forming Christian Habits in Post-Christendom: The Legacy of Alan and Eleanor Kreider*. Waterloo, ON: Herald, 2011.

Meadows, Philip R. *Remembering our Baptism: Discipleship and Mission in the Wesleyan Spirit*. Nashville: Discipleship Resources, 2017.

Murray, Stuart, and Sian Murray Williams. *Multi-Voiced Church*. London: Paternoster, 2012.

Rack, Henry D. "Using John Wesley Today: Some Suggested Principles." In *The Path of Holiness: Perspectives in Wesleyan Thought in Honor of Herbert B. McGonigle*, edited by Joseph W. Cunningham and David Rainey, 8. Lexington: Emeth, 2014

Rainey, David. "The Future of Wesleyan Missional Ecclesiology: Reconciliation and the Eucharist" In *The Path of Holiness: Perspectives in Wesleyan Thought in Honor of Herbert B. McGonigle*, edited by Joseph W. Cunningham and David Rainey, 63–74. Lexington, KY: Emeth, 2014.

Part Two: Towards Kingdom Cultures

Rawlyk, George A. *The Canada Fire: Radical Evangelicalism in British North America 1775-1812*. Montreal, QC: McGill-Queen's University Press, 1994.

Rieger, Joerg. "Between God and the Poor." In *The Poor and the People Called Methodists*, edited by Richard P. Heitzenrater, 83-99. Nashville: Kingswood, 2002.

———. "Margins and the Centre: The Future of Methodist Traditions and Theology." In *Methodist and Radical: Rejuvenating a Tradition*, edited by Joerg Rieger and John Vincent, 23-47. Nashville: Kingswood, 2004.

Runyon, Theodore. *The New Creation: John Wesley's Theology Today*. Nashville: Abingdon, 1998.

Ruth, Lester. *A Little Heaven Below: Worship at Early Methodist Quarterly Meetings*. Nashville: Kingswood, 2000.

Semple, Neil. *The Lord's Dominion: The History of Canadian Methodism*. Montreal: McGill-Queen's University Press, 1996.

Sheffield, Daniel. *The Multicultural Leader: Developing a Catholic Personality*. 2nd ed. Toronto: Clements, 2015.

Sutherland, Alexander. *The Methodist Church and Mission in Canada and Newfoundland*. Toronto: Department of Missionary Literature of The Methodist Church of Canada, 1906.

Treier, Daniel J. *Introducing Evangelical Theology*. Grand Rapids: Baker Academic, 2019.

Wan, Enoch, ed. *Diaspora Missiology: Theory, Methodology, and Practice*. Portland: Institute of Diaspora Studies, Western Seminary, 2011.

Watson, Kevin M. *The Class Meeting: Reclaiming a Forgotten Small Group Experience*. Franklin: Seedbed, 2014.

Wesley, John. "The Character of a Methodist." In *The Works of John Wesley: Volume IX—Letters and Essays*, edited by Albert C. Outler, 30-46. Nashville: Abingdon, 1984.

———. "An Earnest Appeal." In *The Works of John Wesley: Volume XI— The Appeals to Men of Reason and Religion and Certain Related Open Letters*, edited by Gerald R. Cragg, 43-94. Nashville: Abingdon, 1987.

———. *Explanatory Notes upon the New Testament*. London: W. Nicholson & Sons, 1877.

———. "Father Thoughts upon Christian Perfection." In *The Works of John Wesley: Volume XIII—Doctrinal and Controversial Treatises II*, edited by Albert C. Outler, 272-73. Nashville: Abingdon, 1984.

———. "Journal, November 7, 1739." In *The Works of John Wesley: Volume XIX— Journal and Diaries II (1738-1743)*, edited by Albert C. Outler, 119-224. Nashville: Abingdon, 1984.

———. "The 'Large' Minutes." In *The Works of John Wesley: Volume X— The Methodist Societies, The Minutes of Conference*, edited by Henry D. Rack, 844-935. Nashville: Abingdon, 1984.

———. "A Letter to the Rev. Mr. Downes." In *The Works of John Wesley: Volume IX— Letters and Essays*, edited by Albert C. Outler, 350-66. Nashville: Abingdon, 1984.

———. "The Nature, Design, and General Rules of the United Societies." In *The Works of John Wesley: Volume X— The Methodist Societies, The Minutes of Conference*, edited by Henry D. Rack, 62-74. Nashville: Abingdon, 1984.

———. "A Plain Account of the People Called Methodists." In *The Works of John Wesley: Volume IX—Letters and Essays*, edited by Albert C. Outler, 253-80. Nashville: Abingdon, 1984.

———. "The Principles of a Methodist." In *The Works of John Wesley: Volume IX—Letters and Essays*, edited by Albert C. Outler, 47-66. Nashville: Abingdon, 1984.

———. "Sermon 1: Salvation by Faith." In *The Works of John Wesley: Volume I—Sermons 1-33*, edited by Albert C. Outler, 109-30. Nashville: Abingdon, 1984.

———. "Sermon 2: The Almost Christian." In *The Works of John Wesley: Volume I—Sermons 1-33*, edited by Albert C. Outler, 131-41. Nashville: Abingdon, 1984.

———. "Sermon 3: Awake, Thou That Sleepest." In *The Works of John Wesley: Volume I—Sermons 1-33*, edited by Albert C. Outler, 142-58. Nashville: Abingdon, 1984.

———. "Sermon 4: Scriptural Christianity." In *The Works of John Wesley: Volume I—Sermons 1-33*, edited by Albert C. Outler, 159-80. Nashville: Abingdon, 1984.

———. "Sermon 10-11: The Witness of the Spirit." In *The Works of John Wesley: Volume I—Sermons 1-33*, edited by Albert C. Outler, 267-98. Nashville: Abingdon, 1984.

———. "Sermon 15: The Great Assize." In *The Works of John Wesley: Volume I—Sermons 1-33*, edited by Albert C. Outler, 354-75. Nashville: Abingdon, 1984.

———. "Sermon 16: The Means of Grace." In *The Works of John Wesley: Volume I—Sermons 1-33*, edited by Albert C. Outler, 376-97. Nashville: Abingdon, 1984.

———. "Sermon 21-33: Upon our Lord's Sermon on the Mount." In *The Works of John Wesley: Volume I—Sermons 1-33*, edited by Albert C. Outler, 466-698. Nashville: Abingdon, 1984.

———. "Sermon 26: Upon our Lord's Sermon on the Mount." In *The Works of John Wesley: Volume I—Sermons 1-33*, edited by Albert C. Outler, 572-91. Nashville: Abingdon, 1984.

———. "Sermon 30: Upon our Lord's Sermon on the Mount." In *The Works of John Wesley: Volume I—Sermons 1-33*, edited by Albert C. Outler, 650-63. Nashville: Abingdon, 1984.

———. "Sermon 43: The Scripture Way of Salvation." In *The Works of John Wesley: Volume II—Sermons 34-70*, edited by Albert C. Outler, 153-69. Nashville: Abingdon, 1984.

———. "Sermon 45: The New Birth." In *The Works of John Wesley: Volume II—Sermons 34-70*, edited by Albert C. Outler, 186-201. Nashville: Abingdon, 1984.

———. "Sermon 51: The Good Steward." In *The Works of John Wesley: Volume II—Sermons 34-70*, edited by Albert C. Outler, 281-99. Nashville: Abingdon, 1984.

———. "Sermon 62: The End of Christ's Coming." In *The Works of John Wesley: Volume II—Sermons 34-70*, edited by Albert C. Outler, 471-84. Nashville: Abingdon, 1984.

———. "Sermon 63: The General Spread of the Gospel." In *The Works of John Wesley: Volume II—Sermons 34-70*, edited by Albert C. Outler, 485-49. Nashville: Abingdon, 1984.

———. "Sermon 64: The New Creation." In *The Works of John Wesley: Volume II—Sermons 34-70*, edited by Albert C. Outler, 500-10. Nashville: Abingdon, 1984.

———. "Sermon 65: The Duty of Reproving our Neighbour." In *The Works of John Wesley: Volume II—Sermons 34-70*, edited by Albert C. Outler, 511-20. Nashville: Abingdon, 1984.

———. "Sermon 85: On Working Out our Own Salvation." In *The Works of John Wesley: Volume III—Sermons 71-114*, edited by Albert C. Outler, 199-209. Nashville: Abingdon, 1984.

———. "Sermon 92: On Zeal." In *The Works of John Wesley: Volume III—Sermons 71-114*, edited by Albert C. Outler, 308-21. Nashville: Abingdon, 1984.

———. "Sermon 98: On Visiting the Sick." In *The Works of John Wesley: Volume III—Sermons 71-114*, edited by Albert C. Outler, 384-98. Nashville: Abingdon, 1984.

———. "Sermon 101: The Duty of Constant Communion." In *The Works of John Wesley: Volume III—Sermons 71-114*, edited by Albert C. Outler, 427-39. Nashville: Abingdon, 1984.

———. "Sermon 110: Free Grace." In *The Works of John Wesley: Volume III—Sermons 71-114*, edited by Albert C. Outler, 542-63. Nashville: Abingdon, 1984.

———. "Sermon 131: The Danger of Increasing Riches." In *The Works of John Wesley: Volume IV—Sermons 115-51*, edited by Albert C. Outler, 177-86. Nashville: Abingdon, 1984.

———. "Sermon 146: The One Thing Needful." In *The Works of John Wesley: Volume IV—Sermons 115-51*, edited by Albert C. Outler, 351-59. Nashville: Abingdon, 1984.

———. *Thoughts on the Present Scarcity of Provisions*. London: R. Hawes, 1773.

Seeing What the Father is Doing
A Practical and Theological Vineyard Approach to Moving beyond Multiculturalism

BETH M. STOVELL AND MELT VAN DER SPUY

THIS CHAPTER DEVELOPS OUT of the stories, practical experiences, and theological reflection about multiculturalism of two Vineyard church leaders: Beth Stovell, a biblical scholar transplanted from the United States to minister in Calgary, AB, who works at the national level for Vineyard Canada, and Melt van der Spuy, a practical theologian and pastor transplanted from South Africa, who pastors at the Yellowknife Vineyard Church in the highly diverse context of Yellowknife, NWT. In this chapter, Beth and Melt will first tell their stories of the complexities of multiculturalism in the diverse contexts of Austin, TX (for Beth) and of Cape Town and Johannesburg, South Africa (for Melt), and how that has impacted their work towards moving beyond multiculturalism in Calgary and Yellowknife. This chapter will locate these stories in the broader context of multiculturalism within the Association of Vineyard Churches, noting the strengths and weaknesses of Vineyard's historical approaches to these issues. The chapter will examine best practices for engaging the complex questions of multiculturalism from a Vineyard perspective and then discuss a theological framework for moving beyond multiculturalism based on Vineyard theology.

The Association of Vineyard Churches (AVC), commonly referred to as "the Vineyard," developed as a church planting movement in the 1980s in Southern California under the leading of John Wimber

PART TWO: TOWARDS KINGDOM CULTURES

and formed out of a mix of the 1960–70s Jesus movement, Quakerism (Friends), and a charismatically informed Evangelicalism. Vineyard Global/AVC now represents over 2,500 churches on six continents. Due to the multinational nature of the Vineyard, multiculturalism has been an ever-present question for Vineyard churches.[1]

OUR STORIES

Beth's Story

Beth's story with multiculturalism began at birth with a Jewish father and a Western European yet largely German mother. The history of German Nazi hatred and violence against the Jews in the Holocaust and beyond spilled into Beth's family, causing her Jewish family and her German family on each side to equally choose not to be at Beth's parents' wedding and then a rejection by each other's families for a portion of Beth's life. In addition to this, Beth further grew up on the poor side of town in Austin, TX, where she was one of only a handful of *white* students (and the only Jewish one) in a Latinx and African American context. Beth's identity was already bicultural because of her parents. She learned in school how to engage in Latinx, and particularly Mexican, culture and in African American culture as well[2]. In 2002, Beth moved to Canada and became not only bicultural but binational. Across her years in the US and Canada, she could observe the claims to multiculturalism that each country presented and the gaps in how each country actually lived out these values.

Beth joined the Vineyard officially in 2003 when she began attending the Vancouver Eastside Vineyard in Vancouver, BC and soon began preaching, teaching, and leading worship in that context. Since then, she has ministered in Vineyard churches in Canada and the US: specifically

---

1. There should be a distinction drawn between the goal of *being multicultural* and the complexities of multiculturalism at a local congregational level where a community may or may not represent the ethnic and cultural diversity of its neighbourhood. Recently, a new church joined the Vineyard, which is an Asian congregation. They lamented their tendency towards monoculture as *Asian* culture in their church. The need for greater multiculturalism in its local congregational manifestations applies to any monocultural context rather than only predominantly Euro-Canadian contexts.

2. Some of the characteristics of Beth's childhood match with the sociological definition of TCK (Third Culture Kids) (see Pollock and Van Reken, *Third Culture Kids*).

in Vancouver, BC; Cambridge, ON; Doral, FL; and Calgary, AB. She now works with her husband Jon on the Vineyard Canada national team overseeing theological and spiritual formation initiatives alongside her work as a biblical studies professor at Ambrose University.

Melt's Story

Melt's journey into multiculturalism started at seventeen. He was conscripted into National Service in Apartheid South Africa. He served tours of duty in Southwest Africa, Angola, and in the African Townships of South Africa.[3] During these years he was exposed to the ugly reality of Apartheid. This awoke in him a concern for *the Other*. The white family he grew up in was not inherently racist but had a paternalistic attitude toward other race groups since they were regarded as unable to care for themselves. It was an insidious form of racism that never led him to question Apartheid until he served in the military and witnessed the ideology in practice.

A military conflict in Angola converted him from unenthusiastic participant in the system to firm opponent of Apartheid. When two SWAPO (South West African People's Organization)[4] insurgents were killed and two more SWAPO guerrillas were taken prisoner, the prisoners were to be kept awake overnight.[5] Melt shared his two-hour guard shift with a man who was a virulent racist. Instead of waking the prisoners when they nodded off, this young man terrorized them. The terrorizing culminated in him opening a clasp knife and chopping a ten-centimetre gash in the prisoner's leg.

Melt called the medics on a two-way radio to attend to the prisoner. The medics arrived and stitched the wound. No questions were asked about how this occurred. The medics left and someone else came to guard the prisoners. This situation, along with others like it, led to a radical change in the posture of Melt's heart toward *the Other*.

---

3. The South African Border War—also known as the Namibian War of Independence, and sometimes denoted in South Africa as the Angolan Bush War—was a largely asymmetric conflict that occurred in Namibia (then South West Africa), Zambia, and Angola from 26 August 1966 to 21 March 1990.

4. The SWAPO is the liberation organization and current governing political party of Namibia.

5. A fairly common practice by all armed forces since sleep deprivation makes the interrogation process to follow more likely to yield dividends.

Part Two: Towards Kingdom Cultures

Melt's background and involvement in multicultural ministry has spanned more than twenty years. Involvement has been at theoretical and practical levels. He is a white South African with two African Xhosa children and three biological daughters. He pastors the multicultural Yellowknife Vineyard church in the NWT of Canada and pastored the multicultural Kenilworth Vineyard Church in South Africa 2009–2014.

From 2016 to 2018, Melt served as the National Director for Development Associates International (DAI) in South Africa. He assisted in the development of the most recent DAI module, "Culture, Ethnicity, and Diversity," and hosted a pilot workshop in South Africa toward the end of 2017.

STRENGTHS AND WEAKNESSES OF VINEYARD MULTICULTURALISM

Melt and Beth's work with the Vineyard movement has spanned ministry in South Africa, the US, and Canada. As they have walked with Vineyard churches in these diverse countries, they have witnessed the great strengths of Vineyard multiculturalism and the weaknesses in Vineyard's approaches to multiculturalism in these nations.

Strengths and Weaknesses in Vineyard in Light of Melt's Experience

Melt and his wife Anida became first generation Christians in 1990. From 1994 to 2018, they raised their family in the newly free and democratic South Africa. They spent those years making peace with the past and ministering among people of all ethnicities and cultures. They joined the Vineyard movement in 2007 via the New Wine network of charismatic Anglican churches.[6]

In 2009, Melt was called as the Senior Pastor to Kenilworth Vineyard Church (KVC)[7] in Cape Town. Melt inherited a church that, contrary to norms in post-Apartheid South Africa, was fully multicultural with at least seven African ethnicities represented. The church was approximately 45 percent Indigenous African. The church was multicultural due to intentional cross-cultural work done by his pastoral predecessors. KVC

---

6. The New Wine Anglican churches are those that traditionally came under the influence of John Wimber and the Vineyard in the 1980s and 1990s.

7. The KVC was a onetime "flagship" Vineyard church in South Africa.

is located near to railway lines and taxi ranks allowing the poor to access the church. In South Africa, the poor still tend to come from race groups other than white South African.

During the years 1995–2020, AVC South Africa strove to create a multicultural representation at the local church level with limited success. The largest Vineyard congregation in South Africa is a single culture East Indian congregation of approximately 600 people in Chatsworth, an area previously designated for that "people group" to live in. The problem is that people still tend to live in the areas that were designated for them to live during Apartheid. This is changing as the emerging black middle class moves increasingly into what were previously designated *white* areas.

Melt's experience has shown him that people of European origin like him are comfortable in multicultural environments so long as *we are the majority culture*. Our culture seems to have both a blind spot and an inherent superiority complex in this regard. Additionally, linguistic barriers and a generally poorer economic reality for *other* cultures will often translate into feelings of inferiority. Associate professor of sociology at the University of Cape Town, Sharlene Swartz, speaks of South Africa not being able to make significant cross-cultural advances until it loses its inherent "white superiority and black inferiority."[8]

Swartz's observation was illustrated at KVC when Melt noticed that one of the leaders of the church, a Zambian man, never seemed to pray for white people but would pray for black people and would receive prayer from anyone.[9] Over coffee, Melt asked the man about the situation and whether it was the black/white thing. He dropped his head and said, "it is as you say." Melt then asked how it could be so when the man was a professor of molecular biology at a prominent university in Cape Town and held a PhD. His response was, "It makes no difference at all."

Another sad story from South Africa was the attempted handover of a church from a prominent Vineyard scholar and pastor in the early 2000s to a colleague of colour in Bryanston Vineyard Church.[10] The process toward handover was conducted gradually and with great care,

---

8. Swartz, *Another Country*, 93–120.

9. Vineyard practice values body ministry in the sense of praying for one another. Usually, a group of three of four people will pray for one person in a particular way we have of praying for people.

10. Bryanston is an affluent, predominantly white suburb outside of Johannesburg in South Africa.

PART TWO: TOWARDS KINGDOM CULTURES

transparency, and caution, even to the extent of the completion of surveys within the congregation. The overwhelming majority of congregants backed the transition and looked forward to it. Yet, when it came to it, the transition failed, spectacularly scattering the church and leaving both the outgoing (white) and incoming (black) pastor broken and disillusioned.

Making real progress in leading in multicultural contexts requires significant work. Training, along with relational openness and trust, is needed if Vineyard Canada is to make progress in this regard. More concerning is that this type of work is prone to all sorts of misunderstanding and offence. Making a somewhat prophetic plea is the easy part. Doing the work of cross-cultural training and moving beyond multiculturalism is much harder. South Africa comes with its own unique racial tension and baggage. Perhaps AVC Canada could see a more natural transition to diversity?

In November 2018, Melt accepted a call as Senior Pastor to the multicultural Yellowknife Vineyard Church (YKVC). Yellowknife is the capital city of the NWT. YKVC is presently a church of around 200 people. Within those 200 people, approximately twenty-seven different cultural groups are represented.[11]

In two years of ministry, there has not been any significant relational fallout due to cultural tensions. Apart from negotiating a slightly tense Black Lives Matter season early in 2020 where one or two Caucasian people needed to be helped to understand that "you apologize as long as you are alive" for the past, the church has been relationally sound across the cultural divide. It is not coincidental. Melt would like to believe his life and experience brings something to the table in this regard. More than thirty leading adults have been trained in ten sessions of leadership and culture, ethnicity, and diversity. Communication has been regular and fully transparent.[12] Melt hopes that modest progress in

---

11. At last count, the following ethnicities were present in the church: Caucasian Canadian (French and English), Dene, Inuit, Me'tis, Jamaican, Bermudian, Bahaman, Haitian, DRC Congolese, Zambian, Zimbabwean, Cameroonian, Liberian, Ghanaian, South African, New Zealander, Filipino, Cambodian, German, Dutch, English, American, Chinese, East Indian, South Korean, Namibian, and French Guyanese.

12. Because of the tenuous nature of multi-cultural ministry, I am loath to communicate it this way since it sounds like I think I have all the answers. I take nothing for granted. Multiculturalism is always sensitive. Color-blindness is naïve. Culture needs to be recognized and affirmed, and each cultural group, as they mature during training, needs to assess the strengths and weaknesses of their own culture. From a missiological perspective, each group needs to be able to discern what is of God, what

YKVC could serve as a prototype or model for AVC Canada to go beyond multiculturalism.

Strengths and Weaknesses in Vineyard in Light of Beth's Experiences

Beth's understanding of the strengths and weaknesses present in Vineyard multiculturalism is shaped by both her experiences in the Vineyard US and Canada. While the Vineyard movement on the whole is a largely *white* movement in North America due to its roots in Protestant Christianity and its history with the Jesus movement,[13] in recent years, it has shown an increase in multiethnic/multicultural.

While ministering in a teaching and preaching capacity at Doral Vineyard in Doral, FL, Beth experienced a multicultural worship setting. Doral Vineyard had two services in English and Spanish, shared leadership and meetings between English and Spanish pastors, and had bilingual worship (Spanish and English) on a monthly basis as well as monolingual worship services. The leadership teams also foster multicultural connections by periodically switching the English pastor to speak at the Spanish service and the Spanish pastor to speak at the English service with translation where necessary. The church intentionally builds multicultural relationships through food and hospitality with monthly intentionally multicultural meals where the entire congregation brings food representing their home culture and country and speak about their dishes and what they mean to them.[14] While this works in situations where a second culture is large enough to justify such linguistic choices, other multicultural churches have such a high number of diverse

---

is human, and what is darkness in their own cultures. It is not for any other culture to assess this. Each culture does it for themselves. The more mature a cultural group, the easier this exercise is to do.

13. The "Jesus movement" or "Jesus people movement" was a hippie movement in the 1960s and 1970s beginning on the West Coast of the United States. Their revivals consisted of predominantly white youth who were dissatisfied with their parents' spirituality and life-choices. Mary-Catherine Brown notes the lower numbers of multiethnic congregants in Protestant churches compared to within Roman Catholicism (see Brown, "Worldview," 3).

14. Similarly, Melt also experienced bilingual French/English services in his context in South Africa. French is the most spoken language on the streets of Cape Town due to the incoming Francophone African refugees from DRC, Cameroon, Senegal, and elsewhere. Such bilingual churches offer a space for Francophone African refugees to worship alongside Anglophone South Africans.

PART TWO: TOWARDS KINGDOM CULTURES

linguistic groups represented that such an approach would not be tenable and other forms of augmented praxis would work better.[15]

Two other consciously multicultural congregations in the USA, which are also megachurches, are Vineyard Cincinnati, and Vineyard Columbus. Mary-Catherine Brown has done extensive research on the elements that make up these multiethnic/multicultural congregations, pointing to the strengths and weaknesses of each congregation's approach.[16] Brown has several key findings. First, both Vineyard Cincinnati and Vineyard Columbus have integrated multiethnic leadership teams. Such integration has not been tokenistic but instead has honoured the skills and pastoral insight of these specific leaders. Vineyard Columbus offers several ministry contexts to model multiracial/multiethnic interaction. These include the church staff, weekend services, website presence, classes, meetings, the community centre, outreach, and missions activities. Vineyard Cincinnati's multiethnic presence is more limited and focused on the contexts of outreach, conferences, missions, community/healing centre, and website content. In terms of weaknesses, Brown noted that the worldview knowledge areas and the cultural intelligence area of knowledge were the lowest scores for both Vineyard Columbus and Vineyard Cincinnati. Brown pointed out that one of the key areas of low score was a view of race and ethnicity formed by biblical understanding and an awareness of knowledge about other cultures and ethnicities.[17] Brown suggests that churches wishing to transform their multicultural practices need to move deeper below surface level multiculturalism and a general celebration of diversity to growing in deeper knowledge of the cultures that are present in their churches and a deeper awareness of what the Bible says about multiculturalism.[18]

Two further initiatives demonstrate some of the growing work in multiculturalism from Vineyard USA: La Viña and Vineyard Soul. First, in terms of engaging the rising number of Hispanics across the US, Vineyard USA has created a network called "La Viña." This network of churches is overseen by a team of leaders who develop La Viña pastors

---

15. Melt described this situation at Yellowknife Vineyard Church (YKVC) as an example. At YKVC, Filipinos are the second biggest culture, but there are a variety of different dialects spoken by the Filipinos. Thus, they tend to communicate to each other in English, making that the lingua franca at YKVC.

16. Brown, "Worldview Themes."

17. Brown, "Worldview Themes," 201–3.

18. See her other helpful suggestions in Brown, "Worldview Themes," 195–286.

and churches with an awareness of the unique cultural needs of Hispanic communities.

Vineyard USA has also recently addressed one of the core areas of Vineyard praxis as it relates to multiculturalism: Vineyard worship music. At the core of Vineyard practice lies a centrality of sung worship. Vineyard services include extended times of sung worship using music with a contemporary style.[19] Recently, Vineyard USA became aware that one of the hindrances to multicultural worship was a lack of examples of multicultural worship music in the Vineyard worship offerings. Recent albums from Vineyard Music have worked toward filling this gap with the 2017 worship albums *We are Ready* and *Generous God* by Vineyard Soul. Vineyard Soul represents twenty Vineyard multiethnic churches and their worship artists who sing new versions of traditional Vineyard songs and write their own Vineyard worship songs featuring elements of R & B and Gospel music.[20]

Like the rise of concern about multiculturalism in Vineyard USA, Vineyard Canada has also experienced its own set of strengths and weaknesses as it has charted a trajectory for multiculturalism. This can be seen in the Vineyard Canada's national online worship services during 2020. The Easter 2020 service included a powerful call for multiculturalism in the sermon but had limited multicultural representation in the rest of the service. This mismatch was highlighted by some Vineyard Canada congregants. In comparison, the Vineyard Canada Christmas service 2020 provided multicultural representation and leadership that was more explicit, including multilingual worship—English and French for songs; and then a final Christmas wish in a variety of different languages represented across Vineyard Canada. While the call for multiculturalism in the sermon for the Easter 2020 was an important call, the lack of multicultural representation among the leaders made this call feel incomplete. In contrast, the multicultural leadership and worship represented in the Christmas 2020 online service did more than simply show the faces of different ethnicities across Vineyard Canada, it allowed people to sing worship songs in their native language and pronounce worship blessings in their native languages. The Scripture was also read by a person of colour. This brought the *call* of the Easter 2020 service into living colour. Additional recent work with multiculturalism in Vineyard Canada has

---

19. For more on the centrality of worship and its history in Vineyard, see Park et al., *Worshiping*; Hong and Ruth, *Lovin' on Jesus*.

20. "Vineyard Worship Album."

included inviting an Indigenous elder who is a member of Vineyard onto our National team to provide prayer and spiritual guidance.

FINAL THEOLOGICAL REFLECTIONS

So, where do we go from here? Vineyard theology gives a starting point for Vineyard's own practices regarding moving beyond simple claims to multiculturalism. Kingdom theology is an essential part of Vineyard's theology. Kingdom theology provides a possible framework for moving beyond multiculturalism. The basic tenets of kingdom theology focus on the role of the Triune God as the great king and on Jesus' life, death, and resurrection as embodying the kingdom of God. Kingdom theology shows that God's kingdom is an already not yet reality, leaning on scholars such as George Ladd and Derek Morphew, who explore inaugurated eschatology and its place throughout the Scripture, especially as developed during Jesus' time in the New Testament.[21]

We experience God's kingdom in a new way at Pentecost in Acts 2. Here, the language of the kingdom of God is present in Peter's speech, which references the expectations of Joel. Joel's vision of the Day of the Lord as the day when the entire community—young and old, male and female––all participates in God's kingdom through prophesy, visions, and dreams becomes a reality in Acts 2 that shapes what it means for God's kingdom to come, not only to the Jewish people but also to the entire world.[22] Notably, the group present in Acts 2 represents the Jews scattered across the known world. Their kingdom transformation becomes a catalyst for ministry to the ends of the earth in the rest of Acts. As Nicholas Fox has argued in his work on God-fearers in Luke–Acts, Acts 2 shapes the social identity for not only the Jews who become believers but also the Gentiles who become believers.[23] In light of this, kingdom theology encourages us to look beyond a simple picture of multiculturalism where

---

21. Ladd, *Presence*; Morphew, *Breakthrough*. More recently, Vineyard scholars, such as Doug Erikson, have added to these discussions. See Erickson, *Living the Future*.

22. As Derek Morphew states regarding Luke–Acts in *Kingdom Reformation*, "The new or messianic age has dawned, fulfilling the Old Testament expectations and inaugurating the relentless and determined will of God. Its focus is the messianic King Jesus, who by the power of the Spirit brings healing and salvation to all nations. This salvation includes previously excluded groups" (399–400). Here Morphew cites his previous writings in his work (*Mission*, 31–32).

23. Fox, *Hermeneutics*, 44, 67–69.

we include congregants from different cultures and ethnicities. It calls us to include the entire community in the work of the church, not only as those who receive but as those who minister to others. From a leadership perspective, this means that moving beyond multiculturalism involves intentionally cultivating not only a diverse congregation but also diverse leadership. The multicultural nature of the community then needs to be reflected in the worship, teaching, and other practices of the congregation (and the denomination).

The picture of the kingdom of God in Revelation adds to this expectation. Revelation's vision of God's kingdom in the age to come encourages us to imagine a multilingual and multiethnic form of worship rather than a monocultural one. As Beth has explored before, Rev 7 offers us a climactic vision of God's intention for unified worship. As Beth explains, "Without diminishing the diversity of the nations represented, Revelation 7:9 pictures peoples 'from every nation, from all tribes and peoples and language' worshipping before the throne of God and before the Lamb singing together."[24] As J. Daniel Hays explains, this is the climactic "portrayal of the true people of God as multiethnic and multicultural, coming from all of the nations of the earth."[25] The already not yet nature of the kingdom of God allows us to think of this picture of Rev 7 as anticipatory, but also as something we can strive for in our churches today as a way of moving beyond a basic multiculturalism. As the national director of Vineyard USA Phil Strout has stated, the kingdom of God is, therefore, "forward-leaning" in its movement:

> From our beginning, the Vineyard has been committed to proclaiming the Kingdom of God and to bearing witness to the deeds of the Kingdom through healing (physical, emotional, and social), doing justice, and delivering those held captive by evil. Since the Kingdom of God is the future reign of God breaking into the present through the life and ministry of Jesus, we are a forward-leaning movement emphasizing the ever-reforming nature of the church engaging the world in love.[26]

This forward-leaning posture has implications for multiculturalism as we live out the kingdom-to-come in our efforts towards multiculturalism today. Yet, a picture of multiculturalism based on kingdom theology

---

24. Stovell, "Moving."
25. Hays, *From Every People and Nation*, 193.
26. "Core Values & Beliefs."

is not only anchored towards hope and unity. A deeply rooted kingdom theology also provides space for the conflicts that must be faced in order to press into multicultural transformation. Recent work by Vineyard scholars, such as Jon Stovell, has pointed to the need to understand the already not yet framework of the kingdom of God, not only as a picture of hopeful expectation but also to see how struggle and suffering are an intrinsic part of God's kingdom in the world today. According to this vision of kingdom theology, Christ's model as king shows us what it means to seek God's kingdom today. This necessarily involves struggle and pain as it did for Christ: a path of struggle that leads to resurrection life.[27] Similarly, it is necessary for us to move beyond a *nice* surface level multiculturalism through the struggles of intercultural discussion to transform to deeper and more vibrant forms of multiculturalism in our churches.[28] This follows the model of Christ in living out his kingdom in the world today.

CONCLUSION

Melt and Beth's experiences of multiculturalism personally and within the Vineyard have informed how they encourage others to move beyond simple forms of multiculturalism today to a deeper engagement with multiculturalism that acknowledges its complexity. Their experiences in South Africa, the US, and Canada demonstrate that multicultural questions are not unique to the landscape of Canadian churches, but each national context poses its own unique challenges for multiculturalism for the Vineyard movement and for other churches. Theological convictions of the Vineyard provide a helpful starting place for moving beyond a simplistic multiculturalism towards a redeemed multiculturalism that mirrors Christ's transformative power.

BIBLIOGRAPHY

Brown, Mary-Catherine. "Worldview Themes and Cultural Intelligence: A Case Study of Leadership within Two Multiracial/Multiethnic Congregations." PhD diss., Asbury Theological Seminary, 2015.

27. Stovell, "As with the King."

28. Recent studies on intercultural competency discuss the necessity of intercultural conflict competence as part of broader skills in intercultural competency. See Ting-Toomey, "Intercultural Conflict Competence."

"Core Values & Beliefs." Vineyard USA. No pages. Online: https://vineyardusa.org/about/core-values-beliefs.

Erickson, Douglas. *Living the Future: The Kingdom of God and the Holy Spirit in the Vineyard Movement*. Self-published, 2016.

Fox, Nickolas. *The Hermeneutics of Social Identity in Luke-Acts*. Eugene, OR: Pickwick, 2021.

Hays, J. Daniel. *From Every People and Nation: A Biblical Theology of Race*. New Studies in Biblical Theology. Downers Grove, IL: InterVarsity, 2003.

Hong, Lim Swee, and Lester Ruth. *Lovin' on Jesus: A Concise History of Contemporary Worship*. Nashville: Abingdon, 2017.

Ladd, George Eldon. *The Presence of the Future: The Eschatology of Biblical Realism*. Grand Rapids: Eerdmans, 1973.

Morphew, Derek. *Breakthrough: Discovering the Kingdom*. 5th ed. Cape Town: Vineyard International, 2019.

———. *Kingdom Reformation: Rediscover Jesus, Review Everything!* Bergvliet, South Africa: Vineyard International, 2020.

———. *The Mission of the Kingdom: The Theology of Luke-Acts*. South Africa: Vineyard International, 2011.

Park, Andy, et al. *Worshiping with the Anaheim Vineyard: The Emergence of Contemporary Worship*. The Church at Worship: Case Studies from Christian History. Grand Rapids: Eerdmans, 2016.

Pollock, David C., and Ruth E. Van Reken. *Third Culture Kids: Growing Up Among Worlds*. Boston: Nicholas Beasley, 2009.

Stovell, Beth M. "Moving from 'Them' to 'Us': A Biblical Theology for Diaspora Ministry." In *Beyond Hospitality: Migration, Multiculturalism and the Church*, edited by Charles Cook et al., 28–38. Toronto: Tyndale Academic, 2020.

Stovell, Jon. "As with the King, So with the Kingdom: A Christomorphic Eschatology." PhD diss., McMaster Divinity College, 2017.

Swartz, Sharlene. *Another Country: Everyday Social Restitution*. Cape Town: HSRC, 2016.

Ting-Toomey, Stella. "Intercultural Conflict Competence as a Facet of Intercultural Competence Development: Multiple Conceptual Approaches." In *The SAGE Handbook of Intercultural Competence*, edited by Darla K. Deardorff, 100–20. London: SAGE, 2009.

"Vineyard Worship Album 'We Are Ready (Vineyard Soul)' on WorshipTeam." *Worship Team* (July 10, 2017). No pages. Online: https://try.worshipteam.com/2017/07/10/vineyard-worship-album-we-are-ready-vineyard-soul-on-worshipteam.

Part Three

Kingdom Collaborations

In the desire to move beyond government sanctioned multiculturalism toward interculturalism and a deeper interconnected sense of family and home, local congregations can, together, decide to devote themselves to the culture of King Jesus and to collaborate with one another as homemakers and hosts. In addition, they can protect and intercede for those who gather in their *home* in ways that move them from exclusion to embrace.

In Part Three, you will hear the stories of congregations and ministries that have, in Christian vocation, collaborated to nurture the flourishing of life with God. These case studies are reflective of the diverse stages communities of faith may be in as they move towards being intentionally intercultural congregations, and they share the joys and challenges which are part of their journey. As you read their stories, we invite you to reflect on what you can learn from their experiences.

Multivocational Ministry in Multicultural Canada

James W. Watson

It is common knowledge that Canada is a culturally diverse nation, specifically given the globally connected nature of the largest cities. Connecting with grassroots leaders from across the country and listening to their explanations of their context create an opportunity for grounded insight and provoke imagination for the future. While we may never fully appreciate how the Holy Spirit is orchestrating the collective witness to the good news of Jesus Christ, reflecting on different illustrations of ministry at the street level and their missiological implications can assist us in gaining a more complete picture of the whole. Paying attention to the developments in congregational ministry and being open to possibilities for missional engagement assists our collective effort to stay in step with the Spirit.

CANADIAN MULTIVOCATIONAL MINISTRY PROJECT (CMMP)

A mixed methods research project was conducted via a focus group which shaped questions for semi-structured interviews and an established on-line questionnaire. The Wellness Project @ Wycliffe questionnaire addressed the experience of congregational ministry.[1] Weekly schedules, opportunities, challenges of multivocational ministry, the dynamics of the other work, theology of work, and advice for trainers and resource

---

1. Watson et al., "Canadian Multivocational Ministry Project." Regarding the online questionnaire, see Malcolm et al., "Measuring Ministry-Specific Stress," 313–27.

PART THREE: KINGDOM COLLABORATIONS

people were addressed by the interviews, which generated explanations of the ministry contexts. The forty interviewees (twenty-four men and sixteen women) were from a variety of roles of congregational leadership: lead or solo pastors, co-pastors (some spouses were co-pastors), associates (or specialized roles, such as youth), volunteer or lay ministers, and leaders of house churches or incarnational ministries (with an ecclesial identity or direction).

Candidates were selected primarily for diversity of occupations with almost forty distinct roles represented in the study. Some leaders had more than one additional job (thus the multi-vocational terminology rather than bi-vocational) and some had similar roles; there were chaplains for health services, the military, and natural resources industry. These leaders represent congregations of several Christian traditions and, while they represent a wide range of combinations of pastoral and other roles, they should not be considered representative of all tentmaking in Canada.[2] The interviews provide a window into a variety of tentmaking experiences, and because many of the related churches' contexts are multicultural, they also provide access to understand ministry among the diaspora.

Canadian cultural complexity includes many distinct Indigenous cultures as well as English and French influences (and any associated subcultures) for various regions and communities. The focus of this reflection will be on interaction with the diaspora of peoples who have taken up residence in Canada. The CMMP surfaced a collection of examples of multicultural ministry even though diaspora ministry was not the primary focus.

While 20 percent of the interviewees were born in a country other than Canada, there were additional variations of multicultural ministry. It is the nuance of both commonly investigated forms of diaspora engagement and less common examples that surfaced in the explaining of social context or congregational life which are highlighted for further imagining of possibilities. This particular sample of ministry in Canada revealed some patterns of cultural diversity which are worth considering, both to appreciate how the Holy Spirit is inspiring connections and to imagine the implications for the future. Reflecting on both themes from

---

2. Represented in this study were churches of Christian and Missionary Alliance, Baptist, Free Methodist, Mennonite, Mennonite Brethren, and Salvation Army affiliations.

academic literature and Canadian leaders' reflections on ministry allows for a broad perspective grounded in experience.

EXAMPLES OF DIASPORA INTERACTION

In setting the stage for reflecting on examples from the research, some review of the perspective on diaspora ministry in Canada is valuable. Given the dependence of Canadian population growth on immigration, congregational development will be significantly impacted by diaspora ministry for the foreseeable future.[3] Diaspora missiology has brought a helpful focus on many strategic areas of contemporary mission.[4] Identification of helpful frameworks for productive reflection on the realities experienced in Canada makes this integration of mission theory and actual practice beneficial.

Congregations founded by immigrants are a commonly recognized contribution of the diaspora.[5] With the global flows of migration, many Christians bring their commitments to congregational life with them. As might be expected from general awareness of congregational ministry in Canada, one of the leaders in the CMMP study was in full-time employment as well as co-pastoring a recently planted church in the Greater Toronto Area (GTA).[6] As a business analyst for the government with a daily commute, evenings were generally devoted to mentoring, youth, and prayer meetings, and Sundays were devoted to morning worship and a time of food and fellowship (pre-pandemic). This pattern of full-time work alongside a full ministry schedule highlights the discipline and focus required for this approach.

It should be recognized that immigrant-founded congregations are contributing to multicultural congregational ministry, as well as a diversity of monocultural churches. It is understandable that at a certain stage of development a congregation using a language other than one of the official languages (English and French) would strategically enlist someone fluent in the language (and cultural trends) of the second

3. Reimer and Hiemstra, "Gains/Losses."

4. Wan's definition of diaspora missiology is helpful here; he defines it as "a missiological framework for understanding and participating in God's redemptive mission among diaspora groups" (*Diaspora Missiology*, 5).

5. Wan and Casey, *Church Planting*.

6. Watson and Santos, "Tentmaking."

generation.⁷ One youth pastor in a GTA church founded by Korean-Canadian immigrants identified several different cultural backgrounds represented among the teens. Eighty percent were estimated to be second generation, some with parents attending the Korean worship, but others in the group were described culturally as Caribbean, Middle Eastern, and Russian. The shared experience of cultural hybridity as their social identity is important to recognize.⁸ Branching out to the youth of other cultural backgrounds speaks to the opportunity presented by the context and the capacity of the congregation to facilitate the building of bridges with families of other cultural backgrounds.

A more complex account of multicultural ministry initiated by a lower mainland British Columbia diaspora church was provided by a pastor who was ministering in an East Asian language, but for whom their first language was English. While the pastor had lived internationally and learned the language, there continued to be a need for proofreading of sermons by someone who had that language as their first language. A nearby English congregation employed the pastor part-time as a music director. The complexity of the arrangement points both to options for sustainability of churches serving a particular linguistic group, but also the potential for partnership between long established churches and diaspora congregations.

These descriptions of diaspora churches should be well recognized as prevalent Canadian ministry experience. Each expression of intercultural ministry should be celebrated as a contribution to God's desire for every people to contribute to the Church's participation in the *missio Dei*. The CMMP interviews revealed some additional specific multicultural ministry settings which are not specifically initiated by leaders of the diaspora, but point to the opportunities for connectivity in the Canadian context.

One relatively simple example from the GTA is a house church based on what the interviewee described as an ESL (English as Second Language) class. Whether this followed a formal curriculum or was focused on conversational English was not clarified, but it was an ongoing group. The leader mentioned having people from Korea, Japan, and Iran in their group. This points to the simplicity of serving the needs of recent immigrants with a relational focus. Churches can fulfill a relational niche

---

7. Santos, "Mission"; Tang, "Mission."
8. Ybarrola and Tira, "Diasporas and Multiculturalism."

in the settlement sector which overlaps with the primary objectives of the faith community.[9]

Rural Saskatchewan provided an interesting example where the pastor's full-time, seasonal work as a farmer facilitated interfaith relationship building. Muslims who lived in the nearby city, and who appreciated developing a genuine relationship with a producer, would buy meat directly from the farmer/pastor. This progressed to the point where the rural pastor was invited to family weddings of his Muslim friends. This example challenges common assumptions that relationships with Muslim newcomers would be limited to urban encounters. It also points to the role of discernment, openness to someone of another faith, and the initiative on the part of the pastor to foster that relationship.[10]

A Montreal area pastor who owns a small technology company also provided church planting coaching on behalf of a denomination. With the influx of Christian leaders from "Le Francophonie" (countries which use French as a common language), particularly Haiti, it presented an opportunity to offer encouragement and support as new churches were formed. The process of orientation to a new society and diverse metropolitan area offers the experience and connections of the long-term resident to the foreign-born leaders who are starting new churches.

While these examples point to the potential of ministry opportunities with the diaspora, they did not go into detail regarding challenges. Generally, interviewees addressed the negative aspects of multivocational ministry rather than the complications of multicultural ministry because they were specifically asked about multivocational challenges. One notable exception was highlighted by the research. A pastor who was engaged in a broad range of community ministry (food distribution, community agency partnerships) as the director of a social service centre which was integrated with the church in a small city in Quebec did not address the busy schedule of multivocational ministry when asked about difficulties. The concern addressed was with regards to being a long-established immigrant in Canada serving in a predominantly monocultural and unilingual community with their third language. Incorrect assumptions about their ethnicity and complaints about accent were painful as this leader faithfully served both a small congregation and fellow community members, many of whom were marginalized by poverty, homelessness,

---

9. Janzen et al., "Canadian Christian Churches."
10. Bongoyok, "Case Study 3"; Thomas, "Engaging World Religions."

or mental health concerns. "Linguistic peculiarity" as an identifier as a "foreigner" (regardless of actual legal citizenship status) has been raised as a concern for ministry when reactions are negative.[11] Racism is an issue for the church with regards to God's justice transforming society, but there is also a pastoral care concern for the leader in these situations.

IMPLICATIONS

These brief glimpses into the realities of frontline ministry within Canadian communities both affirm the generalizability of many of the missiological themes currently being considered and point to the complexity of multicultural ministry. The omnidirectional influences of culture and the learning curve required to negotiate new encounters are both exciting and intimidating for missionally focused leaders. Diaspora missiology has brought an international perspective to the local dynamics of multicultural ministry. The recognition of the value of transnational theoretical frameworks, what can be learned from the social science literature, and reflection on the potential this raises for mission opportunities can help to provide insight and inspire forward momentum.

International mission perspective can provide the ability to discern new opportunities. In addition to considering skilled immigrants or refugees to Canada as contributors to the economic growth of the country, we can recognize the missionaries (or potential missionaries) which are being gifted to local churches and congregational networks. Celebration of this capacity and finding practical ways to support their leadership development can help orient the Canadian church more towards a positive view of the future rather than an emphasis on unavoidable decline. As has been noted in a previous research project on how Muslim people are exploring faith in Jesus when they migrate to Canada and the US, people born in Canada who have served as missionaries in other countries (and gained language and cultural knowledge in the process) can also be identified as partners in ministry with the diaspora and established churches rather than viewing their task as completed upon their return.[12]

At some point international awareness of potential must be translated into collaboration. How does cooperation take place? Who is responsible? There may be leaders who are positioned to network among

11. Hanciles, *Beyond Christendom*, 367.
12. Watson, "Fruitful Practices."

possible colleagues and initiate collaboration. Diaspora or Canadian born leaders can create opportunities for working together. The example of the shared music director/pastor between the English-speaking congregation and the church worshipping in another language is a partnership which had mutually beneficial outcomes. For the Montreal coach to leaders from the *Francophonie*, an established organization strategically allocated resources for support and training. There will be learning required for working out meaningful relationships across cultural differences, but networks of churches, agencies, and educational institutions can promote connections to foster these relationships and sponsor initiatives. [13]

It should be recognized that local congregations will provide the basis for multicultural ministry. Creativity inspired by the Holy Spirit, healthy cross-cultural relationships, and sometimes pragmatic needs can provide the direction. As noted in these examples, many forms of multicultural ministry will be inspired by the organic development of churches founded by recent immigrants as they relate to the next generations and reach out to their diverse contexts. Intentionally learning from these congregations and applying what is learned into new initiatives may accelerate our adaptation to a rapidly changing world.

CONCLUSION

Discernment of a shared future and the distinct parts played by leaders who have been shaped by God must be an ongoing commitment. The opportunities for shared learning, the witness to Jesus as the one who provides us with the way forward together, and the needs which are present all around us require our common commitment to mission. One of the advantages of the Canadian context is the transnational crossroads it provides within our globalizing world. The lessons learned for multicultural ministry in the midst of Canadian cultural complexity can be shared globally, just as leaders in Canada benefit from what is being reflected upon globally.

---

13. Chapman and Watson, "Common Actions."

PART THREE: KINGDOM COLLABORATIONS

BIBLIOGRAPHY

Bongoyok, Moussa. "Case Study 3: Missions among the Urban Muslim Diaspora in the West." In *Diaspora Missiology: Theory, Methodology, and Practice*, edited by Enoch Wan, 197–208. Portland: Institute of Diaspora Studies, 2011.

Chapman, Mark D., and James W. Watson, "Common Actions: Participatory Action Research as a Practice for Promoting Positive Social Action among and between New Canadian Church Planters and Denominational Leaders." *Ecclesial Practices* 4 (2017) 63–86.

Hanciles, Jehu J. *Beyond Christendom: Globalization, African Migration, and the Transformation of the West*. Maryknoll, NY: Orbis, 2008.

Janzen, Rich, et al. "Canadian Christian Churches as Partners in Immigrant Settlement and Integration." *Journal of Immigrant & Refugee Studies* 14 (2016) 390–410.

Malcolm, Wanda M., et al. "Measuring Ministry-Specific Stress and Satisfaction: The Psychometric Properties of the Positive and Negative Aspects Inventories." *Journal of Psychology and Theology* 47 (2019) 313–27.

Reimer, Sam, and Rick Hiemstra. "The Gains/Losses of Canadian Religious Groups from Immigration: Immigration Flows, Attendance and Switching." *Studies in Religion/Sciences Religieuses* 47 (2018) 327–44.

Santos, Narry F. "A Mission, Migration, and Multiplying Movement." In *From the Margins to the Centre: The Diaspora Effect*, edited by Michael Krause et al., 110–22. Toronto: Tyndale Academic, 2018.

Tang, Timothy. "Mission to, through and beyond the Diaspora." In *From the Margins to the Centre: The Diaspora Effect*, edited by Michael Krause et al., 123–36. Toronto, Canada: Tyndale University Press, 2018.

Thomas, T. V. "Engaging World Religions with the Gospel." In *From the Margins to the Centre: The Diaspora Effect*, edited by Michael Krause et al., 110–22. Toronto: Tyndale Academic, 2018.

Wan, Enoch, ed. *Diaspora Missiology: Theory, Methodology, and Practice*. Portland: Institute of Diaspora Studies, Western Seminary, 2011.

Wan, Enoch, and Anthony Casey. *Church Planting among Immigrants in US Urban Centers: The "Where", "Why", and "How" of Diaspora Missiology in Action*. Scotts Valley, CA: Createspace Independent, 2014.

Watson, James W. "Fruitful Practices." *Jaffray Perspectives*, January 2018, 3–4.

Watson, James W., et al. "Canadian Multivocational Ministry Project: Research Report." *Canadian Multivocational Ministry Project (CMMP)*. Online: https://www.canadianmultivocationalministry.ca/report.

Watson, James W., and Narry F. Santos. "Tentmaking: Creative Mission Opportunities within a Secularizing Canadian Society." In *Mission and Evangelism in a Secularizing World*, edited by Narry F. Santos and Mark Naylor, 131–48. Evangelical Missiological Society Monograph Series 2. Eugene, OR: Pickwick, 2019.

Ybarrola, Steven, and Sadiri Joy Tira, "Diasporas and Multiculturalism: Social Ideologies, Liminality, and Cultural Identity." In *The Human Tidal Wave: Global Migration, Megacities, Multiculturalism, Pluralism, Diaspora Missiology*, edited by Sadiri Joy Tira, 135–49. Pasig City: Lifechange, 2013.

My Journey to Planting a Church of All Nations

Jorge Lin

"Why are you praying about going to other nations, when I have brought the nations here?" This is what I heard on the last day of my prayer retreat in response to my question, "Where should I go to make disciples and reach people of other nations?" My wife, Emily, and I each heard this on the same day. Deep in our hearts, we knew God called us to make disciples and reach people of all nations.

My name is Jorge Lin. I am a church planting missionary with the Lower Pacific District of the Evangelical Free Church of Canada (LPD–EFCC). This is my journey on how God called me to plant a church that reaches all nations—an intercultural church. The journey I tell here starts with me, followed by how others were invited to join. Then, in 2020, we became a larger family, and now, we are journeying together as Church of All Nations[1]—a family of life groups of people of all nations. We are currently in the early stages of our church plant.

Let me start with a few details that will keep the story in context. First, I was born in Argentina to Taiwanese parents, and I definitely look Asian. As many would say, it is when I start speaking that people get confused. I speak English with a Spanish accent, Mandarin with an English-Spanish accent, but I speak fluently without foreign accent both in Spanish and in Taiwanese. I have lived in Canada for most of my life

---

1. The name "Church of All Nations" is fitting for the journey into becoming an intercultural church. It is the project name assigned by the LPD–EFCC district the day I joined as a church planting missionary.

now and I consider myself a Canadian.[2] I cheer for the Vancouver Canucks, my hometown hockey team, with the same intensity and emotion as when I cheer for my Argentine *fútbol* ("soccer") team in the World Cup. My friend Sherman once described me as "a global person with an intercultural worldview." I am telling you all of this not to brag about my diverse cultural background but to preface one of the most important questions that will come up later in my journey.

When I set out on this journey, it was only one year since I had left the Asian church where I ministered for five years as the pastor of the English ministry. The English ministry was made up of both first- and second-generation youth and young adults who were fluent in English but would speak a mix of Mandarin and English during activities. I had established their English ministry from the ground up. I also trained worship leaders and small group leaders. The major work seemed done, and it was time to enjoy the fruits, but something seemed missing. In one of my sermons, I stopped and asked the group to put up their hands if they had close friends who are from different nations than themselves. It was not a surprise to me. Everyone put up their hands. The question that I followed up with was, "Then why aren't they here at church?" The room was silent.

I know the answer may have many layers, but one of them was clear: we were not a church that was reaching people of all nations. We *welcomed* people of all nations, and we *hoped* people of all nations would come, but we never asked ourselves the question, "Do people of all nations feel they are welcomed?" or even more to the point, "Do they feel like they can belong?"

Half a year later, I stepped out of the church to go on missions to make disciples. I thought reaching people of other nations was about going to other nations. After all, I speak many languages. I had open invitations from personal friends to make disciples in Colombia, Peru, Mexico, and Taiwan. All the invitations revolved around the same qualification. They wanted someone who understands and has lived, as one of their own, in their culture. They wanted someone to speak the gospel in their heart language. As you know by now, God already had a plan, and that plan was closer to home than I thought. I heard God clearly say, "Why are you praying about going to other nations, when I have brought the nations here?" God called me to make disciples and reach people of all

---

2. Saying "I am Canadian" means many different things these days, but I mean to say I carry Canadian cultural traits and values.

nations right where I was. And I soon found out, it centered on New Westminster, British Columbia.

Vancouver is indeed a city with people of many nations,[3] but to be a church that reaches people of all nations is not a natural outcome. In the beginning, I was not thinking about planting a church, and even now, my focus is on reaching people in my city with the gospel, a city which happens to have people from different nations. Personally, I am convicted that when Jesus said, "go and make disciples of all nations" (Matt 28:20), he meant everyone in the community where I live and anyone that I can connect with at my school, work, friends, etc., without discrimination[4] for "the harvest is plentiful, and the workers are few" (Matt 9:37, NASB).

I took a step of faith, and I became a church planting missionary to make disciples and to reach people of all the nations here in my city. Another question needed to be answered: "How do I do that?" This is where my background comes into play, but not as I thought it would. See, I realized that no matter how many languages I speak, no matter how many cultures I lived in, and no matter how good I am at interacting cross-culturally or interculturally, I still could not speak enough languages to reach people of all nations in my city. How would I be able to speak the heart language of people of *all* nations? How would I be able to make disciples and reach people of *all* nations in my city? Short answer: it is not about me.

I went into a journey of discovery and came out convicted that making disciples is about transformation. Transformation by the renewing of your mind (Rom 12:2). This is not an outward change but a transformation from the inside out. If it is about transformation, most definitely, it is not about me. Yes, God wants me to do the work, but he is the one that will transform the hearts of people. It became clear to me that my role is not to speak the heart language of all nations but to equip people of all nations to *hear* the gospel in their own heart language.[5]

It was time to invite people into a journey of transformation. A journey where we live as great commission disciples. Our life groups would be the place where we live as disciples making disciples. Every week we

---

3. For simplicity, when I say nations, I mean different ethnicities and different cultures.

4. I know there are issues of ethnocentrism, cultural preference, etc. I will not be addressing these here.

5. In the same way, I heard the gospel in my own heart language—mathematics. A story for another time.

would hear God through Scripture and encourage each other to live in obedience to what we hear. We then send each other out into the mission field (work, school, community, etc.), and every week we gather to share stories of how God showed up and how God is transforming us. We call these "God Stories of Transformation."[6]

My first life group started when a friend told me he and his wife had heard God call them to join me in the journey *to make disciples of all nations*. No doubt we shared the same calling, and I invited them into the journey. Not long after, another friend, whom I had not talked to for a while, reached out to me. He shared how he and his wife were called to make disciples, but they were not able to do so in the church they were part of at the time. Their friends and co-workers, who were from diverse nationalities and cultures, did not feel like they could truly belong in the church they were attending. I invited them into the journey, and we started another life group. A group of Mandarin speakers who had heard me speak about making disciples approached me, too. I invited them into the journey and started my first Mandarin speaking life group. Furthermore, a church called "New Westminster Evangelical Free Church" connected with me through the district of EFCC. As a church with dwindling numbers, they wanted to return to what they envisioned when they started eighty years ago: to the diversity in welcoming people from all nations and be a light in the community. The church had always been attended by a diverse group of people from different nations. They joined the journey as another life group in our church family.[7] There are more life groups now, and some have come and gone as happens in any church plant. While I am writing this, I am about to start a Spanish speaking life group.

A quick pause. I know some are curious, so I will name some of the nations that make up our life groups: Canada, Taiwan, Argentina, Hong Kong, Japan, Philippines, Ethiopia, Nigeria, Barbados, Jamaica, and others. Also, not all life groups have a diversity of nations in them, but as a body (a church), these life groups journey together to become a church family of people of many different nations.

---

6. I am indebted to all those who have gone before me, my colleagues at LPD–EFCC, including my resident coach Steve Sharpe from LPD–EFCC, who helped me "put it all together" in this leg of the journey and continues to journey with me to this date.

7. Truly a testimony for God through a church that gave it all up to return to their calling to make disciples of all nations.

LIN *My Journey to Planting a Church of All Nations*

It was March 2020, and we all got the news in British Columbia, Canada, that the World Health Organization had declared a pandemic, and the city announced a lockdown. Any plans I had to build the body of all nations by joining the life groups through gatherings were not possible as a result. Again, I heard in prayer: it was not about me. To say the least, the first month of the pandemic lockdown was very difficult for everyone. Some life groups moved online while others decided to take a break. By April, one month into the lockdown, life group members started asking me about other life groups. Many wanted to know what God was doing through the other life groups and how God was transforming them during this time. They often said, "We want to meet other life groups and hear their God stories." I recruited leaders from different life groups to plan a gathering. These were the people of different nations that later became members of our Core Team.

Easter 2020 was our first gathering as a large group on Zoom. The screen was a mosaic of faces of people from different nations. People of different nations, who would not normally get together, gathered in a virtual room to worship, to hear each other's God Stories and to celebrate what God is doing in each other's lives. Funnily enough, they were not interested in listening to my sermon. I preached for ten minutes and, as many told me afterwards, they "people watched" for ten minutes. They were more interested in one another. I was not upset at all; rather, I was extremely happy. This was the next step of the journey I was waiting for. A step that I could not artificially create. They wanted to hear the God Stories of the people in other life groups and get to know the people that shared the same calling *to make disciples and reach people of all nations.* This was God's plan. This next step of our journey we came to call "From Strangers to Family" of all nations.

We gathered every other week to hear and celebrate each other's journey. We used breakout rooms as a space for people of different life groups to pray and commit to pray for one another for weeks at the time. Remember, the majority of the life groups and their people had not met one another in person before. As many have indicated, it is one thing to know what a face looks like on a screen and even have a name to attach to it, but it is another to actually meet in person.

When the Christmas season came, the gathering restrictions were still in place. Everyone in the city was feeling isolated, and being unable to see extended family during the holidays added to the sense of loneliness for many of our elderly. Young adults from one of our life groups decided to demonstrate the love of Jesus to the elderly in our community. They each spent hours designing and creating personalized gift baskets for the elderly in our church. Following city COVID protocols, they left each basket at the door and stepped two meters away from the doorways to greet the elderly. What they planned to be a drop-off and greeting turned into fifteen minutes, even thirty minutes in some cases, of chatting away from the sidewalk toward the doorways. They were loving one another despite being from different nations and generations. We have become a family of life groups of all nations.

I want to point out that this journey was an unexpected one. The journey has been about taking a step of faith before another step would open. It was simple but not easy—simple as in a step of faith followed by another step of faith, but not easy as every step required effort to take. It was easier for life groups to gravitate towards their own *nations*, cultures, comfort zones, or long-time friends. Many times, it required effort and encouragement to break down the boundaries of our comfort zones to be authentic and vulnerable with other people. Other times, it required us to break our own barriers of labelling, prejudice, and selfishness. It was not easy to facilitate a place for people to love people of other nations and reach out to one another. It was not easy to be consistently growing in love for one another as Jesus did for each one of us. Our church gathering has become the place where we all learned how to live as disciples whose love for one another shows we are disciples of Jesus. We are still learning. So am I.

Looking forward, I am no longer journeying alone. We, as the church of all nations and as a family of all nations, have decided to journey together and to invite others to join us. We are creating a place where everyone can belong, no matter their age, gender, race, nation, culture, etc. We are learning from one another every time we take steps of faith together. Most of all, we are committed to love one another the way Jesus loved us, so that the world may know we are his disciples (John 13:35).

A Case Study of Crosspoint Church

Rob Chartrand

CROSSPOINT CHURCH RECENTLY CELEBRATED its tenth anniversary. On any given Sunday in 2019, a visitor might see brothers and sisters from the Congo, Sudan, Somalia, Mexico, Ethiopia, China, Korea, the Philippines, Trinidad, Pakistan, First Nations, and many Anglo-European nations. The composition of this three-hundred-person congregation has not always been this way. In the beginning, its ethnic makeup was thoroughly monolithic. What changed in those ten years? This case study explores the intentional, often failing, sometimes accidental, yet providential journey of Crosspoint Church to become a multiethnic[1] church.

IN THE BEGINNING

Crosspoint launched in 2010 from Beulah Alliance Church as a new church plant under Rob Chartrand's leadership (the author). This venture was financially supported by the Western Canadian District (WCD) of the Christian and Missionary Alliance (Alliance henceforth) and Beulah Alliance Church for the first three years. Other Alliance churches[2] also contributed by providing resources and sending people. At the outset,

---

1. There is a semantic range of meaning for this term. Generally, Crosspoint has interpreted this to mean a church that is visibly diverse because it welcomes the stranger, practises hospitality, celebrates ethnic and cultural diversity, empowers diverse leadership, and deepens sacrificial love.

2. Other contributing churches included Sherwood Park Alliance Church, Heartland Alliance Church, and Southgate Alliance Church.

Chartrand scripted seven core values that would guide the formation of this fledgling community. One of these was to be *multiethnic*. This aspirational value would serve as a signpost, pointing Crosspoint toward their desired future:

> Northeast Edmonton has a diverse, multi-ethnic community. We want our church community to reflect and celebrate this rich collection of people groups. We're going to be intentional about developing a mosaic mindset. We believe that God loves all people, regardless of race, gender, height, hockey team, or even coffee preference. The church is to be a kaleidoscope of beautiful colours, sizes, and shapes.[3]

Fulfilling this value was problematic from the beginning. More than one-hundred people joined together to plant Crosspoint Church, but almost all of these were of Anglo or European descent, with a few exceptions. How could a pigment-challenged community ever become a beautiful kaleidoscope of cultures? What would it take to develop a mosaic mindset? Moreover, how would that even look? That it needed to happen was undeniable; how it would happen was undetermined.

This multiethnic value influenced the decision to plant Crosspoint in northeast Edmonton and included the neighbourhoods north of 137th Avenue, between 97th Street and Manning Drive. Census data at the time revealed that many of the neighbourhoods in this region had more diverse ethnic populations and more significant social needs than Edmonton in general. It also had fewer churches per capita, and only a handful of these were experiencing marginal growth. Since Crosspoint's vision was to plant the gospel where there were significant needs and diverse multiethnic populations, this seemed like an ideal location.

THE BEST LAID PLANS

As there was no roadmap for building a multiethnic church, particularly in Crosspoint's unique context, they began with a posture of learning. The planter and leadership team read books, attended workshops and conferences, and consulted with ministry experts. They soon concluded that no silver bullet, no strategy, would inevitably produce a multiethnic church. After launching its Sunday worship gatherings, Crosspoint's priority was to conduct a community needs assessment in partnership with

3. "Our Values."

e4c, a respected community group.[4] They strove to understand how they could best serve the community and build relationships with community stakeholders. They also wanted to sidestep the duplication of other capable organizations' services and avoid local strategies that would inevitably do more harm than good.

This information sparked much experimentation. Within the church, they hosted multiethnic potlucks, encouraged hospitality, and shared testimonies during worship gatherings. They hosted garage sales in the community, helped local agencies, supported a summer basketball tournament,[5] and participated annually in a community festival.[6] These short-term efforts elevated Crosspoint's visible presence in the community, but their lasting effects were difficult to quantify. They soon discovered that the most significant limitation was a lack of permanent geographical presence. As a portable church, they did not have a facility in the region which means they were only in the community for a few hours each week. This limitation led them to find creative alternatives, which often included renting other facilities during the week. Crosspoint also encouraged congregants who lived in the neighbourhood to build relationships with their neighbours and practise hospitality, but not everybody had the capacity or the confidence to do this. Overall, these early efforts did not impact the community as they had hoped, and the church was not becoming more multiethnic.

The one practice that seemed most effective was to re-cast and reinforce a vision for the multiethnic church continually. Sometimes this vision was preached about explicitly, and at other times, it was bolstered using story, illustration, and application. This consistency helped inculcate the multiethnic vision into the DNA of Crosspoint. Crosspoint also invited guest speakers with different ethnic backgrounds to share with its congregation. For example, one teaching series focused on world religions and involved Christian preachers formerly adherent to those religions. Crosspoint's leadership team continually returned to the question:

---

4. *e4c* is a recognized non-profit organization in Edmonton working with people living in poverty (see https://e4calberta.org).

5. "Pride of the Northside 4-on-4 basketball tournament" hosted by Andrew Parker at Londonderry Junior High School each summer (see https://andrewgparker.com/pride-of-the-north).

6. We partnered with other community organizations and *Fusion Canada* to host the Northeast Community Summer Festival for five years. It attracted hundreds from the surrounding community.

Part Three: Kingdom Collaborations

"How do we live out our value of becoming multiethnic?" It became clear that they could not plan or program their way to this future, but they could teach about it—and they could pray about it. They brought this need before the Lord.

While Crosspoint's first experiments seemed fruitless, they helped reinforce the multiethnic vision because they presented opportunities for the church to practise what they were learning. The most successful externally focused ministry that has offered this exposure is Kids Kapers. The first week-long camp launched in 2012 and was designed to be inclusive for New Canadians, especially Muslims. All meals and snacks are Halal, and all camp lessons are based on Old Testament stories, teaching about the goodness and love of God. The primary goal of the camp is to build bridges with families, not to proselytize individual children. Crosspoint recognized this as an essential missional strategy for shame-honour, collectivist cultures. The camp fees are minimal so that they are affordable for low-income families. Only children from Crosspoint and the local community can participate, which requires turning away families from other churches who want to register. Children from various ethnic backgrounds have participated over the years, including those of the Muslim faith. What began as one camp per summer has now expanded to three. Kids Kapers led the way in reinforcing this posture of welcome and embrace.

ACCIDENTALLY PROVIDENTIAL

Eventually, this posture would bear fruit. From the naturalist standpoint, Crosspoint's success at attracting a diverse ethnic population seemed more accidental than intentional; yet, it was providential from a biblical perspective. The hand of God was clearly at work. Over time, Crosspoint became noticeably more diverse as second- or third-generation Canadians began attending. Not long after, some New Canadians also joined. Members of the church community immediately welcomed these families and developed meaningful relationships with them, as the following two stories illustrate.

The Musa family arrived in Canada in 2015 as Congolese refugees who spoke little English and had few possessions. They were looking for a church home, so a community volunteer (unchurched) brought them to Crosspoint, based on a positive review she had received from a friend.

Members of the church welcomed the family, invited them into their homes, and helped them with their needs. The father, Leon, said that, during one of those first worship services, when the congregation sang the chorus to the song, "This Is Amazing Grace," tears flowed from his eyes because he felt like he and his family had found a home. With this support network's help, the Musas would focus on learning English, upgrading their education, and eventually finding employment. The Musas joined a small group, their children joined the youth and kid's ministries, and they started serving with the church. Today, they are an integral part of the Crosspoint community.

The Pia family began attending Crosspoint in 2018. When they immigrated to Canada from the Philippines in 2015, they first joined a predominantly Filipino church. After enrolling their children in the public school system, they soon realized how peers, teachers, and Canadian culture were shaping their young minds. Ian (the father) said they "came to terms with the fact that they were raising Canadians," which catalyzed their search for a church where their children could find peers and spiritual mentors and where the parents could receive deeper discipleship. At first, they were uncertain how Crosspoint would respond to people from a different ethnic background. Ian admits they are shy by nature, but this did not hinder the church community from reaching out to them. Like the Musas, they, too, joined a small group and began serving in the church's ministries. Ian and Joan would eventually receive training to lead a small group of their own.

NEW FACILITY

In 2018, Crosspoint became the owners of a church facility. This property formerly belonged to Beverly Alliance Church (BAC), who voted to dissolve their membership after many years of decline. The WCD then transferred the property to Crosspoint. It was located only ten minutes away from the previous site but was at the periphery of the original target region. As with the previous location, the neighbourhoods surrounding this new campus had diverse ethnic populations and high social needs. In short, the location was a strong fit for Crosspoint's mission, vision, and values. When Crosspoint opened its doors, the remaining BAC members were welcomed, with wide-open arms, to join Crosspoint. Most of them did, and some of these were first- and second-generation Canadians.

Part Three: Kingdom Collaborations

Within the first year, other newcomers from a diversity of ethnic backgrounds also joined. By the end of 2019, Crosspoint was more ethnically diverse than ever before. It was apparent that God's providential hand continued to move.

Since the beginning, Crosspoint's leadership agreed that any building they owned would be a multi-purpose facility that would benefit other ethnic churches and like-minded organizations. When Crosspoint assumed ownership of this new property, they inherited several churches and organizations that were already renting the facility. Crosspoint worked at retaining these partners, and after the first year, most of them stayed. By 2020, five facility partners were using the campus, in varying degrees. Two of these were especially influential in helping Crosspoint embody its multiethnic value.

The first facility partner was Grace Outreach (GO) Ministries, an organization committed to building disciples and training missionaries across western Canada, North Africa, and the Middle East. GO Ministries shared Crosspoint's desire to reach Muslims in northeast Edmonton. The church leadership established a strong affinity with their founder and Canadian Director Joseph Ibrahim, which soon evolved into project collaboration. Together, they hosted a Christmas feast for Syrian Muslims, and when GO Ministries invited these families' children to Kids Kapers, some responded. In 2019, the Ibrahims planted a house church for Muslim background believers in northeast Edmonton. GO Ministries could communicate with Syrian refugees and evangelize them in ways that were impossible for Crosspoint. In return, Crosspoint provided a supportive church in northeast Edmonton and auxiliary ministries (children and youth) for Muslim background believers.

Another facility partner was the South Sudanese Alliance Church (SSAC), led by Pastor Peter Dar. At the outset, Crosspoint's leadership nurtured a strong friendship with Peter by hearing his story and discovering his church's needs. Peter immigrated to Canada in 2004 and established his church with the help of Beverly Alliance Church. He and his congregation are South Sudanese refugees who struggle with English and have lower-paying jobs. Peter is an unpaid volunteer who has a full-time job outside the church. SSAC hosts its worship services on Sunday afternoons in Crosspoint's lower auditorium. According to Peter, the church's greatest need has been to find a guide to help them navigate Canadian systems and policies. When Crosspoint arrived in the facility, SSAC did not have denominational recognition, charitable status, or a bank account; Crosspoint has been helping them obtain these. They have made some efforts at building intercultural relationships between these congregations, including inviting the SSAC choir to sing at Crosspoint's Good Friday service. These interactions have been challenging because of the language barrier. Peter's deepest concern is for the next generation in his congregation. He states that there are "two cultures" living in each congregant's home—Canadian and Sudanese. As a result, the next generation does not want to attend a church where the worship and teaching are in Nuer instead of English. Crosspoint is in dialogue with SSAC about how to create solutions to this problem.

The facility brought partnerships that align with Crosspoint's multi-ethnic vision, but it also brought a new challenge. The church's growth—a fifty percent increase in the first year—has placed Crosspoint's core values in jeopardy. Each new member carries preconceived notions of what a church should value. To avoid these vision disparities, Crosspoint must explicitly re-cast its vision for the multiethnic church. One way to reinforce a multiethnic vision is to foster different cultural articulations of prayer and worship. In the past, Crosspoint has done a poor job at this, so this surfaces yet another challenge.

KEY TAKEAWAYS

Crosspoint did not become more multiethnic because of its ingenuity or masterful planning. Their journey has been more providential than intentional. Still, two discoveries are essential to highlight, as they may help other churches with a similar vision.

First, churches must continue to cast and re-cast their vision for a multiethnic or intercultural community. It has been said on many occasions that vision leaks. A church that wants to maintain an environment of welcome and inclusion must find ways to reinforce this value continually. One way that Crosspoint does this is through its weekly benediction. Each worship gathering ends the same way: "Let me remind you of who you are. You are the people of God, called by God, into his redemptive mission in the world. So be who you are. *Now, meet somebody who does not look like you.*" This simple, weekly reminder is a redemptive rhythm, calling the body of Christ to welcome the stranger and practise hospitality.

Second, small groups serve as helpful pathways of inclusion. Crosspoint discovered that they can be environments where New Canadians learn conversational English, which is a critical amplifier for their integration and contribution to the body of Christ—not to mention career success. Groups also present opportunities for different ethnic groups to break bread, welcome and celebrate cultural differences, share needs, and deepen fellowship. Both the Musas and Pias have attested to the significant role that small groups played in their lives. They also provided significant spiritual blessings to these groups—as their leaders and members will testify.

BIBLIOGRAPHY

"Our Values." *Crosspoint Church*. No pages. Online: https://www.thecrosspointchurch.ca/our-story/our-values.

Willingdon Church
A Case Study of an Intercultural Church Family

JOHN BEST

OVER THE PAST FEW decades, the demographics of the Willingdon Church family have shifted significantly. In 1961, 116 people who could be categorized as both religiously and ethnically Mennonite founded the church. Today, the Willingdon Church family is larger and, notably, multiethnic. Worshiping together are people from over seventy nations. Walking through the lobby on a weekend can either be experienced as a *foretaste of heaven* or as a bustling international airport terminal. There are many people who have immigrated to Canada within their lifetime, and there are many second-, third-, and fourth-generation Canadians in the church family. This transition in demographics has happened for a few reasons. The intent of this case study is to examine how and why Willingdon Church has experienced this significant demographic change. We will also outline the structural model and philosophy Willingdon has engaged and look at the strengths and gaps that exist in Willingdon's current experience.

HISTORY

First, let me present some history to fill in the picture of how Willingdon got to be how it is today. In a tangible way, a tone and foundation were set near the beginning of Willingdon's existence that put the church on a trajectory of becoming multiethnic. Vancouver Mennonite Brethren

PART THREE: KINGDOM COLLABORATIONS

Church (Vancouver MB), a church that worshiped together in German and was predominantly composed of Mennonite immigrants, planted Willingdon Church in Burnaby, BC. Instead of offering services in German, like Vancouver MB did, Willingdon leadership decided to have services in English in order to be able to reach the neighbourhood. This intentional step, along with numerous subsequent decisions by church leadership, has shaped the Willingdon Church family. Over the past several decades, the demographics of Greater Vancouver have become increasingly multiethnic. Willingdon's demographics have shifted as well and reflect the multiethnic makeup of the city.

Here are a couple of date markers related to the development of the multiethnic makeup of the Willingdon Church family: in 1985, a Spanish ministry was formed, and in 1988, a Korean ministry. A quote from *The Story of Willingdon Church—50 Years of God's Faithfulness* fills in the story of the 1990s and 2000s:

> Through the 1990's the church formed many of its international language ministries, including its Cantonese, Japanese, Mandarin, Indonesian and Russian ministries. Each of Willingdon's language ministries began through the initiative of a church member who desired to reach their countrymen living in Vancouver. This led Willingdon to engage the ethnic diversity of the city. International ministries translate sermons live to the sanctuary to unite members of different languages into one church congregation. Both the Spanish and Indonesian ministries went on to plant their own churches . . . The diverse groups of people God brought to Willingdon gave the church a unique platform to preach the gospel to "people of all nations" living in Vancouver . . . Willingdon Church entered the 21st century by adding its Romanian, French and Arabic ministries . . . In 2006, Willingdon began streaming translated video and audio of services on its website. Willingdon translates sermons and worship songs into Korean, Mandarin, Cantonese, Japanese, French, Russian, Romanian, Spanish and Filipino, preaching the Word to people of different languages around the world.[1]

It is important to note that each of these efforts to serve a particular language group was initiated by a member of the congregation that spoke that particular language. Church leadership affirmed and enabled the start of these ministry efforts, by approving the idea, providing space

1. "Willingdon through the Years."

and budget, making it a priority for church staff to have intentional connection with these groups, and establish a model for how these groups would function.

CURRENT REALITY

What is Willingdon's current reality? Up until Willingdon needed to stop meeting in person due to COVID-19, each week around four thousand people gathered for worship. The weekend services are in English, with occasional songs in a different language. When there are baptism testimonies in the services, people can choose which language they want to speak, and English subtitles are added to the video. Eight percent of the church family indicates that they prefer or need to hear the service in a language other than English, so the weekly services are translated into seven languages (live when meeting in-person and overdubbed online). The number of languages translated into has fluctuated over the years as the population has shifted.

Here are a few pieces of data to help fill in the picture. A survey was taken in January 2020 with 2,392 survey responses. The average age of adult attendees was forty-nine years old. Four percent of adult attendees have not yet made a decision to follow Jesus. Forty-nine percent of adult attendees have been attending Willingdon for less than seven years. Seventy-six percent attend four services per month.

A key foundation in our church family is the desire to have people engage relationally in small or mid-sized groups. Thirty-two percent of regular attendees participate in a Life Group (up to twenty people) or a slightly larger Community Group (up to fifty). It is within the context of these smaller groups that more personalized evangelism and discipleship can happen. Within this assortment of groups there are ten International Language Ministry (ILM) groups. Twelve percent of adult attendees regularly participate in one of these ILM groups. ILM groups exist to reach out to the broader community in Greater Vancouver who speak their language, and also to provide discipleship and community in that language. The International Language Ministry groups that exist at the time of writing are Mandarin, Cantonese, Korean, Farsi, Russian, French, Spanish, Portuguese, Japanese, Filipino, and People of Indian Origin.

Here are a few important things to note about Willingdon's ILM groups. First, they meet regularly, usually weekly. These gatherings usually include singing, reflection on the Bible, food, and relationship building. Second, these groups are not separate congregations or churches. Everyone is encouraged to attend Willingdon's weekly church service, and then choose to be involved in an ILM group if it is helpful. Third, most of the International Language Ministries also offer things beyond a weekly fellowship gathering. They offer small groups, classes, or specialized groups (like Chinese Drum Dance, Cantonese Choir, or Portuguese Women's Prayer) that give people opportunities to engage further. In addition to adults meeting, some of the groups provide a gathering for children, youth, or young adults in the particular language. Many second-generation children and youth participate in the English language programming that Willingdon provides.

MODEL AND PHILOSOPHY

As with any evolving enterprise, sometimes the operational model shifts as time goes on. This has been the case with Willingdon's International Language Ministries. There have been a few different models that Willingdon has employed, each with inherent strengths and weaknesses. In the early days of the ILM ministries in Willingdon, efforts were largely volunteer driven, with church staff helping implement translation technologies and caring for the volunteer leaders. In the next season, several pastors were hired to care for a particular language group. This led to significant growth in a couple of the groups. It also led to *siloing*, and, in a couple of cases, the groups deciding to form their own church congregations.

In 2011, the Willingdon Church elders decided to shift the model for International Language Ministries. This is the current model. Here are a few phrases that articulate the model: "one church, worshipping together," "integration and mission," and from Willingdon's Ministry Philosophy, "an intercultural, multi-generational church family in a global city with kingdom impact."[2] Currently, the leadership structure for International Language Ministries is this—a key volunteer who builds a volunteer team around them leads each language ministry. Several of these key volunteer leaders also serve as elders (the core leadership team for the church). There is a small staff team specifically assigned to care for ILM groups, including two full-time pastors. These pastors are not tasked

2. "Ministry Philosophy."

with leading particular groups. Instead, they provide relational support for volunteer leaders, occasional teaching for the groups, and work at equipping the leaders for care, integration, and mission. They also provide care and counsel to members of these groups as needed.

Our goal is to be one church, worshiping and serving together. We desire to be a foretaste of Rev 7:9–12 where there are people from every nation and language bowing before the throne of God in worship. With this vision in view, there are two important words that we use: "integration" and "mission."

When we use the word "integration," we talk of the value of intercultural understanding and connectedness under the umbrella of the same church family. Across our church family, we share a common mission statement, a common central ministry focus, a common ministry philosophy, a common gathering, common ordinances (baptism and communion), common leadership, and a common budget. We also have common curriculum for a variety of discipleship and Bible classes, offered in several languages. So, structurally many things are unified. We want to be relationally unified too. Our desire is for everyone in our church family to grow in interconnectedness, enjoying the diversity that God has orchestrated for this church family, and growing in the ability to understand and care for each other deeply, transcending cultural barriers.

By "mission," we mean this: we want to be a church that effectively and intentionally reaches out to people in our own culture and across cultures, to point people to Jesus. We realize that discipleship and evangelism generally happen most effectively in a person's first language. We also know that for new immigrants, language is often a barrier to participation in English programming. We are blessed to have the resources to provide language-specific and culture-specific engagements for people. Many of the people who have come to faith through the Willingdon Church family over the past several years have been connected to individuals in our ILM groups.

Recently, we have been using the word "intercultural" to describe how we want to be, shifting away from using "multicultural." Our desire is to be a healthy, truly intercultural church family in a multiethnic city. The nuances of this shift in language are well articulated in this quote by the Spring Institute:

> *Multicultural* refers to a society that contains several cultural or ethnic groups. People live alongside one another, but each cultural group does not necessarily have engaging interactions with

each other. For example, in a multicultural neighbourhood people may frequent ethnic grocery stores and restaurants without really interacting with their neighbours from other countries.

Intercultural describes communities in which there is a deep understanding and respect for all cultures. Intercultural communication focuses on the mutual exchange of ideas and cultural norms and the development of deep relationships. In an intercultural society, no one is left unchanged because everyone learns from one another and grows together.[3]

STRENGTHS AND GROWTH OPPORTUNITIES

As we look at Willingdon's current realities, there are some strengths to celebrate and some opportunities for growth to think about. One strength is that the immigrant community that is part of the Willingdon Church family is intentional and fruitful in evangelism. This impacts not only the lives of the people who get to encounter the life transformation that Jesus brings, but also on the whole church family. In 2019, church leadership spent time praying that our church family would lead one thousand people to faith in that year. A survey in early 2020 indicated that God used the Willingdon Church family to lead 1,190 people to Jesus in 2019, 811 in Canada and 379 outside of Canada. In 2019, nineteen percent of respondents led someone into relationship with Jesus. The fact that our church family is so diverse culturally has caused leaders to think with intentionality about how we equip people to share the gospel. Jayson Georges' book *The 3D Gospel*[4] has been a helpful tool for the church family to digest, providing helpful understandings around guilt-based, shame-based, and fear-based cultures—all of which are represented in our church family.

Because of the cultural makeup of the church family, Willingdon can make a unique contribution to global mission efforts. This is another strength worth celebrating. Over the past several years, short-term mission teams and longer-term international partnerships have been formed enabling people from the Willingdon Church family to reach back into the countries from which they have come, or where they know the language. We have been able to work towards intentional engagements

---

3. Schriefer, "What's the Difference?"
4. Georges, *3D Gospel*.

with this in mind in Ukraine, Brazil, China, and Philippines. To be able to send short-term teams as well as long-term workers who speak the language and understand the culture of the place that they are serving enhances impact.

Another special strength to celebrate is that at Willingdon, an immigrant family made up of a couple of generations can worship together, even though they are proficient in different languages. For example, a family immigrating to Canada from China might have parents who are not proficient in English, but also children who have learned English through school and social life. Willingdon has ways to engage with both of these generations, in Mandarin and English.

The final strength to note here—although there are surely more strengths—is that integration happens in truly beautiful ways. Short-term mission teams often have people from four or five cultures represented. The choir that helps lead the church family in worship is culturally diverse. People build relationships with others from different cultures all the time, over a meal in the Willingdon Café or in a Life Group. Cross-cultural relationships are the norm in the Willingdon Church family. It is a beautiful expression of unity in the midst of diversity.

There are also some gaps and opportunities for growth that should be highlighted. First, there is an opportunity to be more intentional about how new immigrants are welcomed and resourced. It is definitely possible for new immigrants to find community at Willingdon, and to encounter the gospel for perhaps the first time. There is room, however, for some more clearly defined "welcome to Canada" resources and care.

Another unique opportunity that Willingdon could think about is how to resource and disciple immigrant families where the experiences of each generation are so varied. Willingdon Church is positioned uniquely to help families navigate these challenges. While we do have a good number of first-generation Canadians, we also have many second and third generation Canadians. So, we have both a rich resource pool from which to glean wisdom, but also a largely untapped opportunity to resource these families at their specific points of need.

One final gap to note here is that the makeup of our core leadership teams (elders and pastors) is lagging behind in reflecting the shift in demographics in our church family. Steps are being taken to expand the cultural makeup of these leadership teams, but the transition is not a quick one.

Part Three: Kingdom Collaborations

CONCLUSION AND QUESTIONS FOR CONSIDERATION

God is doing something special in and through the Willingdon Church family. With some intentionality from church leadership and members, and because of a very evident move of God's Spirit, Willingdon is a church family that reflects, in a special way, that God loves all nations. May we continue to be a glimpse, a foretaste of the vision in Revelation 7, where people from every tribe and tongue and nation are bowing before King Jesus.

To close, here are some questions to reflect upon. What strengths do you see in the model Willingdon has adopted? What is worth celebrating? What gaps should be addressed? What questions does this case study surface for you? What could you apply from Willingdon's experience to your own context?

BIBLIOGRAPHY

Georges, Jayson. *The 3D Gospel: Ministry in Guilt, Shame, and Fear Cultures.* HonorShame.com, 2020.
"Ministry Philosophy." *Willingdon Church.* No pages. Online: https://willingdon.org/about/ministry-philosophy.
Schriefer, Paula. "What's the Difference between Multicultural, Intercultural, and Cross-Cultural Communication?" *The Spring Institute*, April 18, 2016. Online: https://springinstitute.org/whats-difference-multicultural-intercultural-cross-cultural-communication.
"Willingdon through the Years." *Willingdon Church.* No pages. Online: https://willingdon.org/about/history.
"Willingdon Church 2020 Survey Results." Burnaby, BC: Willingdon Church, 2020.

City Church of Winnipeg
A Case Study of a First Generation Intentionally Intercultural Church

Tim and Sue Nielsen

IT IS CHALLENGING TO try to describe City Church of Winnipeg to anyone who has not walked with us for some time. It is like trying to describe Laphet Thoke, a Burmese tea leaf salad, to someone who has never tried this snack of green cabbage, red tomatoes, crunchy brown peanuts, and various seeds, mixed with dark splotches of fermented tea leaves. So is it with our intentionally intercultural church which intermingles many diverse cultures, from Southeast Asia, the Horn of Africa, Central Africa, the Indian subcontinent, northwestern South America, to Indigenous Canadian and European-descent cultures.

Another layer of diversity are the different experiences of war that many have brought with them. Ninety percent of our members are first-generation immigrants from refugee backgrounds. Many of them suffer under the lingering effects of Post-Traumatic Stress Disorder. Most of their children were born overseas, but now, about twelve to fifteen years later, many have additional Canadian-born children, typically with twelve to sixteen babies added to our group annually, resulting in more layers of diversity in worldviews.

Digging deeper into the layers of the City Church "salad," one also finds differing generational worldviews of race, politics, and resistance movements. Our members have different educational backgrounds. Some are well-educated and previously held prestigious positions of

PART THREE: KINGDOM COLLABORATIONS

respect in their communities, although often not allowed to use these skills in Canada. Others were denied even the privilege of any education. As a result, often both groups have had to deal with substandard housing, inner-city school issues, readily available drugs, and gang violence in Winnipeg.

As the years have passed for City Church, our diversity has broadened from primarily focusing on refugees to also including economic immigrants. This newer dimension has added needed strength to our fellowship. Common to most of us, however, is our experience of redemption from sin and our biblical values. Our view of the supremacy of Scripture further unites us and the strong conviction that the intercultural church is not our design but rather is God's original blueprint for the church.

So, how did City Church come into existence in a racially divided world? How can so many diverse culture groups unite in fellowship? The story of City Church can be likened to many small streams running into tributaries that all flow into a river. Suffice it to say that God sovereignly chose to place us, as well as Indiana Salai Cungcin and his wife Ceri, at the headwaters of the many streams that flowed into the creation of City Church.

For more than twenty years before planting City Church, we, the storytellers of this chapter, had a primary focus on ministering to Indigenous people, mostly in an urban context. Prior to our marriage we were associated with two well-known Indigenous ministries in Canada from which we received our specific training for this field of ministry. This three-month training was in addition to our Bible College missions education. The only model that was presented to us was the "Homogenous Unit Principle" (HUP) by Donald McGavran.

After our marriage in 1985, we returned to Illinois for a year where, prior to this, I (Tim) had been applying the HUP in planting a Spanish-speaking congregation. In the fall of 1986, we moved to Winnipeg, MB and again picked up our ministry with Indigenous Canadians by joining and directing a literature ministry as well as concentrating on Bible studies and friendships. In 1996 this led to another attempt to employ the principles of the homogenous church by planting the North End Fellowship.

Questions, however, began to form in our minds regarding this principal. Did Christ not come to earth to break down all dividing walls between us? If so, then why did this missiological principle seem to undermine our unity and create barriers of fellowship? Sadly, we experienced that it strengthened racial bias and created reverse discrimination towards those that were not Indigenous. It also seemed to hinder missional activity outside of the homogenous ethnic identity.

We appreciated the HUP on Indigenous reserves where, in fact, the population was homogenous, but, in an urban context, it failed to address the diversity of cultures that mix every day in the workforce and in the educational system during the week. We could not help but wonder why the church, representing the body of Christ, was not the leader in displaying unity despite diversity, the very issue that the early church wrestled with in Acts 6? Shouldn't it be possible to be a church, unified and equal under Christ, yet be composed of many different ethnic groups? We felt like our thoughts were considered too radical for our ministry co-workers and we did not want to discourage our friends who were Indigenous leaders, yet the questions remained.

Several years into our questioning, we met Brian Seim, Urban Champion at SIM International. Brian's extensive research and writing about the intentionally intercultural church model was foundational to the underpinning of City Church. Brian also introduced us to Dr. Sam Owusu who helped us see that this model was valid and yet the practical outworking required patience and endurance as demonstrated by the intentionally intercultural church he planted.

Indiana Salai Cungcin (Indy), mentioned earlier, is a former Chin refugee from Myanmar, formerly known as Burma. In 1988, he helped organize a pro-democracy demonstration in Yangon (Rangoon). The protests ended with a bloody military crackdown and the death of thousands of innocent civilians. Indy managed to escape the country and became a refugee in Bangkok for nine years. Because he was an illegal resident of Thailand, as were thousands of others from Myanmar, he spent more than two years in immigration detention, in overcrowded and unsanitary conditions.

About the time he had become a refugee, he had given his life to Christ and associated himself with the American Baptist Church of Bangkok. There he established the Burma Congregation, which was composed of ethnic Chin, Karen, Karenni, Mon, Shan, Kachin, Burman, and Nepalese members. Each ethnic group was significantly different linguistically and culturally. While Indy had not heard the term "intentionally intercultural," he practised it by uniting the approximately 500 members.

PART THREE: KINGDOM COLLABORATIONS

In 1997, the church we were attending and lay-pastoring in Winnipeg sponsored Indy, and we formed a meaningful friendship. In 2003, the federal government placed ten Chin refugees in Winnipeg, none of whom spoke English. We, Indy, and his new wife, Ceri, sought to do the settlement work that the government agency was not able to carry out. This included finding employment for these families and securing housing.

With the lessons learned from the initial settlement of these ten families, Indy encouraged other Chin families who had recently come to Canada to move to Winnipeg. We and the Cungcins helped settle these families as well. In 2007, we successfully petitioned the federal government to place 300 Karen refugees in Winnipeg, which number more than 600 today. In the process of meeting the Karen and Chin at a Government Assisted Refugee (GAR) housing centre, we were also introduced to and built meaningful friendships with Congolese, Burundian, Rwandan, Eritrean, Somalian, and other refugee groups who were temporarily housed there as well. At this point, we began to do extensive house visitations, offered hospitality in our home, had Bible studies and conversation circles, organized field trips to parks, and distributed clothing and household goods.

We and the Cungcins were at a crossroad, however, with what to do with these significant contacts, which by this point numbered over 250 people. We had started off by busing many of them to our church weekly, which was in the northwest corner of the city, but what would be the long-term plan? Based on our mutual conviction that the intercultural church is the biblical model, we rejected any thought of splitting our contacts up and planting three or four homogenous unit churches.

The church was elder-led, and Indy and I (Tim) were two of the four elders who pastored the church. We tried to convince our fellow elders that we needed to move to the intercultural church model. We supplied resources and had many lengthy conversations over the course of a year. Unfortunately, the other two elders did not want to embrace this model. We, on the other hand, were not prepared to give up on our new friendships nor a model that we believed was biblical and that could work if we applied ourselves to it. In the spring of 2008, we reached a compromise, and the two opposing elders chose to bless us and the Cungcins in planting City Church as an intercultural church in the core area of the city and to partner with Grant Memorial Baptist Church.

In the fall of 2008, we began City Church as an intentionally intercultural church located in the historic former First English Lutheran church building in the core area of Winnipeg. We offered simultaneous translation services from English into three other languages and incorporated ethnic music into each service, with PowerPoints in English. Our worship teams reflected the makeup of the church in both its participants and music style. Currently, we still ensure that the programming in the service represents most of the ethnic groups.

The problem with planting an intercultural church with first-generation Canadians is the need for them to understand English as the unifying language. Because many of them did not, our response was to offer three ethnic services in the afternoon: in the Chin, Karen, and Tigrinya languages. Eventually a Punjabi service was also added. The Punjabi group is primarily composed of former Sikhs that Akmal Erastus, our Pakistani elder, has led to Christ. The concept of each of these fellowship groups was to supplement the main intercultural service and there was an expectation that each group would continue to participate in the intercultural life of the church.

In order to continue to serve the physical needs of newcomers we opened City Connexions (CCx), which was a church-based ministry centre for former refugees. This centre helped hundreds of people find employment in the first few years of its operation and offered English courses and other workshops. In 2017, CCx transitioned into Naomi House, which continues to be a ministry of City Church. It is a seven-bedroom transitional home for newly arrived refugees. More than fifty refugees have lived there, and several have come to personal faith in Christ. A few of the families have joined the church. In the spring of 2020, Naomi House also became a Sponsorship Agreement Holder (SAH) with the federal government.

Due to the international nature of the church, we have been blessed with the addition of mission-minded families who are Canadian-born. City Church needs these established Canadians to serve as cultural guides to those that are new to Canada. The relationships built between these cultures have been mutually enjoyable. Much of its success is due to hospitality and home visitation.

On March 25, 2012, a transitional leadership team was voted in with one Pakistani, five Chin, three Karen, one Congolese, one Eritrean, and three Canadian-born leaders. Each of these leaders seemed to embrace the intentionally intercultural church model. But, unfortunately, not all the leaders fully understood that the intercultural church was to be the primary focus of their ministry and that the fellowships were meant to supplement the core focus of the church.

The attendance from 2008 to approximately 2015 remained healthy at just under 300 people. Unfortunately, due to the prospect of better paying jobs, three of the five Chin leaders moved to Alberta. The leaders that replaced them also led the ethnic service, but while good in heart, they did not embrace the intercultural movement. They subsequently pulled the Chin out of the intercultural service but continued to use City Church without a fee on Sunday afternoons. Several of the Chin adults remained attached to the intercultural church. The attendance dropped to about 200.

It was at about this time that some of the 1.25 generation of Karen wanted to follow the Chin example and have their own church. The "1.25 generation" is a term Rubén G. Rumbaut has coined. A 1.25 generation is composed of immigrant children who arrived in their teen years (ages 13–17) and are referred to as such because their experiences are closer to the first generation of adult immigrants than to those that were native born second generation in their new country.[1] This movement away from City Church, unlike the Chin, was not followed by all the Karen leaving, but our attendance dropped again and was approximately 130 prior to COVID restrictions. In addition, we have had two breakaway groups within the African Swahili community, one because of questions about the morals of one leader and another because of legalism regarding the issue of social drinking.

Painful as all these departures have been, City Church has taken the position of not shaming the groups that have left. This has left the door open for City Church to continue to work with the children of those that have pulled out. Because the church works based on friendship, relationships with those that left are still maintained, albeit not as strong as they once were. While these departures and shifts have been painful, it has allowed City Church to be more attractive to newcomers from other ethnic backgrounds as they do not feel as outnumbered.

Today the makeup of the church (including the ethnic services) is sixty-five African (DRC, Burundi, Eritrea, and Somalia), ninety-seven Chin from Myanmar, 374 Karen from Myanmar and ninety-one representative of other groups (Indigenous, Pakistani, East Indian, Columbian,

---

1. Rumbaut, "Ages," 1167.

Filipino, and people of European descent). In total we are working with more than 600 people.

City Church continues to endeavour to be intentionally intercultural in its leadership. We currently have seventeen pastors, elders, and deacons. Seven are of European heritage, three Karen, two Chin, two Pakistani, one Columbian, one Congolese, and one Filipino. We also seek to have intercultural Sunday School, youth group, and women's ministries.

Further analysis of the benefits, challenges, and principles learned by City Church needs to be documented. However, City Church, while smaller than its original footprint, remains a vibrant and healthy intentionally intercultural church. It feels more like a family than an institution. Our hope is to always remain strong in disciple-making in an intentionally intercultural context. However, we are learning that for the multi-ingredient "tea leaf salad" to be enjoyed, it tastes best when served in the context of hospitality with Jesus as the guest of honour.

BIBLIOGRAPHY

Rumbaut, Rubén. "Ages, Life Stages, and Generational Cohorts: Decomposing the Immigrant First and Second Generations in the United States." *International Migration Review* 38 (2011) 1160–205.

Cross-Congregational and Cross-Generational Ministries

An Intentional Shift for the Canadian Chinese Church

CALVIN SUN

THE CANADIAN CHINESE CHURCH (CCC) can trace its roots back to the late 1800s—the first CCC was formed in 1892.[1] Today, there are well over four hundred such churches and congregations across Canada.[2] While these faith communities' growth is related to the influx of new immigrants from Asia, there are lingering questions for the different subcultures that reside in these churches. What is the future of these monoethnic churches? Will they continue to be monoethnic, and is that what the next generation of members desire? Is a monoethnic faith community what today's Canadian-born Chinese and new immigrant Gen X, millennials, and Gen Z envision?

While the challenges of the second-generation Canadian-born Chinese of a CCC have been singled out for much research in the past few decades, today's CCC's demographic has grown in its diversity. The CCC of decades past may be broadly divided into the founding Cantonese baby boomer congregation and their adolescent English Gen X congregation. But today, the makeup of a CCC may consist of Chinese subethnicities from Mainland China, Hong Kong, Taiwan, other South Asian countries, and second- and third-generation Canadian-born Chinese. This subethnic diversity is reflected in Canada's 2016 census, where the total Chinese

1. Guenther, "Ethnicity."
2. Wong et al., *Listening to their Voices*, 5.

population is the largest ethnic minority group in Canada, numbering 1,769,195.[3] Furthermore, each of these subethnicities may consist of multiple generations of members, from baby boomer immigrants of the 1970s and 1980s, second- and third-generation Canadian Chinese Gen Xers, millennials, and Gen Zers, to young working-class new immigrants today. No longer are the challenges merely bi-cultural or tri-cultural, but there is a need to look beyond multiculturalism and bring together the CCC's generational diversity.

GENERATIONAL GAPS AND CONNECTIONS

The evidence for this generational divide can be seen in the 2014 Occupy Movement and the 2019 Hong Kong protest. The 2019 Hong Kong protest was instigated by a proposed extradition bill[4] that allowed the Chinese government to extradite fugitives or those the Chinese government deemed criminals to the mainland. Those who are critics of the Chinese government, religious leaders, and missionaries could become targets of this bill. Hong Kong citizens' response was a massive protest unseen before in the city, with an estimated 1.03 million protesters on June 12, 2019. The demonstrations and discontent eventually grew into additional demands, such as an independent probe into police action, amnesty for arrested protesters, a halt to categorizing the protests as riots, and universal suffrage.[5]

The 2019 protest represents more than a difference in political views between the prodemocratic camp and the pro-establishment supporters; it represents a growing divide between the elites and the working class, as well as between the baby boomers and the Gen Xers, millennials, and Gen Zers. For the younger generations, who are now the majority of the working class, the erosion of their economic and political future is perceived to be the baby boomer generation's failures.[6] This frustration against the baby boomers, who are now in charge and in control of the political and economic institutions, can be summarized by Journalist Peter Kammerer, who writes:

---

3. "Immigration and Ethnocultural Diversity Highlight Tables."

4. The proposal is called the "Fugitive Offenders and Mutual Legal Assistance in Criminal Matters Legislation (Amendment) Bill 2019."

5. Arranz and Lam, "From Occupy 2014 to Protests 2019."

6. Harris, "Keynes Was Wrong."

PART THREE: KINGDOM COLLABORATIONS

But they are not alone, of course; leaders of the baby boomer generation are the reason that Hong Kong and the world are struggling with wealth gaps, ageing societies, unaffordable housing, climate change and social welfare dilemmas like flawed pension schemes. It is little wonder that young people, those protesting in our city among them, are so angry about the governments that have given them so little hope in one day being able to get a good job, buy a home and raise a family.[7]

Even though this discontentment by the younger generation is expressed toward their political institution, their perception of leadership (in)competency is a factor we need to consider today as they evaluate church leadership.

As the working-class Gen X and the subsequent younger generation of Chinese migrate to Canada, they also bring their subethnic distinctiveness. Researchers Miu Chung Yan, Karen Lok Yi Wong, and Daniel Lai have also noted this in their study of Chinese immigrants in Vancouver. They write:

> While members of these groups may share similar cultural origins, they immigrated to Canada from different places with distinct social, economic, cultural, and political systems, and display different political tendencies, social values, and economic behaviours. They also differ in educational background, language (Cantonese, Mandarin or other dialects), and time of arrival. This diversity has placed them into different segments within the political, cultural, and economic domains in Canada and generated intra-group boundaries between them.[8]

As these new immigrants settle into Canada and become members of their local Canadian Chinese Church, they also bring their vision of the future and their perceived path toward building a flourishing life in their work, politics, family, and faith. These new members will then need to negotiate their values against the founding functions of the CCC. Aside from evangelization, researcher Enoch Wong described these core functions as (1) a hub where "social bonds are forged, networked established, and material and psychological support offered"; (2) a "venue for preserving ethnic culture, values, and traditions"; (3) a "space where tradition, cultural rituals, languages, and ethnic identity are passed on to subsequent generations. Who in turn negotiate and constitute an identity

---

7. Kammerer. "Why Are Hongkongers So Angry?"
8. Yan et al., "Subethnic Interpersonal Dynamic," 455.

of their own in that context; and lastly, (4) "where male immigrants restore their social status with a leadership role they used to occupy in their countries of origin, mitigating the downward mobility in the host country."[9]

While held for decades and helpful in retaining culture values and traditions, these core functions of CCC may not be the priority of younger generation members. As John E. Chung and Al Tizon expressed in the book *Honoring the Generations*:

> In fact, some of the young interpret the tenacious grip of the first generation to the lifeways of the original culture as prejudicial, even racist—not necessarily intentionally, but ethnocentric nonetheless—as their parents and grandparents try extremely hard to retain the cultural "purity" of the church.[10]

While Park and his cohort describe the second- and third-generation *Asian North Americans*, I would suggest the inclination for diversity, and a different future by the Gen Xers and Millennials crosses national boundaries. In the case of the 2019 protest, the uprising was not contained within the geographical boundaries of Hong Kong as many protests, clashes, and public tensions can be seen across Canada. These clashes of ideology are not just conflicts between subethnicities like Hong Kongers and Mainland Chinese, but also between the older and younger generations. As such, today's younger generations may not be merely looking for a church to maintain or sustain their culture traditions, nor are they looking to (re)establish a male's leadership position once lost in their migration. But they may have a desire to build and forge the next iteration of their faith community that is common to their generational peers. This tension between maintaining or change can be seen in the Gen Xers' to Gen Zers' attitude in their vocal activism in the public space and the baby boomers' desire to maintain order.[11] Reporting on the Hong Kong churches during the 2019 protest, journalist Josephine Ma writes:

> Churches have been criticised in the past, especially by non-believers and young people, for being out of touch with politics and society . . . Many Christians now find themselves questioning the traditional line between church and politics. "Society has changed. People are getting richer and they don't just want

---

9. Wong et al., *Listening to their Voices*, 3.
10. Chung and Tizon, "Extending Grace and Reconciliation," 173.
11. Lorenz, "'OK Boomer.'"

Part Three: Kingdom Collaborations

services. They want to build a fair and righteous society, and this is particularly what the young generation wants," says Reverend Yuen Tin-yau, 68, former president of the city's Methodist Church and former chairman of the Hong Kong Christian Council.[12]

These cross-cultural sentiments and desire to create change in the world together aligns and connects this generation. That is to say, there is much more in common between the younger generations of the different congregations of a CCC than differences. These similarities can be gleaned from research like that carried out by the Barna Group. In *The Connected Generation*, they reported:

> The connected generation is looking for the Church to provide real, tangible, meaningful opportunities for development. They want the church to be a laboratory of leadership, not just a place for spirituality. They want their faith to intersect the realities of life and, as budding Christian leaders, they want to address real life issues.[13]

> The connected generation has global concerns—corruption, climate change, extreme poverty—and eight in ten agree there is a lack of effective leadership. Many want to be part of solutions but aren't sure how.[14]

Their desire to intersect their faith and the church to local and global issues they are reading and experiencing every day is truly what makes the younger generations of differing subethnicities *connected*. Their connection is a common yearning to build and create, and not just maintain and sustain. What they perceive to be lacking is leadership to direct them. And the leadership is lacking the insight to grasp this generation's cross-congregational potential. This potential is not about escaping or discarding the importance of their ethnic heritage, because if that were the case, they would have left the CCC to attend an English-speaking Canadian church. But in many ways, these Canadian-born Chinese believers and their generational counterparts from the other congregations choose to stay and raise their family in a CCC because they desire to live out their faith in the context of their ethnic heritage. They see their ethnicity as

---

12. Ma, "Hong Kong's Protest Pastors."
13. Barna Group, *Connected Generation*, 131.
14. Barna Group, *Connected Generation*, 134.

having potential and being advantageous in building and creating change with their CCC community. They understand their distinctive story as a minority, and they would like to leverage their ethnic heritage and values to contribute to their individual and corporate testimonies. They are a demographic that are truly embracing their "identity-in-progress" or, as the late David Ng described, a "people on the way."[15]

With that in mind, it is essential to note that the younger working-class generation does not choose to stay in CCC because they have no other churches to go to, or because they secretly want to take advantage of what the older generations have built. Unfortunately, these types of critiques and comments often reflect the aforementioned lack of leadership insights and depth of relationships with the CCC's changing demographic. It is important to recognize that if the maintenance and preservation of ethnic values becomes an idol of the church; if it supersedes the church's missional and reconciliation mandate, such a community will eventually become a cultural center rather than a gospel empowered transformational space. CCC is not just a multi-congregational church that caters to its subethnic audiences; its corporate testimonies come alive when each congregation, along with the different generations, can celebrate each other's distinctiveness and, at the same time, can sacrifice their subethnic values for the sake of the others; for the unity of the body.[16]

INTENTIONAL CROSS-CONGREGATIONAL AND CROSS-GENERATIONAL MINISTRIES

If the younger generations have cross-congregational aspirations, is the CCC ready for such a shift? And where do the older generation—the baby boomers—fit in? As a Canadian, we are exposed to multiculturalism and diversity in our daily lives. This Canadian value provides a glimpse of Rev 7:9–10. Here, a future where all nations gathered under God's reign is not impossible but very much a reality by God's design. This vision of a cross-cultural future is reinforced as the younger generations interact in an education system that is diverse in ethnicities and where their workplaces consist of multiple cultures. As such, the Canadian social landscape forces many of us to ask how we are effectively reaching out to our neighbours and if our church is as inviting and accepting as it could

---

15. Chung and Tizon, "Extending Grace and Reconciliation," 172.
16. Hiebert, *Transforming Worldviews*, 281.

PART THREE: KINGDOM COLLABORATIONS

be. For this generation, the question is not how can we protect our ethnic traditions, but how can we all leverage our heritage as minorities to further the kingdom of God by living out glimpses of the passage in Rev 7? In conjunction, the question remains for the baby boomer leaders: Are they willing and ready to loosen their grip on some of the CCC's founding core functions and walk alongside their younger generation leaders as they forge the next iteration of the CCC together?

While the concept of a cross-congregational and cross-generational ministry is not new, many CCC may not be set up structurally for an intentional cross-congregational and cross-generational church culture. Historically, CCC is segmented by languages; that is, by Cantonese, Mandarin, and English. Language is an essential factor in creating deep relationships and fellowships within the wider church. Still, over-prioritizing languages in a church's ministry organizational structure may deprecate and reduce the CCC's distinctiveness. To add to the challenge, joint congregational events or ministries are not often lived out as the norm, but instead as exceptions primarily because of its difficulty in facilitating multiple languages.

An intentional and strategic cross-congregational and cross-generational CCC may require an organizational culture shift. Rather than automatically distributing church ministries and programs by languages as a default, we should consider a shift toward prioritizing joint congregational programs and ministries, thus mobilizing the church's mission with greater unity, resource, and effectiveness. This is not a call to dismantle individual subethnic congregations, but rather to intentionally instill a cross-cultural and cross-generational value into the institution's soul. In this model, we may still have Sunday services divided by a primary language, but each service may incorporate an aspect of the other subethnicities. For example, an English Sunday service may use Mandarin or other languages for their scripture reading with English translation provided on the screen. Cantonese services might incorporate one English song in their praise and worship segment. The idea is to integrate into its practice the diverse subethnic cultures of a CCC into each congregation and create a norm for cross-cultural and cross-generational ministries, fellowships, and missions. The hope and goal of this shift is to help CCC move toward a greater acceptance of other ethnicities—non-Asian ethnicities—into its church body.

Furthermore, the Gen Xers and millennials' passion for engaging with social concerns, such as poverty and institutional corruption, provides the Church with an opportunity to develop cross-congregational ministries in these areas and to teach on these issues from a biblical framework. Here, we find the older generation's experience and wisdom to be invaluable as they can mentor and guide the younger generation who may lack resilience and endurance. Mentoring ministries are impactful, especially on the Canadian Born Chinese demographic, as researcher Enoch Wong noted in his study. If CCC can leverage and redirect the baby boomer generations into such a ministry, we may help each generation find a renewed function in today's CCC.

CONCLUSION

As Chinese immigration to Canada continues to grow, and the CCC continues to be home to many generations of believers, leaders and pastors of these Canadian Chinese congregations will need to look beyond its present monoethnic make-up. The CCC is primed for diversity because of the generational trends today. No longer are CCC only expected as a multi-congregational or as separate *churches* unintentionally bound together under one roof by ethnicity and family ties, but rather, an intentional cross-cultural and cross-generational testimony of God's reconciling power in us and for us here in Canada; a future where CCC moves beyond multiculturalism and toward a cross-cultural and cross-generational body.

BIBLIOGRAPHY

Arranz, Adolfo, and Jeffie Lam. "From Occupy 2014 to Protests 2019." *South China Morning Post*, December 1, 2019. https://multimedia.scmp.com/infographics/news/hong-kong/article/3030696/from-occupy-to-hong-kong-protests.

Barna Group. *The Connected Generation: How Christian Leaders around the World Can Strengthen Faith and Well-Being among 18–35-Year-Olds*. Ventura, CA: Barna Group, 2019.

Chung, John E., and Al Tizon. "Extending Grace and Reconciliation: From Broken Households to the Ends of the Earth." In *Honoring the Generations: Learning with Asian North American Congregations*, edited by M. Sydney Park et al., 169–96. King of Prussia, PA: Judson, 2012.

Guenther, Bruce L. "Ethnicity and Evangelical Protestants in Canada." In *Christianity and Ethnicity in Canada*, edited by Paul Bramadat and David Seljak, 365–414. Toronto: University of Toronto Press, 2008.

Part Three: Kingdom Collaborations

Harris, Malcolm. "Keynes Was Wrong: Gen Z Will Have It Worse." MIT Technology Review, December 16, 2019. https://www.technologyreview.com/2019/12/16/102389/keynes-was-wrong-gen-z-will-have-it-worse.

Hiebert, Paul G. *Transforming Worldviews: An Anthropological Understanding of How People Change*. Grand Rapids: Baker Academic, 2008.

"Immigration and Ethnocultural Diversity Highlight Tables: Ethnic Origin, Both Sexes, Age (Total), Canada, 2016 Census—25% Sample Data." *Statistics Canada* (2016). No pages. Online: https://www12.statcan.gc.ca/census-recensement/2016/dp-pd/hlt-fst/imm/Table.cfm?Lang=E&T=31&Geo=01.

Kammerer, Peter. "Why are Hongkongers So Angry? Because their Baby Boomer Leaders Are Living in a Parallel Universe." *South China Morning Post*, November 18, 2019. https://www.scmp.com/comment/opinion/article/3038067/why-are-hongkongers-so-angry-because-their-baby-boomer-leaders-are.

Lorenz, Taylor. "'OK Boomer' Marks the End of Friendly Generational Relations." *New York Times*, October 29, 2019. https://www.nytimes.com/2019/10/29/style/ok-boomer.html.

Ma, Josephine. "Hong Kong's Protest Pastors: As Violence Escalates, Churches Struggle to Find a Place between Religion and Politics." *South China Morning Post*, November 16, 2019. https://www.scmp.com/news/hong-kong/politics/article/3037977/hong-kongs- protest-pastors-violence-escalates-churches.

Wong, Enoch, et al. *Listening to their Voices: An Exploration of Faith Journeys of Canadian-Born Chinese Christians*. Markham, ON: CCCOWE Canada, 2018.

Yan, Miu Chung, et al. "Subethnic Interpersonal Dynamic in Diasporic Community: A Study on Chinese Immigrants in Vancouver." *Asian Ethnicity* 20 (2019) 451–68.

Part Four

For King and Kin

THE GOVERNMENT OF CANADA has announced its plans to continue to welcome significant numbers of new permanent residents to Canada. Yet, this announcement comes as citizens are increasingly wary of outsiders and historical abuses of racial power are being reviewed. This presents the local Christian church with a challenge to reassess the practice of hospitality in its modern form that often resembles a temporary hospice based on modern utopian ideals. Juxtaposed to this idealism are thousands of communities of faith located in neighbourhoods across the nation endowed with the valuing, welcoming, and embracing DNA of King Jesus. If what people really long for goes beyond a commodified concept of meeting the modern ideal of multiculturalism and even a functional idea of *reaching out* for numbers or a cause, then faith communities must commit to kingdom goals over national ideals.

In this final part of the volume, the insights of an ethnically diverse group of contributors, call for honest, though difficult, introspection as well as Spirit-guided action. This is a simple yet profound undertaking—requiring self-giving action that prefers the model of King Jesus and preferences kin in Christ over self and tribe. As you read these invitations to move towards greater unity in the body of Christ, we invite you to prayerfully reflect on what this means for you.

Diversity

A Means to a Greater End

Ashwin Ramani

I HAVE A FIRM conviction that an intercultural church is best suited to reach a multicultural city. Being intercultural is not about looking trendy, being inclusive, or being politically correct. Our interest in being intercultural should be for the sake of the gospel. A person who lives in a diverse city but goes to a monocultural church is confronted with a major problem. Their church is incapable of reaching the diverse people groups in their city and fulfilling the Great Commission of discipling the nations. Bishop Lesslie Newbigin wrote these persuasive words:

> How is it possible that the gospel should be credible, that people should come to believe that the power which has the last word in human affairs is represented by a man hanging on a cross? I am suggesting that the only answer, the only hermeneutic of the gospel, is a congregation of men and women who believe it and live by it.[1]

What Newbigin implies here is that one can come to a greater understanding of the gospel of Jesus by looking at the believing community in a local church. If the relationships within a local congregation serve as the lens through which we understand and interpret the gospel of Jesus, then an intercultural church depicts the full intent of the gospel.

When a person walks into a church community where everyone looks identical, they have a skewed understanding of the gospel message.

---

1. Newbigin, *Gospel*, 227.

They will mistakenly conclude God so loved this one people group that he gave his one and only Son. But imagine walking into a church that has a wide variety of diversity in the congregation—ethnically, generationally, culturally, and socially. Despite their major differences when such a congregation embodies love for one another and serves one another, they become the hermeneutic of the gospel. People who walk into this church will understand God loved the whole world that he gave his one and only Son.

In the New Testament, Jesus envisioned an intercultural church and so did the apostle Paul. Granted it would be easier for a church to stick to one group of people, as they have a lot in common making it easier for them to amicably get along with one another. While it may be true from a convenience point of view, it certainly is not an appealing missional strategy. More importantly, such an approach fails to reflect the heart of Jesus or the apostle Paul.

When we become followers of Christ, he does not erase our culture or make us all uniform. For example, as an East Indian, I love spicy food. This did not change when I decided to become a follower of Christ. Our entire family, including our kids, love spicy food. Embracing Jesus Christ does not necessarily change our cultural values provided they are not sinful. But a transformation happens deep inside our hearts, and we start accepting and valuing the good in every culture. Consequently, even though we may be of different cultural backgrounds, we can worship together as part of one church because we value our common bond in Christ over our differences. The beauty of the gospel is seen in diversity.

PAUL: AN ADVOCATE FOR THE INTERCULTURAL CHURCH

It is fascinating to note that one of the most vocal advocates of the intercultural church is the apostle Paul who once used to be a zealous Pharisee. Strongly rooted in his Jewish convictions and being far ahead of all of his contemporaries, Paul used to be exclusive and narrow-minded. Yet, the incredible turning point in his life came when he met Jesus on the road to Damascus, and that encounter changed the trajectory of Paul's life forever. The persecutor became a preacher of the very truth he tried to discredit. The zeal to destroy the church was now channeled to build the church. The man who once looked down on Gentiles and considered them less than humans will now become the apostle to the Gentiles and the foremost proponent of ethnic harmony in the church.

Persecution and suffering became part and parcel of Paul's apostolic ministry. We often assume that Paul was persecuted for preaching the gospel. But further reflection would reveal there was more to why Paul faced such stiff opposition in his ministry. It is because of his conviction that through the gospel the Gentiles shared the same promise of Israel, making all of them equal before God. This view was unacceptable in Paul's time and earned the wrath of the religious Jews.[2] If Paul had stated that the Gentiles were beneath the Jews and reinforced the existing hierarchy, he could have bypassed most of the persecutions. By starting separate Jewish and Gentile churches, Paul could have avoided the hostility from religious leaders. But Paul knew this was a battle worth fighting for because it encapsulated the essence of the gospel.

MYSTERY OF THE GOSPEL

In Eph 3:6–12, Paul refers to the mystery of the gospel that was revealed to him. The Bible does not use the word "mystery" in the same way as we would use the word "mystery" today. A mystery in the Bible is not a puzzle we solve by our own efforts; rather, it is made known only through God's revelation. Paul claims that this mystery that was hidden all through the ages for generations has now been disclosed to him. What is the mystery Paul is referring to in his letter to the Ephesians? It is stated clearly in Eph 3:6: "This mystery is that through the gospel the Gentiles are heirs together with Israel, members together of one body, and sharers together in the promise in Christ Jesus" (NIV). This is a critical verse that requires our undivided attention. The word "together" is used three times in Eph 3:6. As we unpack the content of God's mystery, we see that the wide rift or chasm between Jews and Gentiles has now been bridged. Those who were once divided have now been brought together.

The term "Gentile" in Eph 3:6 refers to everyone who is a non-Jew. It is the Greek word *ethnos*, and it refers to the nations. It is the same word Jesus used to refer to making disciples of all nations in Matt 28:19. Paul claims that the nations share the same promise as Israel. The Gentiles through adoption share with Israel the same promises of God. This verse is alluding to our riches and inheritance in Christ. Legally speaking, an

---

2. DeYmaz, *Building a Healthy Multi-Ethnic Church*, 31.

adopted child is no less than a biological child and has the same rights and privileges. In the same way, the nations are now co-heirs with Israel in sharing the same heavenly inheritance through Christ. Paul goes on to convey that both Jews and Gentiles are now members of one body in Christ. When we place our faith in Jesus, we become part of his body of which Christ is the head.

The fact that the nations along with Israel are part of one body in Christ speaks not just of equality but also of integration. The apostle Paul declares emphatically that there is only one body—the body of Christ. He eagerly desired for the mystery of the gospel of diverse people groups as part of one body in Christ to be comprehended and live out in the context of the church[3]. In contemporary terms, we do not have a separate section in the body of Christ for Whites, Blacks, Aboriginals, Asians, and Latin Americans. We do not have any distinction here between Anglicans, Baptists, Pentecostals, or any such denominational associations. The one body of Christ comprises all of us from various backgrounds who have placed our faith in Jesus Christ. Lastly, Paul communicates in Eph 3:6 that we are sharers together in the promise in Christ. The promises of God are yes and amen in Jesus and this is made available for all believers. No Christian believer is excluded from the promises of Jesus because of their ethnicity.

GOD'S ETERNAL PLAN

To summarize what I have stated so far, God's eternal plan involves racial harmony. The mystery of the gospel is that the nations are co-heirs with Israel through adoption. All races become members of one body in Christ and share in the same promises of God. Now we come to the key verse of our passage and the main point of the text in Eph 3: "His intent was that now, through the church, the manifold wisdom of God should be made known to the rulers and authorities in the heavenly realms, according to the eternal purpose that he accomplished in Christ Jesus our Lord" (vv. 10–11, NIV). God's eternal plan is to create a new humanity, a new society, a new community called the church that will include all ethnicities of people.

The church will be the new creation of God representing his kingdom ideals. Through the church, the manifold wisdom of God is made

---

3. DeYmaz, *Building a Healthy Multi-Ethnic Church*, 32.

known. The word translated "manifold" or "multifaceted" in Eph 3:10 is used only once in the entire New Testament and conjures the images of being many coloured. Interestingly, the Greek translation of the Old Testament uses this very word to refer to Joseph's coat of many colours.[4] The manifold wisdom is speaking of God's glorious plan of redemption in creating the church that comprises all the people groups of the world. When Jesus died, when his body was bruised, when he was nailed to the cross, the blood that he shed was to redeem people of all colours. They are from every tribe, every tongue, every nation, and every language. It is through this ransomed community of people who come from all backgrounds God will demonstrate his manifold, multi-coloured wisdom. What God has done in redeeming us will reflect God' glory and reverberate his praise all through eternity.

All this leads me to conclude that diversity is not the end; it is a means to a greater end. It ultimately results in the eternal praise of our God. We eagerly look forward to this grand culmination of our hope. If indeed heaven will be multiethnic, it should motivate us to replicate this reality here on earth. Jesus taught us to pray, "your kingdom come, your will be done, on earth as it is in heaven" (Matt 6:10, NIV). When believers from diverse backgrounds, ethnicities, and ages worship together in one place and fellowship together in one local church we are living out this future vision and bringing heaven down to earth.

INTERCULTURAL CHURCH: LIVING PROOF OF THE GOSPEL

An intercultural local church is the best apologetic to the gospel; we are living proof of the message we proclaim. If we were to ask the apostle Paul for the proof or evidence of the gospel, he would have pointed us to the local churches of his time. In the first-century local churches, Jews and Gentiles, who once were enemies, despised and hated one another, were functioning as a spiritual family by laying aside their differences. In a society where social segregation was huge, this was a radical demonstration of the power of the gospel to break all barriers. Perhaps, the church in the first century was the only place where people of different backgrounds came together for meaningful fellowship.

---

4. Arnold, *Ephesians*, 197.

PART FOUR: FOR KING AND KIN

Ephesus was a multicultural, cosmopolitan city represented by many people groups like the Romans, Jews, Egyptians, Persians, and Greeks.[5] Paul's church planting strategy did not target a separate church for each people group. Instead, Paul insists on believers of different backgrounds worshipping together to signify the walls of hostility have been demolished. This was made possible because the members of the early church valued their identity in Christ more than their ethnicity of birth.

Could this become true today in our major North American cities full of ethnic diversity? I hope we can prove the gospel's power to unite us by pointing people to our intercultural local churches as evidence. When diverse people come together to worship Jesus as part of a local church, we demonstrate what defines us is not our difference, but what we have in common—our love and commitment to Jesus. It is normal to gravitate towards people who culturally resemble us, but an intercultural church with diverse cultures and ethnicity serves as proof it is a supernatural entity created by the Holy Spirit. Let us issue a compelling invitation to the nations who live in our city to come to know Jesus and be part of this multicoloured family of worshippers.

BIBLIOGRAPHY

Arnold, Clinton E. *Ephesians*. ZECNT. Grand Rapids: Zondervan, 2010.
DeYmaz, Mark. *Building a Healthy Multi-Ethnic Church*. San Francisco: Wiley, 2007.
Newbigin, Lesslie. *The Gospel in a Pluralist Society*. Grand Rapids: Eerdmans, 1989.

5. Arnold, *Ephesians*, 177.

The Body of Christ—Becoming Who God Is Calling Us To Be

Vania Levans

A GREAT SHALOM IS coming that is unceasing in its unfolding. Like yeast mixed into dough that cannot be eradicated (Luke 13:20–21), Jesus, in his birth, inaugurated a kingdom which, in reaching its fullness, will bring wholeness, healing, and reconciliation beyond anything anyone could dream of or imagine—a shalom that will imbue and transform every iota of the cosmos.

One of the most arresting expressions of this great shalom is the picture given in the book of Revelation, where a multitude from every nation, tribe, people, and language worships at the throne of God (Rev 5:9–10; 7:9–10). Christ, who is reconciling all things to God and putting everything in its right place, is calling forth a bride that will be stunning to behold. Myriads of different cultures and peoples will bring their gifts as they celebrate, worship, and live for the One at the centre of all things (Col 1:15–20). They will be a beautiful tapestry of culture, ethnicities, languages, and nations, and the primary locus where this great transformation is in the midst of being worked out is the church. Although no culture is perfect and every culture and people are comprised of aspects that must be redeemed and submitted to the way of Christ, every culture will have something beautiful and God-given to contribute.

This trajectory the church has been set on is in full alignment with the character and identity of Jesus. Even the briefest reflections on the life of Jesus highlight these aspects of his character. Christ, in the few years that he spent preaching the gospel, called all sorts of people to himself.

Among them were the rich and the poor, Samaritans, Jews, lepers, fishermen, tax collectors, centurions, Pharisees, thieves, children, Romans, women, lame, and the demon-possessed (see the Gospel books). And while the vast array of people that Jesus called into relationship with him was extraordinary, especially when one considers the various ethnicities and socio-economic circumstances that they came from, what is even more remarkable is that not only did Jesus call these people to himself, but he called them to each other.

This mix of people, used to walking in completely different circles of power, had to learn a completely new way of being. Whether slave or free, landowner or beggar, all new believers were called into the family of God where they had to learn to recognize each other as brothers and sisters (Acts 2). Their previous way of relating and making their way in the world was made completely defunct. A motley group of people who did not choose to be together but were chosen to be together in Christ was called together in love to function in such a way that they worked like a body. Each part was needed, and each had value, and was honoured and celebrated so that there was room for them to contribute.

First Corinthians 12 communicates that God has arranged the parts of the body and that each part of the body matters. It draws attention to the absurdity of one part of the body (e.g., the foot) denying its need for another part of the body (e.g., the hand). In Christ, the various parts cannot say to each other, "I don't need you," and yet, too often in the church, the intrinsic need the various parts of the body have for one another is not recognized or is easily dismissed. Consequently, little energy is put into opening up ways so the voices of all God's people, both powerful and powerless, can be valued and heard. And yet, it is invigorating to wonder what would happen, if church communities really came to believe they needed their seniors, shut-ins, people who struggle to speak English, children, and everybody. What happens when leaders and congregants in the church believe and behave as though every person were needed and that the body is less when the contributions or voices of others are missing?

Recognizing and including the various parts of the body takes time and energy. It is often easier, and more efficient, to let the voice of the majority or the more powerful dominate. Consequently, many faith communities, while being multiethnic, are usually monocultural or bicultural. A lack of intercultural community in no way denotes a lack of the presence of the Holy Spirit, or an indication that the kingdom of God is not growing; perhaps, its absence is an indication that there is more room to grow. If the goal for any church community is to come to maturity in Christ, then it is worth asking the question: "Is it possible for a faith community that has grown to maturity in Christ and is flourishing to be anything but intercultural, reflecting in some way the diversity of those who are a part of it—a diversity that comprises not only cultural aspects, but is a rich mix of ages and socio-economic backgrounds?" Undoubtedly, there would be other marks of maturity to look for, but because of Christ and who he is, and what he is calling his church to become, is a growing intercultural ethos not essential?

NURTURING AN ENVIRONMENT FOR AN INTERCULTURAL ETHOS

Leaders in faith communities often want to know what they can do to help their church become more multi- or intercultural. While it can help to do things like having Scripture read in different languages, or having a community learn a worship song from another culture, often it can be amidst the simple acts of caring and loving each other wholeheartedly that intercultural worship and ethos emerge, and unique, meaningful, and appropriate expressions of an intercultural community arise that build up the body of Christ and glorify Jesus. Two practices that any faith community could adopt as a means of beginning or continuing to nurture an environment in which intercultural community and worship abounds and flourishes are as follows:

Acknowledging Preferences with Sacrificial Love and Humility

The first practice is one of openly acknowledging and expecting the diversity of personal preferences and experiences that will be present within any community. Often, over the course of getting to know someone, people will discover particular preferences of the one they are getting to know, their favourite colour or meal, ice cream flavour, or preferred love language.[1] These things, when held in an appropriate balance, are part of the joy of getting to know someone. They help us know how to best spend time with the individual or discern what kind of gift or surprise might best delight them. Generally speaking, preferences are not things

---

1. Chapman, *Five Love Languages*.

to be feared or suppressed. However, if someone whose favourite colour was green went around trying to persuade everyone that they encountered that their favourite colour needed to be green as well, that could be problematic. Suppose they demanded that all the events they were participating in had to have a certain amount of green in them.

This type of behaviour would, for most, be cause for concern, and yet, particularly in corporate worship settings, personal preferences like a person's favourite colour can be enforced and propagated as if they were great theological truths or the *right* way. When stylistic preferences for music and liturgy are discussed this way, significant harm can be done to the body of Christ.

There is certain amount of courage and humility that is expressed in statements "I like . . ." or "I prefer X, Y, or Z." As soon as one names something as a preference, and not an objective truth or mandate from God, they make room for the possibility that other preferences may exist. Will not individuals in the body of Christ, who are seeking to grow in love for one another and who acknowledge that others may be better able to engage in corporate worship with a different style of song or type of prayer, engage in aspects of corporate worship that may not be to their liking, just for the sake of the sister or brother worshipping beside them? Is this not part of what it means to love each other as the body of Christ?

Teachers, in their training, are often made aware of the various preferred learning styles their students may have. The average student will learn best in one of three ways: auditory, visual, and kinesthetic.[2] A teacher who is working towards being able to help all their students learn and grow will be intentional about crafting lessons that contain all three of these styles of learning. One of the things that the gathered children of God do in their corporate gatherings in addition to worship is to learn. Consequently, if one of the primary loci where the people of God gather, remember, and participate in the story of God is the corporate worship gathering, then a discussion about nurturing an intercultural ethos would naturally give attention to a diversity of communication media.

There are multiple ways an intercultural ethos can be nurtured within a community, and yet, that is not the ultimate goal. The ultimate goal for faith communities is to continue to mature in Christ and to one another deeply as exhorted through Scripture (John 15; 1 Pet 1:22; 4:8;

---

2. Christison, "Learning Styles."

1 Thess 3:12). If they do this, they will be intercultural, while remaining Christ-centred.

Yes, those who lead such gatherings will likely always be asking such questions as "How do these songs and words align with Scripture? What will help this community learn and grow? What will help this community engage and sing? What will help this community connect with the living God and each other? Is the story of God being told?" The answers to questions like these will help in the sifting process for a corporate worship gathering, and yet, within these questions, there is still so much room for the beauty and diversity of God's people to come to fruition in myriads of aspects, such as tempo, art, medium, song style and choice, use of instruments, etc.

Thus, naming and acknowledging the reality of personal preferences in the body of Christ and being able to name one's own personal preferences are crucial first steps in nurturing an intercultural community.[3] Assuredly, it is pointless to engage in this practice without maintaining postures of humility and sacrificial love. Without humility, the primary concern will become a corporate worship service tailored to one's personal preferences, rather than one that is crafted for the gathered community of God's people. It takes time and energy to do the reflecting work of acknowledging and discerning one's own preferences and recognizing those of others. This gift and sacrifice of time is also a needed companion for the next practice that can serve to nurture an intercultural ethos in community—the act of listening.

Listening in Order to Value and Celebrate

One of the best ways to engage in the commandment Jesus gave ("Love one another") is to practise becoming good listeners. Listening is an act of love. And it is only through truly listening to someone that we can value and celebrate them. Church communities would do well to equip their people with listening skills not only in one-on-one conversations

---

3. One way of helping people appreciate the diversity of experience that happens when a group of people participate in the same corporate worship gathering is by inviting a group of five to ten people to gather on a regular basis (weekly or bi-weekly) for 30–45 minutes and reflect on two questions regarding how they experienced the gathering: "What was most life-giving for you?" and "What was most life-draining for you?" Listening and paying attention to the points of resonance and difference participants hear from each other will open people's eyes to the diversity among them.

but also in groups. When someone is listened to uninterrupted within the safety of a confidential small group, it is amazing to see what can happen in terms of their sense of being known and loved, and the group being able to value and witness the part of that person's story they have heard, as well as God's activity in their life. Even five minutes of intentional listening can have tremendous impact on the person being listened to and on the person listening; both can be transformed in the process.[4]

CONCLUSION

As 1 Cor 12 exhorts us, we seek to recognize each person as a unique part of the body of Christ. Differences are not cause for ostracization; rather, they are valued and celebrated. Thankfully, the hand is not an eye because it plays such a critical role. But how would the hand manage without the eye, or the ear? Each plays an important and interconnected role in the way our physical body functions. Similarly, in Christ, every part has something that is unique and needed by the rest of the body.

It is fascinating to think about the repercussions of that—not only does the church, the bride of Christ, need all the beautiful cultures and ethnicities present within it, but she needs her elderly, her children, her singles, and marrieds. She needs those struggling to make ends meet in its communities, and she needs those who have plenty. She needs people who are differently-abled. She needs lawyers, homemakers, and dentists, landlords, tenants, and the homeless. And she needs more voices. As we, the church, acknowledge our differences and preferences, and practise listening in a posture of valuing, respecting, and celebrating one another, inevitably space will be made for more voices to be heard, particularly voices that have been muted in the past. Our faith communities unified in Christ, by the Holy Spirit, will be places of shared culture.

---

4. One simple practice to help demonstrate this would be invite people to get into groups of two, and each one takes a turn of listening to the Other for 5 minutes uninterrupted, and then to have both debrief on what it was like to listen, and to be listened too. Another helpful aid, in helping people explore the value of uninterrupted listening would be to facilitate a discussion about some of the reasons we feel compelled to interject in conversations and what is happening in us when we do that.

BIBLIOGRAPHY

Chapman, Gary. *The Five Love Languages: The Secret to Love That Lasts.* Chicago: Northfield, 2015.

Christison, Mary Ann. "Learning Styles and Strategies." In *Practical English Language Teaching*, edited by David Nunan, 267–88. New York: McGraw Hill, 2003.

The Correlation between Forgiveness, Reconciliation, and the Trinitarian Unity of the Church and its Impact on Missional Efficacy

Clint Mix

J ESUS' PRAYER FOR UNITY in John 17 can be used to proactively address the inevitable conflict that will take place as the church seeks to move beyond multiculturalism and become an intercultural expression of the body of Christ. This chapter will explore this idea as well as examine how this type of Trinitarian unity should result in an increase of the missional efficacy of the church. This topic is timely in our current Canadian context as there continues to be an increase in the diversity of nations coming to Canada. When the apostle Paul was dialoguing with the Athenians on Mars Hill, he reminded them, and us today, that God determined the times and the exact places where people live (Acts 17:26–27).

THE TRINITY AS A MODEL FOR CHURCH UNITY

John 17 records Jesus' *deathbed* prayer which demonstrates the priority that Jesus placed on unity. In v. 11, Jesus says, "protect them by the power of your name—the name you gave me—so that they may be one as we are one" (NIV). He goes on to say:

> I pray also for those who will believe in me through their message, that all of them may be one, Father, just as you are in me and I am in you. May they also be in us so that the world may believe that you have sent me . . . may they be one as we are

Mix *Forgiveness, Reconciliation, and the Trinitarian Unity*

one—I in them and you in me—so that they may be brought to complete unity. Then the world know that you sent me and have loved them even as you have loved me (vv. 20–23, NIV).

The prayer of Jesus is that *we (the church) would be one as (the Trinity) is one*. Jesus prayed that the relationship existing between God as Father, God as Son, and God as Holy Spirit would be mirrored/replicated in the church today.

In *The Great Dance*, C. Baxter Kruger states, "The Trinity is not three highly committed religious types sitting around some room in heaven. The Trinity is a circle of shared life, and the life shared is full, not empty, abounding and rich and beautiful, not lonely and sad and boring . . . The great dance is all about the abounding life shared by the Father, Son and Holy Spirit."[1] This dance of the persons of the Trinity is a great example of how we should live with one another in interdependence and mutual submission.

Miroslav Volf poignantly brings this concept together when he writes about the *perichoresis* (the "dance of the Trinity") and how this refers to the interiority of the Trinitarian persons. He goes on to explain how this should be a model for the church to follow in that just as the Father is in the Son and vice versa that they are also in us, the church.[2] Volf also states it this way: "Jesus' high priestly prayer, that his disciples might become one . . . presupposes communion with the Triune God, mediated through faith and baptism . . . the relations between the many in the church must reflect the mutual love of the divine persons."[3]

Richard Rohr, in his book *The Divine Dance*, reminds us, "At the heart of Christian revelation, God is not seen as a static Monarch but . . . *a divine circle dance*, as the early (parents) of the church dared to call it (in Greek, *perichoresis*, the origin of our word *choreography*). God is the holy One presenced in the divine in the dynamic and loving action of the three."[4] This image of the divine circle or dance shows itself in replicable ways for the church today. In this dance the persons of the Trinity live in mutual submission to one another. This is demonstrated to us by Jesus' pre-betrayal prayer, "yet not my will, but yours be done" (see Luke

---

1. Kruger, *Great Dance*, 22.
2. Volf, *After our Likeness*, 209.
3. Volf, *After our Likeness*, 195.
4. Rohr, *Divine Dance*, 31.

22:39–46). In the same context, Jesus recognizes that the Father would intervene and stop this if he would ask (Matt 26:47–56).

Honouring the Other is also seen in this Trinitarian dance. This is demonstrated at the baptism of Jesus where the Father spoke words of identity, "This is my Son, whom I love; with him I am well pleased" (Matt 3:17, NIV). We know, too, that the Holy Spirit descended then as well, and in the upper room discourse (John 13–16), Jesus honoured the Holy Spirit. Additionally, Scripture is full of examples of the Son and the Spirit honouring the Father and seeking to lift him up. How much greater unity in the local and catholic church would we experience if we took the posture of honouring the Other instead of correcting others' *wrong* perspectives.

Scripture is clear that the church is to be one, even as God, Father, Son, and Holy Spirit are one. The unity of the church is to mirror the unity of the Trinity. We, like the Trinity, are called to live in interdependence with one another, in mutual submission to one another, and honour one another. As much as this is the ideal, we also know that humanity is not sinless, therefore, it is important to consider some of the causes and results of conflict and disunity.

THE CAUSES AND RESULTS OF DISUNITY/CONFLICT

Conflict is as old as the church itself. Even before the church started in Acts, the disciples fought over who would get the prestigious positions in the new kingdom (Matt 20:20–28). There was conflict when the Hellenistic widows were being marginalized in the distribution of food (Acts 6:1–7). The first *General Assembly* (Council of Jerusalem) was called to navigate some early theological disagreements (Acts 15:1–35). Paul and Barnabas had conflict in Acts 15:36–41, and 1 Cor 3 describes a leadership conflict. The church at Philippi had interpersonal challenges (Phil 4:2–3), and there are many more biblical examples of conflict.

Causes of Conflict in an Intercultural Church

There is considerable work done on conflict in any church; areas such as control, vision, leadership, theology, interpersonal relationships, values, to name a few, can be contentious.[5] For the multicultural church, and one

---

5. Reed, "Leadership"; Mix, "Leading through Conflict."

MIX *Forgiveness, Reconciliation, and the Trinitarian Unity*

that is aspiring to become an intercultural church, there are additional and unique areas for potential conflict.[6] The following list highlights a few significant areas which may be sources of conflict in some churches.

Time

My wife is Latina, and I have travelled with her to her birth country of Chile, where a start time and an end time are quite relative fixtures. Years ago, when I served in district leadership in the Greater Toronto Area (GTA), we were late in starting a meeting in the downtown area because people had not yet arrived. My culturally fluent boss noted that in the Canadian First Nations culture we honour people by waiting for them to arrive. I quickly noted that, in the GTA culture, we honour people by showing up early.

Food

In a former ministry role, I gave oversight to our operations team and the church's outstanding intercultural ministry. Food is obviously a big part of culture. There was ongoing tension between our operations team's commitment to a contracted caterer and the ministries' need to explore food and culture. Additionally, some cultures perspective on food, waste, parenting, etc. create internal conflicts.

Governance

Several years ago, I spent a couple of weeks in a First Nations context in Northern Quebec. There was a church building in the same parking lot as a cultural centre. Even though the church was for First Nations people, it was constructed and run in a majority culture way (this was part of my being there). Out of interest, I went into the cultural centre and noted how they had a room where they would sit in community and listen and decide. The church ran on typical Roberts Rules, even though they could simply gather and govern in a way that made sense to their cultural context. Many cultures follow the *spiritual leader*, who is most often the *man* (gender exclusivity intentional) *of God*. This clashes with

---

6. This list is compiled from my own experience, consultation with Dr. Charles Cook; Hibbert and Hibbert, "Managing Conflict."

various models of governance such as a board governance model, a congregational model, or the Carver model.

Communication

Communication can involve cultural differences relative to direct and indirect communication. Also, in a multicultural church, it can simply be difficult to understand one another and pick up on the subtleties of language that a person using their first language would be able to pick up on.

Education

Different cultures place a significantly different value on education. Even within one denomination there can be diverse requirements based on ethnicities' relative prerequisites for ordination. In a multicultural church setting the disparity between groups creates an obvious point of tension.

How to Address Conflict

An irony relative to this topic is how conflict itself is actually a source of conflict. Those from an honour/shame cultural background tend to be less upfront with concerns. Whereas those from a predominantly Western world view tend to be much more confrontational.

Ethnocentric Hermeneutic of Scripture

Our theological perspectives are shaped by our cultural background. For example, many from the Global South embrace liberation theology,[7] while those from a Western cultural background have a challenging time grasping the emphasis on liberation.

---

7. Elwell, *Evangelical Dictionary*, 635–38.

MIX *Forgiveness, Reconciliation, and the Trinitarian Unity*

Our Identity as Followers of Jesus versus our Identity Based on our Cultural Upbringing

An observation that I have seen in many homogenous churches (Caucasian included) is that our cultural way of doing things—consciously or subconsciously—can trump our way of doing things. Having had the privilege of working with almost as many ethnic specific churches as there are in Canada, I have often been told, "You don't understand, this is the (fill in your ethnicity) way of doing things." In earlier days of my ministry life, I would often simply defer; in more recent years, however, I have concluded that just because it is not Western (my culture) does not mean it is Christian.

Results of Conflict and Disunity

The North American Evangelical church's inability to walk in Trinitarian and intercultural unity is one of the significant reasons why there has been a sharp increase in the "rise of the nones."[8] Several of the conflict scenarios that I was involved in mediation reinforce this.

One church had two groups that were vying for control, and both called the police to evict the other group. The police officer looked at me with confusion as to what to do; I looked at him and was struck with a deep sadness that this public servant would likely be lost to the kingdom of God for all eternity because of what he walked into. Similarly, another congregation located in the downtown/university area of a major urban centre was fighting so loudly that those passing by on the street called the police to the church building. How can those who placed the phone call and the first responders ever believe our message? In one extreme case, a very engaged physical altercation broke out between two women on opposite sides of a conflict. Police arrived and observed a fight taking place, as did the young people and children present. How can they ever believe our message?

David Fitch, in his book, *The Great Giveaway*, states, "Evangelicals often preach that what the culture needs is absolute truth, but what culture needs is a church that believes the truth so absolutely that it actually lives it out."[9] The learning relative to the topic of missional lethargy

8. White, *Rise of the Nones*.
9. Fitch, *Great Giveaway*, 57.

Part Four: For King and Kin

intercultural disunity is that when we fail to demonstrate the truth of the gospel by how we treat one another we invalidate our message. We are called to Trinitarian unity. We have and will have conflict. But endeavoring to *move beyond multiculturalism* means we will have potential for further conflict and disunity and missional ineffectiveness. Because of this, it is necessary to consider how to respond to conflict with forgiveness and reconciliation.

FORGIVENESS AND RECONCILIATION

Forgiveness

Much has been written on the topic of forgiveness. As such, limited attention will be given to it here beyond a reminder about biblical forgiveness and reconciliation. In his powerful book, *Exclusion and Embrace*, Miroslav Volf reminds us, "That the injustice of oppression must be fought with the creative 'injustice' of forgiveness."[10] This insightful reminder articulates the teaching and life of Jesus. On the cross, Jesus prayed, "Father, forgiven them, for they do not know what they are doing" (Luke 23:34, NIV). Jesus taught that we *should forgive "seventy times seven times"* and that those who have been forgiven much should also forgive others (Matt 18:10–35). Jesus' teaching on prayer reiterated that as we receive forgiveness, we should also reciprocate it to others (Matt 6:9–15). And, while there are some offences that we can never forget we are called to live debt free (including forgiveness) and that when we forgive, there is nothing owing to us from the offender (Matt 18:10–35; Rom 13:8–14).

Reconciliation

Forgiveness is a unilateral process, and reconciliation is a bilateral process.[11] As challenging as forgiveness can be, reconciliation is usually even more difficult. This emphasis on reconciliation is pertinent for a few reasons. In *The Missional Church and Missional Life*, Howard Snyder ties together the concepts of Trinity, reconciliation, and mission when he says, "God the Father sends the Son into the world in the power of the Holy Spirit to bring salvation in all its dimensions, including ultimately

---

10. Volf, *Exclusion and Embrace*, 121–22.
11. Mix, "Leading through Conflict."

the reconciliation of all things, the kingdom of God in its fullness."[12] Scripture reminds us that reconciliation is core to who we are and that we are commissioned to this ministry (2 Cor 5:11–21). So, even if one or both (or more) parties forgive but continue to walk separately, at a minimum, it appears to the watching world that *forgiven people cannot forgive*, and we demonstrate that the gospel may not be true. The opposite is also true; when we move beyond forgiveness to reconciliation, we then give testimony to the truth of the message we proclaim.

To dig deeper into the challenges of reconciliation, I conducted a phone interview with Dr. Cheryl Bear, who serves an Indigenous Canadian Christian leader. She has spoken wisdom into the Canadian Truth and Reconciliation Commission (TRC). Cheryl poignantly noted, "an apology is appreciated, but until we walk together as equals, are we truly reconciled?"[13] She has also suggested, "Reconciliation cannot stop with people but must also include the land." She also added, "Reconciliation is or has become a distraction, we talk about it, but its business as usual ignoring rights and treaties . . . while land acknowledgment is a positive baby step, it is not enough." She rightly noted that reconciliation is "an awkward dance with an often unwilling partner."[14]

When we take a step past forgiveness to reconciliation—meaning we walk again, together, as equals—the church will experience far greater missional effectiveness. Thus, it is important to explore the missiological implications of Trinitarian unity.

THE MISSIOLOGICAL IMPLICATIONS OF THE CHURCH'S TRINITARIAN UNITY

The words of Jesus are clear. One of the ways we can be great apologists for the validity of the gospel, how we can see the church move forward in mission, is by replicating Trinitarian unity. This is what the earlier quote from David Fitch reminds us of: "Evangelicals often preach that what the culture needs is absolute truth, but what culture needs is a church that believes the truth so absolutely that it actually lives it out."[15] When we live out Trinitarian unity, we proclaim the truth of Jesus. David Bosch in

---

12. Snyder, "Missional Church," 1.
13. Dr. Cheryl Bear, interview by Clint Mix, January 2020, transcript.
14. Dr. Cheryl Bear, interview by Clint Mix, January 2020, transcript.
15. Fitch, *Great Give Away*.

his seminal work *Transforming Mission* ties together the Trinity and missional effectiveness, saying "Until the sixteenth century the term [mission] was used exclusively with reference to the doctrine of the Trinity, that is, of the sending of the Son by the Father and of the Holy Spirit by the Father and the Son."[16]

The psalmist writes, "How good and pleasant it is when God's people live together in unity . . . there the lord *bestows his blessing, even life forevermore" (Ps 133:1, 3b,* NIV). If we would practise forgiveness and reconciliation, then we should experience a greater blessing from God. In Ephesians, we are given another call to intercultural unity when Paul instructs the church that "the dividing wall of hostility" has been broken down (Eph 2:11–22). Paul goes on to describe that this does not simply validate the truth of the gospel to our physical world, but it does the same to the unseen world as well. Paul states, "through the [united] church, the manifold wisdom of God should be made known to the . . . heavenly realms" (Eph 3:7–13, NIV).

WAYS TO WALK IN TRINITARIAN UNITY DESPITE SIGNIFICANT INTERCULTURAL AND THEOLOGICAL DIFFERENCES

Trinitarian unity—being one as God: Father, Son, and Holy Spirit are one—is a challenging and elusive goal that fallen humankind cannot fully achieve. However, the Evangelical church can make significant movement towards unity that should see us achieve a far greater kingdom impact than we currently have. The following are a few insights which some within Evangelicalism could explore and possibly embrace.

A Biblical Line in the Sand

A mark of Evangelicalism is our commitment to Scripture as our authority for faith and practice. So often we have used our understanding of Scripture as the line in the sand to create disunity. But consider again our guiding passage: "I in them and you in me—so that they may be brought to complete unity. Then the world will know that you sent me and have loved them even as you have loved me" (John 17:23, NIV). Jesus provides us with the *line in the sand*. Jesus himself is the answer; he is where we

---

16. Bosch, *Transforming Mission*, 1.

draw the line. As we are in Jesus and Jesus is in us, we must be united. Andreas Köstenberger in his book on the Trinity reminds us, "the Son is the means to accomplishing this end of unity."[17] Dietrich Bonhoeffer reiterates this idea when he states, "Christian community means community through and in Jesus Christ. On this presupposition rests everything that the Scriptures provide in the way of directions and precepts for the communal life of Christians."[18] Regardless of what our theological and intercultural differences are, if someone claims to be a follower of Jesus, we are called to live in unity with them.

A More Christ-like Disciple

Disciple making is gaining fresh traction. When we claim *success* in the discipleship process we usually point to an example where we created an upper-middle class Evangelical who reads their Bible and prays. However, true disciple making means that we live Christ-like lives and empower others to live just like Jesus lived. What if a true disciple majored on the things that Jesus majored on (Matt 22:34–40; Luke 4:14–30) and minored on the things that Jesus minored on, and maybe gave even less attention to the items Jesus did not even address?

Another powerful example of what it means to be Christ-like was demonstrated by Jesus in the upper room. He knew he was about to be betrayed, denied, and abandoned and yet he still washed the disciple's feet and broke bread with them. So often in conflict we say, "I am taking the high road, I am being Christ-like," yet we condemn the other and exalt ourselves.

The Trinitarian Dance as a Model for Achieving Unity

C. Baxter Kruger reminds us that "our inclusion in the great dance of the Trinity is not a goal for us to attain. It is the way things are. And we must learn to see ourselves and others . . . as people caught up in the fellowship, camaraderie, the glory and joy and love and life of the Father, Son and Spirit."[19] As amazing as the dance is, the reality that we are already a part of this divine dance is even more incredible. What if we acted like it?

17. Köstenberger and Swain, *Father, Son and Spirit*, 176.
18. Bonhoeffer, *Life Together*, 24.
19. Kruger, *Great Dance*, 57.

I have wondered what the back story is to the few windows we are given in Scripture about the dance of the Trinity. In Genesis, when God decides to make humanity in his image, did a conversation—a dance—take place? I wonder, when the Father postulated the idea of creating people, if the Advocate responded, "You know they will fall . . . and what that will cost the Son." I also wonder if the Father said, "My Son, just say the word and we will scrap the idea!" and the Son used the same words he did in the garden and said, "you know I want your will more than mine!" Was there an ebb and flow, mutual submission, and communal decision? None of us know how these things happened, but if there truly is a dance, and we are a part of it, and if we are to replicate the Trinitarian relationship, we could probably respond differently to those we are in conflict with.

In my discussion with Canadian theologian Dr. Bernie A. Van De Walle, he noted that a mark of the divine is humility. Citing Phil 2:1–11, he suggested that Jesus' model of humility should be one we emulate when it comes to dealing with conflict and pursuing unity.[20] Rather than condemning those we find ourselves in disunity with, could we listen, understand, submit, honour, and dance? Will we come to agreement on everything? No, however, when we grasp the reality that we are a part of the *perichoresis* and a part of each other, we may be able to get to the point of forgiveness, reconciliation and walking in Trinitarian unity.

CONCLUSION

The good news, the gospel message of which we are stewards, is too important for us to allow it to become marginalized because we will not walk in Trinitarian unity with others. The prayer of Jesus is a call for those of us who have, and will, find ourselves in conflict scenarios to seek forgiveness and pursue reconciliation. We need to stay in the dance. The prayer of Jesus is a call for all of us who name Jesus as Lord to walk in unity with those who have differing views on theological, moral, and cultural issues. We can be an answer to the prayer of Jesus by being, *one as God is one so that the world will know that God loves them and that God sent Jesus* (John 17:20–23).

---

20. Dr. Bernie A. Van De Walle, personal conversation, February 2020.

BIBLIOGRAPHY

Bonhoeffer, Dietrich. *Life Together: The classic Exploration of Faith in Community*. New York: Harper and Row, 1954.

Bosch, David J. *Transforming Mission: Paradigm Shifts in Theology of Mission*. Maryknoll, NY: Orbis, 2011.

Elwell, Walter. *Evangelical Dictionary of Theology*. Grand Rapids: Baker, 1986.

Fitch, David. *The Great Give Away: Reclaiming the Mission of the Church*. Grand Rapids: Baker, 2005.

Hibbert, Richard, and Evelyn Hibbert. "Managing Conflict in a Multicultural Team." *Evangelical Missions Quarterly* 53 (2017) 18–23.

Köstenberger, Andreas J., and Scott R Swain. *Father, Son and Spirit: The Trinity and John's Gospel*. Downers Grove, IL: InterVarsity, 2008.

Kruger, C. Baxter. *The Great Dance: The Christian Vision Revisited*. Vancouver: Regent College Press, 2000.

Mix, Clint. "Leading through Conflict." Lecture given at Tyndale Seminary, Toronto, ON, 2019.

Reed, Eric. "Leadership Surveys Church Conflict," [n.d.]. *Christianity Today*. https://www.christianitytoday.com/pastors/2004/fall/6.25.html.

Rohr, Richard. *The Divine Dance: The Trinity and your Transformation*. New Kensington, PA: Whitaker House, 2016.

Snyder, Howard A. "The Missional Church and Missional Life." Lecture given at the Faculty Retreat of Tyndale University College & Seminary, 2010. Online: https://www.tyndale.ca/sites/default/files/SnyderMissionalChurchandLife.pdf.

Volf, Miroslav. *After our Likeness: The Church as the Image of the Trinity*. Grand Rapids: Eerdmans, 1998.

———. *Exclusion and Embrace: A Theological Exploration of Identity, Otherness, and Reconciliation*. Nashville: Abingdon, 1996.

White, James Emery. *The Rise of the Nones: Understanding and Reaching the Religiously Unaffiliated*. Grand Rapids: Baker, 2014.

The Intercultural Leader

Sam Owusu

THE GROWING ETHNIC DIVERSITY of our communities provides rich and often untapped resources for the church's mission. Leading in an ethnically diverse community is a new and daunting experience for many Western Christian leaders. The intercultural leader is the key to addressing these problems and developing the capacity to reach out to these communities. Too many Christian books on leadership today are written from a monocultural perspective interspersed with Bible verses and marketed as universal biblical principles of leadership. Leadership models, although they may differ from person to person and method to method, generally have a common bias toward Western or European influenced ways of thinking. Thus, contemporary leadership theories exclude the enormous contributions, potential learning, and valuable insights that come from leaders in diverse communities. As a result, most church leaders are often not adequately prepared to deal with the rapid growth in their communities' cultural diversity. How will they lead others who are different from them in their communities and their churches? How will they create safe environments so that those who are different from them will feel comfortable in their churches?

For the purposes of this chapter, an intercultural leader is defined as the one who leads with an inclusive approach and philosophy that incorporates Scripture and the values of diverse cultures in a respectful manner to equip people to fulfill their God-given mission. It is the future of the church. There are a few elements to this kind of leadership which we will examine below.

AUTHENTICITY

The effectiveness of the intercultural leader is ultimately dependent on their authenticity. First, it is the authenticity of having a deep relationship with Jesus Christ, and consequently, their obedience to the Scriptures. Secondly, they have chosen to live in a cross-cultural setting. It is more than a church role requirement; they need to desire to be fully immersed in living life with people from other cultures. It is in playing together, learning together, and worshipping together that the intercultural leader leads the church in authenticity. Their lifestyle choice is motivated by a genuine love for all people, valuing others regardless of ethnicity or background.

TRANSFORMATION

The intercultural leader aspires to maximize their leadership capacity through a deeply personal, and sometimes painful, transformation. This can only be done in cooperation with the Holy Spirit. As a leader and as a member of the dominant culture, I had to learn about and accept the reality of my privilege and consider how I can use that privilege to empower minorities in my church. I have also had to unlearn much of the conventional wisdom about church growth because it relies heavily on a homogeneous model. In fact, building an intercultural church at times may be very slow as people wrestle with whether they are willing to let go of preferences to serve someone else.

SCRIPTURAL AUTHORITY

An intercultural leader must rely on Scripture as the authority for the church and life. The Bible must be the church's reference manual. It will be the only defence in the face of enormous adversity when the church begins to move towards the reality of becoming an intercultural church. Numerous obstacles will be thrown in one's path, but the Bible provides a pattern and an encouragement to those who walk this less-travelled path. One of the primary obstacles will be church versus cultural tradition, and only the Bible will serve as the ultimate standard against generations of tradition. When the apostles were faced with a volatile racial division between Hellenistic and the Hebraic widows in Jerusalem's early church, they devoted themselves to prayer and Scripture (Acts 6:2, 4). Whenever a racial conflict occurred in the early church, Scripture was used as a reminder and instructor on exactly how to proceed. When conflict came up between Peter and Paul concerning Peter's withdrawal from table fellowship with the gentiles, Paul reminded him of the equity of both the sinfulness and the salvation for Jews and Gentiles. Even in the Old Testament, when the Jews neglected or refused to include the Gentiles in God's salvation, a word from God would correct and remind his chosen people that they were instruments to reach the entire world (Jonah 4:9–12; Isa 49:6).

The Bible is the basis for building this new humanity and must be central to the ministry of the intercultural church. The leader must understand the ongoing dialogue that warns the church about the pitfalls of pluralism and multiethnicity. Syncretism will be easy to detect and deal with. For example, this was the issue of discipline in our church. In some of the cultures represented in our church, losing face in front of a congregation is an offence. Yet, the agreement among the leadership of our church was that scripture must be the determining factor in dealing with sin and error. We also evaluate our worship in light of Scripture. Culture should not be the last word in determining how worship is carried out in the church. The Bible must be the leader's positioning, rather than trends and social context. This does not mean that the leader ignores scripture, but rather that the leader's position on scripture forces him to do theology in the milieu of a diverse community.

HUMILITY

When stepping into any kind of intercultural situation, the leader must humbly admit to themself (and others) that despite their ministry experience, academic pedigree, or extensive global travel, they do not know diverse cultures sufficiently, and have so much to learn from them. Humility helps us to reflect on our experiences and perspectives through the lens of our own culture. Humility also opens the door to recognizing our ethnocentrisms that need to be overcome, to make room for others' experiences as just as valid and valuable.

The attitude of humility will bridge the relationship gap and endear the leader to the community they are called to serve. They need to spend time with the people, ask meaningful questions, listen to the answers, learn their histories, and educate them. This will go a long way toward deepening their ties with the new community. In addition to learning new things, the leader must be ready to suspend their judgment of the way things are said, done, or implemented. Keep in mind, that some in the community might be outraged that the Other is wrong: "They do not do things the way we do them." But in reality, the adage "It's not wrong; it's just different" is the key to finding understanding and developing an attitude of acceptance. When we can realize that we truly have many things to learn and that we do not know everything, we can take the first steps forward in closing the culture gap and building relationships.

VISION

The intercultural leader has a conviction to establish a community that would bring diverse people groups together. They also solicit and engage other leaders to join in this vision. They *sell* the vision to the congregation and to the staff that will eventually own it. And they are committed or willing to carry the full burden of this process for many years. They shepherd the flock to understand that God has entrusted the congregation to them (Acts 20). Their call is to develop a congregation toward a new humanity founded on Christ and take on this mission challenge in that context. And one of the ways is the expression of preaching. There are so many different preaching styles, ranging from monotone reading word-for-word of a manuscript to an extemporaneous, rhythmic, and interactive dialogue between an animated preacher and an engaged audience. The intercultural leader's strategy is to expose and expand their people to different preaching traditions and expressions. The goal is to provide a variety of preaching, backgrounds, training, and styles.

WORSHIP

The intercultural leader must be committed to intercultural worship. In our contemporary landscape of the struggle between contemporary and traditional styles, it may seem like adding intercultural worship will further complicate the dialogue. Instead, we are aiming to reflect God's intention and purposes.

One of the most challenging areas of struggle in an intercultural church is music. Each culture and tradition feel strongly that their heart expression of worship is the best expression and sometimes the only acceptable form of worship. When believers focus so much on their cultural expression of worship, their worship will flatten out and lose its potential racial harmony. The church needs the fullness of the cultures to enrich the harmony of the heavenly choir. When we begin to listen to and, in time, sing one another's songs, we may have a new and renewed ecclesiology that will favour more unity.

At Calvary Worship Center, our approach to intercultural worship is choosing a default liturgical or music style to guide and accompany our worship. At the same time, we continue to explore the boundaries of our default style with the hope of representing the nations within the church and the target audience of our evangelistic ministry.

We also encourage diversity in our worship team. Some may suggest that it borders on tokenism. But this practice is a strategy to fulfill God's mission for the church. It parallels that of the apostles who chose seven Greek deacons to serve the Greek widows (Acts 6).

God's intercultural choir singing in harmony announces to the world the harmony that He has brought to the fragmented cultures in the body of Christ. We indeed reflect Rev 7:9–10, which says, "After this, I looked, and there before me was a great multitude that no one could count, from every nation, tribe, people and language, standing before the throne and before the Lamb. They were wearing white robes and were holding palm branches in their hands. And they cried out in a loud voice: 'Salvation belongs to our God, who sits on the throne, and to the Lamb'" (NIV).

EVANGELISM

The intercultural leader understands that there is no option in the matter of evangelism. The intercultural leader must have an evangelistic heart for all races in order to grow the church. And the most effective way to grow an intercultural church is through the conversion of new believers. The context of their evangelism is their neighbourhood, and in their community live diverse people who need to know the good news about Christ's amazing love and acceptance. This good news must be presented with sensitivity toward their culture. We are faced with the biblical reality that God is no respecter of persons and that we are to serve the world with God's love and compassion (Acts 10:34). Because of God's sufficient grace, a Ghanaian, Korean, Chinese, or Hispanic is saved. And it is the responsibility of the local church to bring the new Christian into the fold with joy and celebration of what the Lord has done. The combination of evangelism and new Christians hungry to learn about Christ provides the church with growth and empowerment to continue the work of Christ in a mission context.

AMBIGUITY

The leader must come to terms with ambiguity, uncertainty, and generally a lack of timely knowledge. Other cultures value different things. This means the leader may not always have the information they want in the time frame that makes them comfortable. To succeed in those situations, they must find some way to manage their emotions and intellect when things are not presented to them as they would prefer. In general, there is always a cultural reason for the perceived ambiguity that they may not know and must learn. The more questions they ask and the stronger their relationships become, the more they will be able to see the reasons for the ambiguity and become more comfortable. This takes time, effort, patience, and a genuine desire to learn and submit to local authority. Some of us will never feel comfortable in ambiguous circumstances. But if they can manage themselves when this type of situation arises, they will be able to deepen their understanding of a relationship with a new culture.

ADAPTIVENESS

This starts with your deepest core values, who you are as a person or church. The leader needs to ask, "What is the adaptation that will enable us to live out our calling as God's people in this changing world?" The nature of intercultural leadership is always a state of flux. Changing global migration patterns impact the cultural diversity of churches and their neighbourhoods. The leader seeks to adapt as they are aware of these cultural trends and empower the church to respond to these developments.

THE HOLY SPIRIT

Finally, the intercultural leader must lean mightily on the Holy Spirit. I have yet to witness an intercultural church that minimizes the role of the

Holy Spirit. Instead, each church I have witnessed has discovered that the Holy Spirit is the one who brings and holds together a people of nations. In addition, each one has affirmed the Holy Spirit's active role in the worship of God's people. So, we need to pray continuously to the Holy Spirit to shape us into a church of all nations.

Intercultural leadership is hard work. It can be complicated, messy, and almost always harder than ministry in homogeneous environments. You will be challenged, and at times frustrated. But it is all worth it as we partner with God to create a new reality that the apostle Paul calls the "one new man" (Eph 2:15, NIV), a community of faith where "there is neither Jew nor Greek, slave nor free, male nor female" (Gal 3:28, NIV). The vision for an intercultural church must be deeply rooted in our conviction to live as the reconciled people of God, committed to breaking down the barriers that separate and divide us from one another.

The Stories We Share
An Intersectional Approach towards Family and Home

Lorajoy Tira-Dimangondayao

6:00 AM

My father is a storyteller. When we were small, he would call out from the bedroom that he shared with our mother, "Nak! Nak!"[1] and we would break out of our sleep to run down the stairs into our parents' room. It was always in the early mornings, before 6:30 am, so we would drag our duvets with us, and plop down onto the floor, beside our parents' bed. There, in the twilight of the early Alberta morning, our father would tell us where we were from and who we were becoming.

There was the animated story of a "brilliant" uncle, who was called home from university in Manila to their *hacienda* in South Cotabato, "on the southernmost point of the Philippines, so close to Indonesia, you can row your boat across." The summons arrived at the outbreak of war in the Pacific. "Uncle lost his wits" and spent the remainder of his life singing hopeful songs to the full moon, while knotting together threads of his own hair before eating them.

Then there was the macabre story of a cousin, who hid in an armoire while armed *Bangsamoro*[2] men invaded their home in defence of their

---

1. "Nak" is an abbreviation of the Tagalog word, "anak," meaning "my child."

2. The Bangsamoro people are a Muslim-majority ethnolinguistic group native to the Southern Philippines. "Bangsamoro" is the modern and preferred term for the

sister who had been unjustly taken by the Christian master of the house as his mistress. In hiding, while his mother was at the market, the cousin survived the massacre of his father (the master), his *querida*[3] (the armed men's sister), and the household of *katulong*.[4] "The Christians from the northern islands who had, under the fledgling American-backed Filipino government, displaced people and settled parts of Mindanao—on Muslim *Moro* soil,"[5] my dad recounted, "had a an ironic saying: Never walk ahead of a *Moro*."

In the early hours of the morning, my father told us stories meant for family. They were stories from another time and space—bizarre and broken, some marked by sadness and shame. For a child raised in the suburbs of Alberta, the stories were like fairy tales, but as an adult-now-parent looking back, I appreciate the intent. "You cannot know where you are going if you do not know where you are. You cannot chart a future, if you do not know where you have been," counselled my father in between early morning tales.

I

I have come to realize that *I* think and speak in stories. Naturally, this mode of self-inspection and self-revelation spills into my writing—I write in stories, too. I came to this realization during the summer of 2021, during a summer of attempting to write a different way—the way I was taught to write in 1993—"academic essays and papers are written in the third person. And never, should it ever, be about *you*." Since my tenth grade English class, I have followed this rule.[6]

Spanish-coined term, "Moro"—it refers to a people group as well as to the Bangsamoro Autonomous Region in Muslim Mindanao.

    3. In the Philippines, the "querida" is the mistress of a married man.

    4. "Katulong" is literally translated to "helper." In the Philippines the term refers to household helpers or servants, though one should not think of "katulong" in the sense of a slave.

    5. Mindanao in the southern Philippines is the traditional home of Muslim Filipinos—historically referred to by the Spanish and their colonies as "Moros," who actively resisted foreign occupation. This region of the Philippines was not fully occupied by Spain. To read more about the migration of Christian settlers to Mindanao during the American colonial period (see McKenna, *Muslim Rulers and Rebels*).

    6. I do not know, however, where this rule derived from.

In the summer of 2021, I became comfortable with *I*, "the epistemological and ontological nexus upon which the research process turns."[7] It is also the summer that I gave in to the *story* as valid knowledge. Demanding a response, writers including Kwok Pui-Lan, Grace Ji-Sun Kim, Susan M. Shaw,[8] Delores S. Williams,[9] Shawn Wilson, and E. J. R. David share stories.

E. J. R. David, Filipino-American Associate Professor of psychology at the University of Alaska in Anchorage, employs letters to his Filipino-Athabascan family in *We Have Not Stopped Trembling Yet*[10] to elucidate his experiences of living in the aftermath and in the midst of colonialism, oppression, racism, intergenerational trauma, and internalised oppression. In *Research Is Ceremony*, Wilson uses narratives in letters to his sons to describe the task of making Indigenous ontology and epistemology known.

In a similar way, works relevant to the study of postcolonial multicultural societies establish the narrative as an authentic way of communicating, even in the academic realm—a way in which people located outside the dominant culture can represent themselves as themselves, from their own place in time and space. While encountering these personal stories, readers perhaps question why the narratives are considered relevant. Why are they even necessary; are they not making the topic on hand all about the author? In *Postcolonial Imagination & Feminist Theology*, postcolonial womanist theologian Kwok Pui-Lan writes:

> Women's articulation of their experiences of colonization is so new; these women have been much represented, but until fairly recently have not been allowed the opportunities to represent themselves. Even if they have "spoken," their speech acts are expressed not only in words but also in forms (storytelling, songs, poems, dances, and quilting, etc.) that the academic and cultural establishments either could not understand or deemed insignificant. These knowledges have been ruled out as nondata: too fragmented, or insufficiently documented for serious inquiry. How do we come to know what we have known?[11]

---

7. Spry, "Performing Autoethnography."
8. Kim and Shaw, *Intersectional Theology*.
9. Williams, *Sisters*.
10. David, *We Have Not Stopped Trembling Yet*.
11. Kwok, *Postcolonial Imagination*, 30.

PART FOUR: FOR KING AND KIN

"How do we come to know what we have known?" is a question Shaw Wilson wrestles with. However, forwarding a robust explanation of the value of personal narrative, Wilson exhibits story as a culturally authentic way of sharing information. It is a manifestation of relationships. Wilson believes, for the Indigenous scholar, "there may be multiple realities . . . rather than the truth being something that is . . . external, reality is in the relationship that one has with the truth."[12] Wilson believes that reality is "not an object but a process of relationships."[13] In a rejection of dominant (Western) epistemology and ontology, he asserts that the knowledge communicated via story is valid data and sufficient for serious inquiry, for it is born of relationships, and embodiment of these relationships. Apart from *giving* the marginalized a voice, Wilson says that stories are authentically grounded in the Indigenous culture and experience.

In the academic world, storytelling has found its place in the research method of *autoethnography*. With the focus of connecting the personal to the cultural, "Autoethnography asserts itself against the dissociative, dispassionate, and disembodied orthodoxy of social science writing."[14] With the potential to uncover "a more intimate and emotionally rich narrative than other data-gathering techniques," the reflexive work "inspire[s] readers to deeply reflect on their own experiences and positionalities."[15] Using the autoethnography method, the researcher-participant interprets and analyses their own narratives and experiences, and not the "researched other." There is no separation between research and researcher, thus the autoethnography lends itself effectively to polyvocality. The *I* as locus of being and knowing in the autoethnographic process validates the voices at the margins.

For the context of the local congregation in a diverse society, I ask, "Where am *I* located in this?" As a person of mixed race, hybrid, migrant culture, born to a perpetually colonised and occupied people (i.e., the Filipino), I am inexplicably drawn to the stories of others as a way of knowing. Deeply personal, a far cry from the preference for third-person perspective in dominant Western academic literature, and narrative, I am seeing story acknowledged as valid data to communicate the ways of being and understanding of non-dominant societies. It is a way, as

12. Wilson, *Research Is Ceremony*, 73.
13. Wilson, *Research Is Ceremony*, 73.
14. Bochner and Ellis, "Autoethnography."
15. Spry, "Performing Autoethnography."

well, to make myself known to others. We cannot truly be known until we allow ourselves to be known. We cannot make home until we find safe places in which our selves, shared in stories, resonate with others, and where we are known and loved. As one located outside of dominant culture (though, admittedly, in many ways privier to it than others, hence the intersectionality), stories are a way that I make myself known and in listening careful to the stories of others, I contribute to the making of home with them.

Daniel Bogert-O'Brien, a professor of Hebrew Scriptures, describes that individuals are all travelling in "vehicles." There are "windows all around," but while they reveal the landscape, the window frames and the doors that surround them, continue to obstruct the view. To truly engage with the landscape, one must exit the vehicle and walk around to meet the others who are also on the journey. I propose that stories are a way to invite others into our different cars.

7:30 AM

Once, as a young mother, I tried to fill out a family tree for my children. I wrote out my father's name and those of his siblings, and his father's name, and his father's name, and his father's name, but then, it became a challenge. On my father's maternal side, I listed my grandmother, her sisters, and her parents. On my mother's side, names became sparse—my mother's generation, and her father's, plus one—Hugo—my mother's grandfather. Never mind my mother's maternal side. In the summers, I would fly to Honolulu to spend weeks to a month with my mother's family—established Hawaiians, but they told no stories. My family tree was sparse, and genealogy sites like ancestry.com[16] did not help. Still, apparently, I could fill in more leaves on the tree than many other Filipinos.

For all the things I knew about my family tree, I could not fill out the branches in the way that many of my Euro-Canadian friends could. I have friends who have family records dating back to the 1700s, to the Loyalists who migrated to Ontario from the US, following the American Revolution. In 2005, I wrote on my Tumbler blog, "I have no history; I've been robbed by invaders." I was a child of empires—living in the *wake* of

---

16. Genealogy sites are populated with European surnames and histories (see Balonon-Rosen, "Not White?"; Weiss, "Looking for Your Roots?").

galleons and destroyers. A *Nowherian*[17] falling and existing in the spaces between boundary lines.

What I did have were the family stories told in the early mornings in my parents' room, that I write of here. My father, the storyteller, had a deep faith in family and much hope for something *more*—with stories of loss and of death, there were ones of life and redemption, too. When all the stories were told, and it was time for the day to move on, he would lay his hands on our heads and pronounce the priestly blessings: "May the lord bless you and keep you . . ." All at once, I was rootless but planted, was unhoused but *at-home*.

THOU

People are never as simple as they seem. The Filipino[18] one walks by in a Canadian grocery is never just "a person who arrived from the Philippines." People of Philippine origins can never be captured by the occupations that have become their common descriptors— "worker," "nanny," "nurse," or "custodian." Not even "student," "dentist," "lawyer," or "priest." These words render people reified[19] objects of productivity, but they are not flat characters or objects, but persons living and engaging with the world.

This is the point at which my acceptance of the *intersectional approach*, as sharply defined, must be refined. By definition, the *intersectional approach*, is to be applied for the liberation of those oppressed, dominated, and marginalized. At this point in history and in this location, it is plain to see that it is exclusively used to advocate for the people who live in my immediate context (i.e., gender, racial, and economic minorities), with a subject's location in whiteness seeming to preclude the reality of their oppression. However, I would propose, in the words of my colleague: "we have all been othered at some point." In my interaction with others and in my readings of history, I have seen this to be true. Dominance is a dynamic force that flows from the temporal power of those who currently hold it. At the intersections of my multiple locations,

---

17. Iyer, *Global Soul*, 23–24.

18. I use Filipino here, because this is what people living in the Philippines refer themselves as; however, I do recognize that, particularly in the diaspora located in the west and concerned with "post-colonial" realities, the term is hotly debated (see Cabigao, "Are You Filipino or Filipinx?").

19. See Rosa, *Uncontrollability*, 28. See also "reification."

I am both colonised and coloniser, settled upon and settler, a member of a marginalised group and of a dominant one. I represent the underserved in as much as I benefit from extreme privilege.

Thus, for my work as a Christian, I would suggest an expansion of intersectional theologian Kwok Pui-Lan's call for readers to see diasporic people as "multiply located, always displaced, and having to negotiate an ambivalent past, while holding on to fragments of memories, cultures, and histories in order to dream of a different future."[20] She explains that their experience may leave them at a loss for words, and so "when [they] speak, [they have] to constantly spin and weave . . . a complex tapestry of memories . . . across generations, with both continuities and ruptures and elements from here and there."[21]

Though perhaps unpopular, given pressing postcolonial concerns, I would propose that all people be viewed in the context of their self-revealing stories, and all stories, when told in authenticity, be valued and called into the service of building the visionary *home*. In a Vancouver School of Theology class, theologian Miroslav Volf was asked, post-lecture, "how do we not focus on the evil?" Volf answered, "We must work towards the primacy of the good."[22] In the context of the gospel of Jesus Christ that informs my thought and practice, the primacy of the good is stipulated in the counter-cultural words of Jesus, the Christ, "forgive us our debts, as we also have forgiven our debtors" (Matt 6:12, NRSV) and in a reading of the writings of the early Christ-followers that acknowledges the radical transformations of family and household codes. (e.g., see the book of Philemon). The journey from *I* to *Thou* is long,[23] but I believe that the radical community of God—a new vision of *home*—is the goal of the Christ-follower and the sharing of stories paves a way.[24]

---

20. Kwok, *Postcolonial Imagination*, 46.

21. Kwok, *Postcolonial Imagination*, 46.

22. Volf, "Home of God."

23. Articulation of the I–Thou relation is attributed to Martin Buber (1878–1965), whose best-known work is *Ich und Du* (1923; *I and Thou* [ET, 1937]).

24. Shmemann, *For the Life of the World*, 36, who writes that Christians "have been called to come together in on to bring their lives, their very world with them and to be more than what they were: a new community with a new life."

Part Four: For King and Kin

11:30 AM

In the hospitals where my father was confined for over six months in 2020, I witnessed the most amazing thing—I witnessed, at the height of the pandemic, nurses sharing meals. In one of these instances, I observed the exchange intently.

"*Ate*,[25]" said a hijab-wearing nurse to a crucifix-bearing one, "here is your chicken." The Filipino nurse pushed a plastic container onto the table, "and here is your *pancit*."[26] The lounge filled up with chuckles and banter, the scent of their lunch penetrated my mandatory surgical mask.

I remembered the ugly saying "Never walk ahead of a *Moro*." Yet, there, in that lounge, with the exchange of kinship terms and nourishment, these historical enemies, existing in the liminal space of multiple locations, presented evidence that they had become more than friends—they had become family, and they were, together, building a *home*.

US

How does a community of faith go beyond a societal ideal of hospitality towards something *more*? How does a local congregation go from being a *stop before leaving* to a *home*? An *intersectional approach* permitted by the telling of stories is important in the formulation of my response to these questions, for in the stories of others, we come to hear our own voice.

Kwok Pui-Lan observes: "A diasporic consciousness finds similarities and differences in both familiar territories and unexpected corners: one catches glimpses of oneself in a fleeting moment or in a fragment in someone else's story."[27] I also find similarities and differences, catching glimpses of myself in the stories of people recorded in Christian scriptures. I wonder how these disparate people, combed from the far reaches of the Roman Empire cobbled together community in a location at which even their Indigenous ways of dining were intentionally dismantled and reshaped into Roman fashion.[28]

---

25. "Ate" is a Tagalog kinship term for "older sister."
26. *Pancit* is a Filipino dish made of noodles.
27. Kwok, *Postcolonial Imagination*, 50.
28. "Meals."

I wonder how much the dining together—the joining of selves around the early Christian meal[29] instituted by Jesus and carried on to this day by his followers—was a countercultural move towards a new code of community; that is, the meal was made available to all Jesus followers, breaking the bounds of the Roman social strata. It was marked by the welcome of the formerly marginalised into community, not to be assimilated, but welcomed into family, defined by new household codes.[30] Did they listen to each other's stories as they sat lounged around the family-style meal? Are shared meals something like the sharing of stories? Places of vulnerability, of trust, of hope?[31]

The push towards reconciliation in a postcolonial age presents the Canadian church with a challenge to rethink the practice of hospitality in its modern standard that more resembles a temporary hospice based on reified ideals. An *intersectional approach* forwarded by storytelling encourages the sense of community that people long for, beyond a commodified concept of meeting the modern ideal of multiculturalism, and even, a reified idea of "reaching out" for number's or cause's sake. What people actually long for is the deep life-giving relationships of a flourishing family.

10:30 PM

En route to Guayaquil, Ecuador for The Alliance World Fellowship's Quadrennial Convocation in 2021, I left Edmonton on October 15, then checked into the Calgary airport at 4:30 am on October 16. From there I flew into Dallas–Forth Worth, then boarded a plain for Miami. The planes were packed, and for the first flight I was seated beside a thoughtful but talkative gentleman who was curious about my studies. I had answered his question, "What do you do in Edmonton?" and he had provided me with a commentary of his many interests and engagements.

On the second flight, I was seated between two Spanish speakers who persisted in talking through me, until giving up on my work, I joined their conversation. They had assumed that I was *una China* and

---

29. In the first century, it was not yet institutionalized as the highly liturgical sacrament—it was also known as the Eucharist, the Lord's Supper, or Communion.

30. See MacDonald, "Kinship."

31. The early Christian meal is a developing interest of mind and continues to be examined through different perspectives.

had mentioned me a few times in their conversation. It surprised them to discover that I understood their conversation. After their shock wore off, I chatted with the woman who had commented on my copy of Kwok Pui-Lan's book. She, too, was working on a graduate degree and was fine tuning her thesis proposal on the use of Theatre of the Oppressed in working with poor women in Colombia. It struck me that two hours before, at takeoff, we had been complete strangers to each other, and perhaps may have even been irritated with one another.

What had transpired to bring us to a place of mutual appreciation? I am convinced that the shift in tone changed when we were given the opportunity to share a story about ourselves, and we actually listened to one another. For an hour suspended in the air, a stranger became a collaborator, a friend.

Finally, on the last leg, I boarded the plane in Miami headed for Guayaquil. I was assigned the last row and looked forward to the serenity of silence after a long day of broken up travel and crowds. However, hopes for solitude were shattered when an irritable tattooed man took the seat beside me. He was, to my observation, short with the crew, and annoyed with the plane full of people. When he turned to me and discovered that I was from Canada, he started up an initially one-sided conversation that would take the length of the flight.

He was Quechua, born then abandoned by his mother in New Jersey, who started to work when he was fourteen. His "father hit her and life in the US was like being a slave. Work, work, work, work, work." He was, in his words, "always seen to be aggressive and bad because of the tattoos, when I am just trying to be good." It was initially a difficult sit. I was annoyed, and I wondered if I would ever get to my reading but was reminded of the call to be fully present to the world and its inhabitants, to partner with God in making this place more habitable for each person, so, I put my book away and listened for four and a half hours to a Stranger named William.

William described a lifetime of suffering and marginalisation, shared his dreams for his daughter with some special needs and his joy in learning new languages. At some point, perhaps three hours into the flight, the tone of his voice had changed—calmed. A transformation occurred in my own mind as well: William became, to me, a person whose stories were precious to God, and so had become, precious to me as well. I have a sense that in sharing his stories with someone who was intently present, William was also transformed.

CONCLUSION

Our Father is a storyteller. The Christian God calls people from slumber to waking in the flourishing of family and the belonging of *home*. There is a mystery in the stories—even the bizarre and broken, often marked by sadness and shame—that we vulnerably share with others, and that they vulnerably take in. The stories mark where we have been and they invite us into being, beyond functional occupations, to very much alive.

Therefore, in the interests of *family* and *home*, stories invite the historically othered and silenced unto the platform and validates their own words as song. Qualitative narratives should be seen as valuable ways of communicating in traditionally exclusive forums (e.g., academia), and space be made for them alongside the quantifiable.

"You cannot know where you are going," my earthly father would say, "if you do not know where you are. You cannot chart a future, if you do not know where you have been," counselled my father in between early morning tales. In a diverse Canada, I am learning that the stories we tell pave a way into the family we long for.

BIBLIOGRAPHY

Balonon-Rosen, Peter. "Not White? Ancestry Services Don't Work So Well . . ." *Marketplace*, May 25, 2018. No page. Online: https://www.marketplace.org/2018/05/25/23andme.

Bochner, Carolyn, and Arthur Ellis. "Autoethnography, Personal Narrative, Reflexivity." In *Handbook of Qualitative Research*, edited by N. Denzin and Y. Lincoln, 733–68. Thousand Oaks, CA: Sage, 2000.

Cabigao, Kate. "Are You Filipino or Filipinx?" *Vice*, January 7, 2021. Online: https://www.vice.com/en/article/qjpwnm/filipino-vs-filipinx-debate-language-philippines-culture-identity.

David, E. J. R. *We Have Not Stopped Trembling Yet: Letters to my Filipino-Athabascan Family*. Albany, NY: State University of New York Press, 2018.

Iyer, Pico. *The Global Soul: Jet Lag, Shopping Malls, and the Search for Home*. Toronto: Random House Canada, 2001.

Kim, Grace Ji-Sun, and Susan M. Shaw. *Intersectional Theology: An Introductory Guide*. Minneapolis: Fortress, 2018.

Kwok, Pui-Lan. *Postcolonial Imagination and Feminist Theology*. Louisville: Westminster John Knox, 2005.

MacDonald, Margaret Y. "Kinship and Family in the New Testament World." In *Understanding the Social World of the New Testament*, edited by Dietmar Neufeld and Richard E. DeMaris, 29–43. London: Routledge, 2010.

Part Four: For King and Kin

McKenna, Thomas M. *Muslim Rulers and Rebels: Everyday Politics and Armed Separatism in the Southern Philippines*. Los Angeles: University of California Press, 1998.

"Meals in the Early Christian World." *YouTube*. https://www.youtube.com/watch?v=RdZ46_0f6ak.

"reification." In *Oxford Reference*. Online: https://www.oxfordreference.com/display/10.1093/oi/authority.20110803100412880.

Rosa, Hartmut. *The Uncontrollability of the World*. Medford, MA: Polity, 2020.

Shmemann, Alexander. *For the Life of the World: Sacraments and Orthodoxy*. Yonkers, NY: St. Vladimir's Seminary Press, 2018.

Spry, Tami. "Performing Autoethnography: An Embodied Methodological Praxis." *Qualitative Inquiry* 7 (2001) 706–32.

Volf, Miroslav. "The Home of God: A Brief Story of Everything." Lecture Given at the Vancouver School of Theology, Vancouver, BC, July 5, 2021.

Weiss, Elizabeth. "Looking for your Roots? For Asians, Blacks and Latinos, DNA Tests Don't Tell Whole Story," *USA Today*, December 3, 2018. Online: https://www.usatoday.com/story/news/2018/12/02/asians-blacks-latinos-genealogical-tests-dont-tell-full-story/2132681002.

Williams, Delores. *Sisters in the Wilderness: The Challenge of Womanist God-Talk*. Maryknoll, NY: Orbis Books, 1993.

Wilson, Shawn. *Research Is Ceremony: Indigenous Research Methods*. Winnipeg, MB: Fernwood, 2008.

Conclusion

Lorajoy Tira-Dimangondayao and Lauren Umbach

There is an unusual image depicting a group of two dozen friends sitting around an elongated dining table, composed of smaller individual tables set up end to end, in the middle of a city street. Included are old friends who had set the table with table linens, dishes and drinks, and new friends—just joined, with food contributions in tow. In the photo, this multigenerational, multiethnic group is eating and conversing, facial expressions and hands animating words. It looks, on the grey concrete, between the man-made buildings, to be the most inviting place in the world: the idealised family home.

When the editorial team set out to conceptualize the symposium that would result in the voices reflected in this volume, the second in the Jaffray Centre for Global Initiatives's series inviting Canadian churches to go *beyond* societal expectations and examine the church's role, they had in mind an image much like the one described above. A multigenerational and multiethnic group gathered around a virtual *love feast* that intentionally sought to listen to the words each participant brought to the table.

The voices included in this volume emphasise relationships and making a home for all—addressing issues of prominence and obscurity (i.e., dominant culture versus non-dominant culture), but ultimately moving on to a beautifully harmonious song made up of many equally essential voices. The multivocality demonstrated in this *gathering* of family voices, communicates a variety of perspectives reflecting the intercultural, intergenerational nature of Canadian society.

Though the words brought together by the Canadian family are varied in tone and texture, the desire to share, to see, and to listen are here. It is our prayer that this resource will be in the spirit of the Ephesian church, inviting readers to join in a movement going beyond a culture-specific understanding of God, and embracing a richer, fuller understanding of the kingdom.

We believe that it is through our interactions with those from other cultures that we are able to expand our understanding of the fullness of Christ and begin to nurture greater insight into the multifaceted grandeur of God.[1] Each of us is deeply shaped by our cultures, and as such we meet Jesus and come to understand God in very distinct cultural ways. Our God is infinite and grand, and we, in our human culture bound ways, only experience aspects of who He is. Therefore, we need to be attentive to the fact that each of us understands God through our own cultural lens. Our kin from different cultures and backgrounds also experience and comprehend God in their own distinct ways. Imagine how robust our faith journeys would be if we took the time to listen and share our insights of God with our broader kingdom family; what a gift to each and all of us. This posture encourages us to step into our roles as Inbetweeners—agents of transformation who bridge across cultural differences to develop God-honouring relationships with the Other.[2]

THE PATH FORWARD

The authors of *Beyond Multiculturalism* reflect on Canada's rich heritage of welcoming cultural diversity while recognizing many of its limitations and challenges. The church has a unique role to play in this context, for in society it is the only institution which has any possibility of bringing people together to break through the power of cultural fragmentation and live out a true expression of the kingdom. As we seek to make this a reality, the authors of these chapters have suggested a number of practices we need to be attentive to.

> Build Genuine Relationships: We need to take the time to get to know the Other by spending time together, sharing meals together, and celebrating together. Intentionally welcome those who are different than us into our lives in meaningful ways.

1. Cook, "Multifaceted Grandeur."
2. Cook, "Introduction."

Listening: We can learn a lot from the stories and experiences of others, but we need learn to listen. We need to learn about each others' preferences and create safe spaces to share the difficult stories. We must get to know people more deeply.

Lament: We need to lament together as a community of faith. Without acknowledging the suffering, grief, loss, and injustices experienced by those in our communities we can not heal or move forward. We must wade through the discomfort and pain together.

Notice and Work to Change Power Dynamics: As uncomfortable as it may make us feel, we need to be aware of how power and privilege are at work in our communities and address these issues with humility as we work to move forward.

Cast a Vision: To create intercultural communities of faith we must know what we want our communities to be and intentionally work to create them. Leadership needs a clear vision of where they are going and need to regularly recast that vision with those they are leading.

Develop Strong Spiritual Practices: By intentionally focusing on Christian practices, such as prayer and fasting, we position ourselves well to build relationships with others from diverse backgrounds and support one another.

NOW WHAT?

This conversation is far from over, and we invite you to be a part of this ongoing journey as we continue to reflect and challenge each other to move beyond multiculturalism. Jesus reminds us of the importance of loving God and loving our neighbours (Mark 12:29–31). While this sounds simple, we all know that it is not; loving the Other is profound. Although we would like it to be easy, we acknowledge that it requires time, intentionality, and hard work. For most of us, if not all of us, it will require some kind of risk as we step out of our comfort zone. Missiologist Ralph Winter observed, "Risks are not to be evaluated in terms of the probability of their success, but in the value of the goal."[3] We submit to you that developing intentional intercultural congregations a is worthy

3. Butler, "Loving God."

goal. It is our prayer and hope that as readers reflect on the contributors' experiences, stories, and insights, they will add their own voices to the conversation. May we influence and shape each others' lives and ministries for the flourishing of our Canadian home and beyond.

BIBLIOGRAPHY

Butler, Robby. "Loving God through Heart Obedience in Seeking First his Kingdom: Life Principles of Dr. Ralph D. Winter, December 8, 1924-May 20, 2009," *Mission Frontiers*. Online: https://www.missionfrontiers.org/uploads/documents/rdw-booklet-r-butler.pdf.

Cook, Charles. "Introduction." In *Beyond Hospitality: Migration, Multiculturalism and the Church*, edited by Charles Cook et al., x–xiv. Toronto: Tyndale Academic, 2020.

———. "Multifaceted Grandeur of God." October 2022 (Unpublished).

Index of Modern Authors

Airhart, Phyllis, 53
Anderson, Gerald H., 60
Arber, Ruth, 17
Ares, Alberto, 17
Arnold, Clinton E., 133, 134
Arranz, Adolfo, 119
Arrowsmith, Colin, 17

Baker, Ken, 22
Balonon-Rosen, Peter, 165
Barna Group, 122
Bear, Cheryl, 31, 33, 34, 149
Bergquist, Linda, 48
Bhatti, Deborah, 57
Blevins, Dean, 55, 59
Bochner, Carolyn, 164
Bogert-O'Brien, Daniel, 165
Bongoyok, Moussa, 85
Bonhoeffer, Dietrich, 151
Bosch, David, 149, 150
Bramadat, Paul, 118
Bratton, Amy, 81
Brousseau, Laurence, 5
Brown, Mary-Catherine, 71, 72
Buber, Martin, 167
Burns, Michael T., 52
Butler, Robby, 175

Cabigao, Kate, 166
Cameron, Helen, 57
Campbell, Ted A., 52, 53
Carter, Warren, 35
Casey, Anthony, 83
Chapman, Gary, 137
Chapman, Mark D., 81, 85, 87
Charles, Claire, 17

Chilcote, Paul W., 60
Christian, Jayakumar, 14, 15, 17
Christison, Mary Ann, 138
Chung, John E., 121, 123
Cloonan, Anne, 17
Coetzee, Karen L., 81
Cook, Charles A., 75, 145, 174
Cousins, Robert, 23, 25, 84, 85
Cragg, Gerald R., 54, 55
Cross, Shaun, 48
Crowder, George, 6
Cunningham, Joseph W., 51, 54, 59

David, E. J. R., 163
Dayton, Donald, 55
Deardorff, Darla K., 76
DeMaris, Richard E., 169
Denson, Nida, 17
Deusen Hunsinger, Deborah van, 47
Dewing, Michael, 5
DeYmaz, Mark, 3, 131, 132
Draper, Marilyn, 81
Dube Shomanah, Musa W., 32
Duce, Catherine, 57
Dyrness, William, 24

Ellis, Arthur, 164
Elwell, Walter, 146
Escobar, Samuel, xxiv, 24
Erikson, Doug, 74

Fernandez, Mercedes, 17
Fernando, Ajith, 60
Fisher, Elizabeth A., 81
Fitch, David, 147, 149
Fox, Brandi, 17

Index of Modern Authors

Fox, Nicholas, 74
Francis, R. Douglas, 6

Georges, Jayson, 108
Goldbeck, Lauren, 75, 174
Guenther, Bruce L., 118
Gunter, W. Stephen, 53, 58

Halse, Christine, 17
Hammer, Mitchell R., 15
Hammond, Geordan, 54
Hanciles, Jehu J., 86
Harris, Malcolm, 119
Hartung, Catherine, 17
Harvey, Thomas, 22
Hays, J. Daniel, 75
Heitzenrater, Richard P., 53, 56
Hibbert, Evelyn, 145
Hibbert, Richard, 145
Hiebert, Paul G., 60, 123
Hiemstra, Rick, 83
Hong, Lim Swee, 73
Hung, Kwing, 118, 121

Im, Chander H., 22
Iyer, Pico, 166

Janzen, Rich, 59, 85
Jedwab, Jack, 5
Jenkins, Philip, xxiii
Johnson, Robert K., 55
Johnson, Steve, 54
Jones, Richard, 6
Joseph, Bob, 33

Kammerer, Peter, 119, 120
Kim, Grace Ji-Sun, 163
Kim-Cragg, HyeRan, 36
Knight, Henry H., 53, 57, 58
Koester, Jolene, 31
Köstenberger, Andreas J., 151
Krabill, James, 51
Krause, Michael, 23, 84, 85
Kruger, C. Baxter, 143, 151
Küster, Volker, 41
Kwok, Pui-Lan, xviii, 163, 167, 168, 170

Ladd, George, 74

Lai, Daniel W. L., 120
Lam, Jeffie, 119
Lingenfelter, Sherwood, 25
Livermore, David, 25
Long, Thomas G., 29, 30
Lorenz, Taylor, 121
Lustig, Myron W., 31

Ma, Josephine, 121, 122
MacDonald, Margaret Y., 169
Mahoney, Caroline, 17
Malcolm, Wanda M., 81
Mansouri, Fethi, 17, 18
Marzouk, Safwat, 6
Mayers, Marvin, 25
Mayfield, D. L., 48
Mbiti, John, xxiii
McGavran, Donald, 41, 112
McKenna, Thomas M., 162
McPartlan, Paul, 21
Meadows, Philip R., 54
Meneses, Eloise Hiebert, 60
Mix, Clint, 144, 148
Modood, Tariq, 18
Moltmann, Jürgen, 45
Moodian, Michael A., 15
Moreau, Scott, 15
Morphew, Derek, 74
Moss, Julianne, 17
Murray, Stuart, 51, 57

Naylor, Mark, 3, 83
Neufeld, Dietmar, 169
Newall, Marvin, 23
Newbigin, Lesslie, xxiv, 14, 18, 129
Ng, David, 123
Niebauer, Michael, 48
Nunan, David, 138

Ohi, Sarah, 17
O'Mara, Joanne, 17
Outler, Albert, 51, 52, 53, 54, 55, 56, 58
Ovenden, Georgia, 17
Owusu, Sam, 4, 113

Palmer, Parker, 11, 15
Paradies, Yin, 17
Park, Andy, 73

Index of Modern Authors

Park, M. Sydney, 121, 123
Perkins, Larry, 3
Peterson, Eugene, 45
Phan, Peter C., 47
Pollock, David C., 66
Priest, Naomi, 17
Pullenayegem, Chris, 23

Rack, Henry D., 51, 54, 58
Rah, Soong-Chan, 3, 121, 123
Rainey, David, 51, 54, 59
Rawlyk, George A., 59
Reed, Eric, 144
Reimer, Sam, 83
Rethmeier, Cindy, 73
Riedel, Bill, 48
Rieger, Joerg, 53
Robinson, Elaine, 53, 58
Rohr, Richard, 143
Rosa, Hartmut, 166
Rumbaut, Rubén G., 116
Runyon, Theodor, 59
Ruth, Lester, 52, 73

Santos, Narry F., 23, 25, 81, 83–85
Schreiter, Robert J., 42
Schriefer, Paula, 107, 108
Seim, Brian, 113
Seljak, David, 118
Semple, Neil, 51
Shaw, Gary, 17
Shaw, Susan M., 163
Sheffield, Dan, 12, 15, 25, 55, 59
Sheffield, Kathleen, 12
Shmemann, Alexander, 167
Siebert, Jared, 81
Singh, Jennifer, 30
Slater, Victoria, 43
Smith, David, 24
Smith, Donald B., 6
Snodderly, Beth, 15
Snyder, Howard, 148, 149
Springsteen, Bruce, 29
Spry, Tami, 163, 164
Stobbe, Alethea, 85
Stovell, Beth, 75
Stovell, Jon, 76
Strano, Beth, 18
Strout, Phil, 75

Sutherland, Alexander, 53
Swain, Scott R., 151
Swartz, Sharlene, 69
Sweeney, James, 57

Tang, Timothy, 83, 84
Tam, Jonathan, 118, 121
Taylor, Charles, 15, 16
Thomas, T. V., 22, 85
Thorstenson, Timothy A., 44
Ting-Toomey, Stella, 76
Tira, Sadiri Joy, xvii, 22, 84
Tira-Dimangondayao, Lorajoy, 75, 174
Tizon, Al, 121, 123
Travis, Sarah, 30
Treier, Daniel, 51
Trudeau, Justin, xvii
Tsui, Tommy, 118, 121
Twiss, Richard 31, 34

Van De Walle, Bernie A., 152
Van Reken, Ruth E., 66
Vincent, John, 53
Volf, Miroslav, xviii, 16, 27, 143, 148, 167

Walls, Andrew F., xxvi
Wan, Enoch, 60, 83, 85
Watkins, Clare, 57
Watson, James W., 20, 81, 83, 85, 87
Watson, Kevin M., 55
Weerakoon, Kamal, 41
Weiss, Elizabeth, 165
Wells, Paul, 6
Wesley, John, 51–60
White, James Emery, 147
Whiteman, Darell L., 60
Wildman, Terry M., 34
Williams, Delores S., 163
Williams, Sian Murray, 57
Wilson, Shawn, 163, 164
Wimber, John, 65, 68
Winter, Ralph, 175
Wong, Enoch, 118, 120, 121, 125
Wong, Karen Lok Yi, 120
Wong, Wes, 118, 121
Woodley, Randy S., 37
Woods, Paul, 21

Index of Modern Authors

Wright, Lesley, 17

Yamamori, Tetsunao, 12, 22
Yan, Miu Chung, 120

Ybarrola, Steven, 84

Zizioulas, John, 21

Index of Ancient Sources

OLD TESTAMENT

Genesis

2:18	7
3:15	8
12:3	21

Exodus

12	8
29:45	7

Leviticus

19:33	7

Deuteronomy

17:9	7

1 Samuel

9	7

Psalms

133:1	150
133:3b	150

Isaiah

49:6	156

Ezekiel

37:11–14	9

Jonah

4:9–12	156

Zechariah

1:4	7
9:9–13	7

NEW TESTAMENT

Matthew

3:17	144
6:9–15	148
6:10	133
6:12	167
9:37	91
18:10–35	148
20:20–28	144
22:34–40	44, 151
22:37–39	xxvii
26:47–56	144
28:19	131
28:20	91

Mark

3:13	7
12:29–31	175
15:34	35

Index of Ancient Sources

Luke

4:14–30	151
7	35
7:13	35
9:23	7
9:23–24	9
10:25–37	xxvii
13:20–21	135
18:10–35	148
22:39–46	143, 144
23:34	148

John

1:14	22
4:1–42	8
11:1–44	8
11:43	9
13–16	144
13:35	94
14:16–17	23
14:26	23
15	138
16:13	23
17	142
17:11	142
17:20–23	142, 143, 152
17:23	150

Acts

2	74, 136
6	113, 158
6:1–7	144
6:2	156
6:4	156
7	34
8:29	23
10–11	16
10:17–23	23
10:34	158
15:1–35	144
15:36–41	144
17:26–27	142
20	157

Romans

12:2	7, 91
12:3–5	16
13:8–14	148
15:7	16

1 Corinthians

3	144
9:19	23
9:22	23
12	22, 136, 140
12:13	22

2 Corinthians

5:11–21	149
5:14	xxvii
5:18–19	22
5:20	7

Galatians

2	16
3:28	160

Ephesians

2	16, 42
2:11–22	150
2:15	160
3:6–12	131
3:6	131, 132
3:7–13	150
3:10–11	132
3:10	133
4:5	4

Philippians

2:1–11	152
4:2–3	144

Colossians

1:15–20	135

Index of Ancient Sources

1 Thessalonians

3:12	139

1 Peter

1:11–12	14
1:22	138
2:17	16
4:8	138

Revelation

5:9–10	135
5:9	3
7	59, 75, 110, 124
7:9–12	107
7:9–10	42, 123, 135, 158
7:9	3, 75
21	59

www.ingramcontent.com/pod-product-compliance
Lightning Source LLC
Chambersburg PA
CBHW070325230426
43663CB00011B/2220